DIVINE, DEMONIC, AND DISORDERED

DIVINE, DEMONIC, AND DISORDERED

WOMEN WITHOUT MEN
IN SONG DYNASTY CHINA

Hsiao-wen Cheng

UNIVERSITY OF WASHINGTON PRESS

Seattle

Divine, Demonic, and Disordered was made possible in part by grants from the Association for Asian Studies First Book Subvention Program; the China Studies Program, a division of the Henry M. Jackson School of International Studies at the University of Washington; and the University of Pennsylvania.

Additional support was provided by a Taiwanese Overseas Pioneers Grant from the Ministry of Science and Technology, Taiwan.

Composed in Warnock Pro, typeface designed by Robert Slimbach

25   24   23   22   21   5   4   3   2   1

Printed and bound in the United States of America

UNIVERSITY OF WASHINGTON PRESS
uwapress.uw.edu

LIBRARY OF CONGRESS CATALOGING-IN-PUBLICATION DATA

Names: Cheng, Hsiao-wen, author.
Title: Divine, demonic, and disordered : women without men in
    Song Dynasty China / Hsiao-wen Cheng.
Description: Seattle : University of Washington Press, [2021] |
    Includes bibliographical references and index.
Identifiers: LCCN 2020020422 (print) | LCCN 2020020423 (ebook) |
    ISBN 9780295748313 (hardcover) | ISBN 9780295748320 (paperback) |
    ISBN 9780295748337 (ebook)
Subjects: LCSH: Women—Sexual behavior—China. | China—History—Song
    dynasty, 960–1279—Anecdotes. | Celibacy—China.
Classification: LCC HQ29 .C43 2021 (print) | LCC HQ29 (ebook) |
    DDC 306.70820951—dc23
LC record available at https://lccn.loc.gov/2020020422
LC ebook record available at https://lccn.loc.gov/2020020423

To my professors

CONTENTS

ACKNOWLEDGMENTS

I owe my deepest gratitude to Patricia Ebrey, my mentor to this day and my role model. I am grateful to my teachers and friends at University of Washington, where I learned to be a historian and became interested in gender history: R. Kent Guy, Tani Barlow, Shih-shan Susan Huang, Madeleine Yue Dong, Kyoko Tokuno, Jordanna Bailkin, Sumei Yi, Jeong Won Hyun, Erin Brightwell, Cheng-shi Shiu, Chong Eun Ahn, Juned Shaikh, Li Yang, Gladys Ge Jian, Yu Huang, Hsun-hui Tseng, Jason Chan, Chad Garcia, Xi Chen, Xiaolin Duan, and Shuxuan Zhou. Charlotte Furth's pioneer research on gender in Chinese medicine and Tze-lan Sang's work on female sexuality in Chinese literature were important inspirations. I am also in debt to my teachers at National Taiwan University, especially Chang-pwu Hsia, who trained me rigorously in Chinese philology and sparked my interest in intellectual history.

I am grateful to the many sharp and uplifting minds that I have encountered as this book evolved: Jen-der Lee, Ping Yao, Cong Ellen Zhang, Robert Hymes, Yujen Liu, Chih-hua Chiang, Tomoya Yamaguchi, Angelina Chin, Wayne Soon, Howard Chiang, Margaret Ng, Fei Deng, Ann Braude, Amanda Izzo, Jacquelyn Williamson, Lihi Ben Shitrit, Sarah Bracke, Yan Liu, Shigehisa Kuriyama, He Bian, Man Xu, Jingyu Liu, Beverly Bossler, Stephen Boyanton, Yunju Chen, Ronald Egan, Jessey Choo, Elena Valussi, Sue Takashi, Alister Inglis, Barend ter Haar, Zhaohua Yang, Paul Smith, Edwin Van Bibber-Orr, Zhengming Luo, Nirmala Salgado, Pierce Salguero, Hilary Smith, TJ Hinrichs, Yi-Li Wu, Marta Hanson, Bridie Andrews, Clarence Lee, Hsin-yi Lin, Yaju Cheng, Robert Campany, and Jean DeBernardi.

I am lucky to be surrounded by wonderful colleagues at Penn, who have been supporting me in so many ways, and many of whom have read parts or even the entirety of the book manuscript: Paul Goldin, Nancy Steinhardt, Victor Mair, Christopher Atwood, Ayako Kano, Linda Chance, David

Spafford, Eugene Park, Adam Smith, Ori Tavor, Brian Vivier, Justin McDaniel, Jolyon Thomas, Siyen Fei, Heather Love, Josephine Park, Beth Linker, Nathan Sivin, Isabel Cranz, Daniel Gillion, Kathryn McDonald, Megan Robb, Jamuna Samuel, and Mauro Calcagno. I would also like to thank Guy St. Amant, Brendan O'Kane, Debby Chih-Yen Huang, Helen Teng, and my students in the Gender, Religion, and China seminar—I benefit greatly from our discussions in class and their feedback on my works in progress.

Many institutions have supported the research and writing of this book, including the Institute of History and Philology at Academia Sinica, the Women's Studies in Religion Program at Harvard Divinity School, the Center for East Asian Studies, the Alice Paul Center for Research on Gender, Sexuality and Women, and the University Research Foundation at the University of Pennsylvania, and the Taiwanese Overseas Pioneers Grants by the Ministry of Science and Technology, Taiwan.

I am grateful to the editors and staff at the University of Washington Press, especially Lorri Hagman, Beth Fuget, Neecole Bostick, Margaret Sullivan, and Christopher Pitts. I thank the two anonymous reviewers for their meticulous reading of the manuscript and kind suggestions. I also thank Brill for permission to include portions of my article "Manless Women and the Sex–Desire–Procreation Link in Song Medicine" in chapter 1 (*Asian Medicine* 13 [2018]: 69–94).

I thank my parents, who have never treated me differently from my brothers. To Ko, Shun-Yu, Li-Hsin, Margaret, Isabel, Lisa, Sinwoo, Lin Lei, and Leonar, thank you for being there. And to Riley, who has become an important person in my life and has had to put up with all of my political commentary, thank you for your love and company.

DIVINE, DEMONIC, AND DISORDERED

INTRODUCTION

THIS IS A BOOK ON WHAT WE DO NOT KNOW ABOUT WOMEN. IT IS about navigation through uncertainties and, particularly, through failures to know and to stabilize female bodies that were unavailable to men. Three Chinese sources from the seventh, tenth, and eleventh centuries contain similar depictions of women who, for various reasons, refrain from sharing a room with their husbands. In source A, a certain kind of woman tends to avoid people and prefers her own company, yet when alone, she talks and laughs as if someone else is present. In source B, a husband is suspicious when he hears conversation and laughter coming from his wife's secluded room at night. In source C, a woman refuses to share a bed with her husband, yet while she is sleeping alone, people hear her whispering as if speaking to someone.

Source A is the seventh-century medical text *On the Origins and Symptoms of Various Illnesses* (Zhubing yuanhou lun), compiled by a Sui-dynasty imperial physician, Chao Yuanfang. The description appears among the symptoms of women's "intercourse with ghosts" or "dreaming of intercourse with ghosts."[1] Source B is the tenth-century Daoist hagiography *Continued Traditions of Transcendents* (Xu xian zhuan) compiled by Shen Fen (937–975). The woman was Pei Xuanjing, a Daoist adept who was said to have ascended to heaven in 854. She requested a separate room from her husband almost immediately after marrying.[2] Source C is the childhood recollection of the Northern Song literatus Liu Fu (fl. mid-11th c.) about a woman he had seen in his hometown who was possessed by a fox spirit.[3] Although they were written in different centuries, in different genres, and for different purposes, these sources contain strikingly similar depictions of women who stayed alone and were thought to have some sort of relationship with spirits.

3

This book does not assume dichotomies of male fantasy versus female resistance, or elite men's representation versus women's true experience. Nor is the analysis about women's choice or agency—whose choice is it if a woman asserts that she is chosen by the gods to practice celibacy and she has to obey? What kind of agency is it if a woman interacts with ghosts or speaks in the voice of spirits? The focus, instead, is on epistemology—the sets of vocabulary and conceptual frameworks available to both men and women to understand what they see and to describe what they do or who they are. This book further situates the epistemology of manless women in a historical context where the discursive nature of medical knowledge and the power of the state were radically different from their modern counterparts, and neither medical knowledge nor state regulation nor any particular system determined the truth about the human body. Scholars of premodern China have made significant contributions to the critical analysis of women and gender in literary representation, medicine, religion, art, elite culture, the legal system, as well as the material culture of everyday life. They have presented evidence of women's engagement both in the family and in society at large.[4] This book, however, shifts attention away from women's much-discussed reproductive body and familial roles. It turns instead to women who did not procreate, whose bodies were not accessible to men (including and especially their husbands), and whose social significance thus remained unstable. Consideration of such women's bodies and lives prompted new questions about normalcy, desire, sexuality, and gendered identities.

The subject of this book is not simply women without sexual contact with men. The main focus here is on women whose sexual and reproductive bodies were not available or were made inconvenient to present, future, or late husbands: a maiden who was deemed possessed by a demon and therefore unable to marry until the demon was expelled; a married woman who requested a separate room and avoided sexual contact with her husband; or a woman who left her home to become a renunciant while still at a marriageable age or while her husband was still alive. Although this was not an explicitly delineated category at the time, historical sources provide very similar descriptions of and attitudes toward these "manless women." Such women faced similar social scrutiny and were often treated differently from women whose sexuality remained in line with the family system. Various diagnoses and solutions might have been applied to these women, but it was their manlessness, among other things, that required explanation. In some cases the sexuality of manless women was so different from that of other women that the former no longer considered themselves, or were considered by others, as women—they could be religious devotees who rid themselves of the "female body" or the "female self" (*nüshen*), which did not always entail physical sexual transformation; they could also be considered demons that had assumed female form. Manless women by this definition usually did not include widows, who were expected to be celibate not because their sexual bodies belonged to no one but precisely because their sexuality still belonged exclusively to their deceased husbands. Widow chastity is thus relevant here only when a few medical authors draw peculiar connection between widows' sexual status, desire, and their reproductive bodies. "Manless women" does not fit modern classifications of sexual identity or sexual orientation, nor was it an established concept in premodern Chinese sources. But it is a productive category for analyzing the distinct configurations of gender, sexuality, illness, divinity, and subjectivity in my sources.

MANLESS WOMEN AND SONG SOCIETY

The main sources of information on manless women are medical treatises, "bedchamber" (*fangzhong*) literature, manuals of exorcism, literary tales, anomaly accounts (*zhiguai*), anecdotes, and Buddhist and Daoist hagiographies. Although this book covers the period from the Southern Dynasties (420–589) to the Yuan (1271–1368), its main focus is on changes that occurred during the Song dynasty (960–1279). During this time, most of the characteristics of later imperial Chinese society began to emerge—including urbanization and commercialization, increased production and circulation of printed books, diversification of popular culture and religion, the rise of local gentry and their communities, emergence of professional religious services, and increasing numbers of elite physicians or scholar-physicians (*ruyi*). Manless women were rarely included in official biographies or epitaphs.[5] But other sources show increasing awareness of such women in Song society, illuminating pertinent social and cultural conditions and the changing epistemologies.

Such textual sources are treated here as narratives—stories told with specific purposes, framed under certain values and worldviews, and situated with reference to particular historical settings. The fact that one text is fictive or anecdotal does not mean that it cannot reveal significant historical facts. Scholars have made use of hagiographies to study the social history of Daoist adepts,[6] and *biji* (miscellaneous jottings) and anecdotal writings help historians understand the lives of those who are not recorded in official histories.[7] These are particularly useful regarding the social and cultural environment of manless women during the Song.

Record of the Listener (Yijian zhi), a substantial collection of anecdotes compiled by Hong Mai (1123–1202), is an especially rich source for reconstructing the material conditions of and people's interactions with manless women in Song society. Hong Mai compiled and published *Record of the Listener* installment by installment during the last forty years of his life in the second half of the twelfth century. Fourteen out of at least thirty-two installments survive today. In compiling *Record of the Listener*, Hong sought to include extraordinary incidents that his contemporaries had witnessed. Each story in the collection has unusual elements, although not always supernatural by modern standards. All of the stories are presented as happening in the ordinary, everyday settings of Hong's time. Hong insisted not on the factuality of all his collected stories, but rather that someone had witnessed the incident and the *possibility* that such things did happen. For Hong Mai, his informants, and his intended audience, these extraordinary incidents were likely true events, and that was precisely what fascinated them. For Hong's contemporary audience to accept that a certain story could have been true, the setting had to make sense. A story that took place in urban America in the 2010s, for instance, would not be believable if none of the characters went online or used smartphones. Scholars differ in their approaches to *Record of the Listener* as a historical source, but they agree that it contains substantial information about Song people's everyday life and that many of its accounts preserve oral narratives of the time.[8]

Three social and cultural developments during the Song were particularly germane to manless women. The first was the emergence of scholar-physicians and the discussion of desire among Confucian scholars. Scholar-physicians wrote for those who read. The burden was on physicians or medical writers to convince others that their theories were correct, and yet there was not a uniform or standardized method to test their theories. Medical knowledge did not automatically enjoy the authority of dictating the truth as it does now. The Neo-Confucian discussion of desire, especially the urge to distinguish desire from necessity and spontaneity, influenced medical discussions of manless women from the Southern Song on, as medical writers began to use the Neo-Confucian vocabulary to explain medical theories. Prior to the Song, medical texts (except for bedchamber literature) were not as interested in women's sexual desire. According to Neo-Confucian ethics, women were responsible for controlling their own desire. In order for women to be moral subjects, they had to be deemed as subjects rather than simply objects of desire.

The second significant change was the rising interest seen in Song sources in the lives and experiences of nonelite people, a phenomenon related to the growing elite population and the overlap of elite and commoner cultures.[9] It was also related to the thriving local cults and temples during this time. Local temples were not simply places where people of different social strata prayed for their fortunes, but also served as both community centers where local leaders held meetings and as cultural symbols through which the gentry constructed their regional identities.[10] Witnesses and testimonials were important for local temples not only because word of mouth attracted offerings and pilgrims, but also because efficacy was a crucial criterion for the Song state's recognition of local cults.[11] Stories of efficacy—spiritual experiences of men and women from all walks of life—circulated orally and were included in temple inscriptions as well as collections such as *Record of the Listener*.

Finally, urban and commercial developments made it more possible during the Song than earlier for women without men to live independently, especially those women who did not belong to a monastic order. A gazetteer of Putian (in present-day Fujian) records that an unmarried woman moved there with a substantial fortune and funded the construction of a weir; after death, she was worshiped as a local deity. Another gazetteer of Funing (also in Fujian) records two unmarried women who accumulated money through textile work.[12] There is also plenty of evidence in *Record of the Listener*. "Yong's Daughter" tells the story of a quasi-marital relationship between a deity and the daughter of an official in Jiankang (present-day Nanjing). The relationship lasted for many years until the father finally managed to find a powerful exorcist to send the deity away. Even though the deity was gone, the story says, no one dared to marry the daughter and, after her parents passed away, she sold wine to earn a living on her own.[13] What made this story "extraordinary" and thus fit for Hong's collection was the relationship between the daughter and the deity and the exorcism, not the fact that a single woman could fend for herself by selling wine. Judging from the degree of details given in the account, there was likely a man named Yong Zhang who served as a "specially appointed administrator of official wineries" in Jiankang at that time, as this story records. He probably had a daughter who never married, and people gossiped about why she remained single.

Two other accounts relate strange incidents about several manless women who did not belong to a religious institution but were sheltered by their family or the community. The women were not the focus of either narrative and the strange incidents had little to do with their manless state. The first account records that Wen, the daughter of a local official, returned to her natal home after divorce. Another woman, called "Yang the Person of Dao" (Yang Daoren) and also from an elite family, lived together with Wen; the two of them practiced the Dao together. The main story is not about the relationship between Wen and Yang but a ghost-haunting incident that took place in 1154, when the whole family stopped in southern Quanzhou en route to Zhangzhou (in southern Fujian), where Wen's father had been assigned to a new position. One night Yang's maidservant was found hanging under the roof beams by an invisible rope, and a mysterious young man who did not belong to the family appeared next to her. Wen's father heard a sound and rushed to investigate. The young man claimed that Yang owed him a large sum of money for the medicine that she once acquired from him. Wen's father wielded his sword and the young man disappeared. The father summoned a priest from a Daoist temple, but the maid had returned to normal before the priest arrived, and the young man did not appear again. Yang was only in her twenties at that time, and some thought that what the young man claimed might have happened in her previous life.[14] This story's intriguing background—that a divorced woman stayed at her natal home and practiced the Dao with an unrelated woman, who traveled with the family when the father moved from one post to another—was not what the narrator expected to impress the Southern Song audience.

The other story tells that in Fangcheng County (in present-day Henan) the locals put together money and built a "hall of the Dao" (*Daotang*) on a mountain to accommodate women who practiced the Dao (*Daonü*).[15] A village woman named Liu renounced her family life and entered the Dao. One night she dreamed that her married daughter came to her weeping, saying that she had just died after a fight with her husband. Liu went to her in-laws' home and confirmed that her daughter indeed had died the day before of the said cause. She wanted to press charges against her son-in-law in the county court, but the villagers convinced her not to disrupt her renunciant practice, and the head of the village complied. "The injustice that was done to the daughter was not redressed," the story ends.[16] The fact that the villagers cofunded a nunnery was only the backdrop. Liu was likely a widow, judging from the absence of the daughter's father at her death. The narrative can be read as a criticism of the compliance of the villagers and lament for the daughter's death. But the existence of a community nunnery was not remarkable to the narrator.

Manless women who were not sheltered by a family or a recognized community often aroused suspicion and were sometimes associated with demonic forces, despite or perhaps precisely because of their economic independence. Another *Record of the Listener* story tells about an adult woman and two young girls who sold medicine in the market of Quanzhou in 1147. They were probably itinerants and unknown to the locals; the group of three females without obvious familial or religious affiliation must have drawn unusual attention. The account records that "for several days, some busy-bodies secretly followed them." They found that the three women lodged alone in a separate house in a Buddhist temple complex. Some said they heard the sounds of processing medical ingredients come from the house every night. One day a monk in the temple peeked into their house and saw that each of the women had only one leg. The next day all three of them disappeared.[17] References to manless women as vendors, ritual and healing service providers, or small business owners exist in pre-Song sources as well. But the growth of cities, the development of water transportation, interregional trade, and a money economy increased the opportunity for those economic activities.[18] During the Song, we also begin to see more uncertainty and bewilderment in discussions of manless women.

COMPLICATING DISCOURSE AND AUTHORSHIP

While many significant social developments in late imperial China began during the Song, a market for published women's writing had not yet materialized. In contrast to the large number of women's writings from the Ming-Qing period (1368–1912), extant texts from the Song-Jin-Yuan (960–1368) were predominantly written by elite men.[19] Yet those sources are by no means monolithic, nor do they speak only for elite men. Beyond representations of male anxiety, fantasy, and androcentric gender discourse, we can glimpse in these texts unstable meanings attached to manless women's bodies, lives, and stories. To do so, this book adopts a three-part strategy. First, it emphasizes the inconsistent and heterogeneous nature of "discourse," of ways of constituting knowledge. For instance, when the twelfth-century physician Chen Ziming crafted *guafu* as a distinct medical category denoting all "husbandless women," his theory was based on a mixture of sources truncated and taken out of their original contexts. The theory also inadvertently contradicts Neo-Confucian notions about female fidelity, and yet it was precisely his Neo-Confucian colleagues whom Chen attempted to impress with his medico-philosophical writing.

Second, this book diversifies and complicates the questions it asks of male-authored sources. Historians cannot claim access to unmediated, authentic female voices, even through women's own writings; nor can ethnographers do so even through direct interviews with women.[20] Similarly, elite men's writings are not simply straightforward representations of elite men's voices. Authorship is not tied only to those who eventually write a text down, but is a long and complex process. For example, the most recent scholarship on *Record of the Listener* suggests that it contains diverse voices and conflicting worldviews, even though it was compiled by Hong Mai. Comparison of Tang tales and Song anecdotes about women's "enchantment disorders" reveals that many Song anecdotal writings, especially those in *Record of the Listener*, are fundamentally different from Tang literary tales in their multivocality and lack of omniscient voice. Another tool for complicating the reading of male-authored sources is the juxtaposition and comparison of sources from different genres. One finds, for instance, that medical treatises, hagiographies, literary tales, and anecdotes depict women who had some sort of connection to spirits in an almost identical fashion. This phenomenon speaks to a popular perception of female sexuality and subjectivity that was not single-handedly shaped by a small circle of elite men. Sources such as *Record of the Listener* and hagiographies adapted from popular anecdotes reveal traces of how people at that time navigated through uncertainties.

Third, this book calls attention both to the frustration of not knowing— or the inadequacy of established language and epistemology to describe certain forms of experience—and to the instability of claimed discoveries of truth. In "narratives of failure," no method of treatment for women's enchantment disorder works and no one knows for certain what has happened. Repertoires of female transcendents and enchanted women overlap, generating both anxieties and possibilities.

RECONFIGURING SEXUALITY

Sexuality, as we have come to use the term, is a result of various forms of state and colonial control and the development of modern science since the nineteenth century. In Victorian England, for example, scholars argue, sexuality was produced by the state's "decisions to protect and regulate some bodies and not to regulate and protect others." While legislators were often reluctant to regulate the sexuality of British men as opposed to women and the racial Other—since that would mean violating British men's right to protection from undue state control—the state did not hesitate to interfere in its male subjects' private lives in the case of sodomy laws. Women were rarely prosecuted under sodomy statutes in Victorian England, and that made English sodomy laws "a rare instance of the Victorian state exerting control over men but not women." Women were not subject to regulations that were equivalent to the sodomy laws "not because those laws assigned women greater sexual freedom, but because legislators and judges tended to be unwilling to recognize women as capable of having sex with one another." Marriages between women were neither prohibited nor protected by the state. Thus, the Victorian state created sexuality by designating the kinds of desires and behavior that had to be constrained or eliminated and those that could be ignored.[21]

Similarly, as historian Matthew Sommer argues, the new legal definition of illicit sex (*jian*) in eighteenth-century China revealed the priorities of the Qing state. The Yongzheng emperor (r. 1723–36) sought to legislate uniform standards of sexual morality applicable to all, regardless of social status. This shift from the "age-old paradigm of status performance" to a "new one [of] gender performance" had much to do with anxiety about "the growing crowd of rogue males" at the bottom of Qing society who lacked wives, family, and property.[22] But unlike sexuality as created in nineteenth-century Western Europe and North America, *jian* as defined by the Qing did not become naturalized. It remained a legal and moral category. Sexuality as a naturalized universal phenomenon and an object of modern scientific study was introduced to China in the early twentieth century. An old term, *xing*, was used to translate this new concept and has become the standard term for both sex and sexuality in modern Chinese.[23]

The formation of sexuality as a modern concept has been analyzed by many scholars.[24] Historians have come to recognize that *sex* as a naturalized category does not determine what matters; instead, what matters determines what sex is. References to sex in a particular time and place are not cultural representations of a natural phenomenon; rather, our perception of sex as a natural phenomenon is itself a cultural and historical construct. By exploring how things we consider sexual today were construed differently in a different time and place, we learn what things mattered, and how they mattered, to people of that other time and place.

Sexuality and its modern assumptions sometimes make us see things that were not there or prevent us from seeing things that were. Assumptions about a sex–desire–procreation link could prevent historians from seeing certain significant nuances and developments in Song medicine. Similar assumptions also create problems in the study of anomaly accounts from premodern China. Literary scholar Liu Yuan-ju, for instance, studies stories about sexual anomalies from the Six Dynasties (220–589) and divides tales dealing with "relationships between the two sexes" (*liangxing guanxi*) into six categories according to their relation to marriage and procreation.[25] Liu further argues that the stories all carry the same moral message that "deviant sex [*weichang de xing*] is definitely ineffective sex and cannot result in children," and serves to "reinforce the traditional ethics of 'generating life' [*shengsheng*]."[26] Liu's argument is flawed. In the literary and social worlds of the Six Dynasties, marriage and procreation were not the criteria according to which sexual relationships were classified or evaluated. At best, they were necessary but insufficient conditions for the legitimacy of a woman's position within the patriarchal family.[27] A man, especially a man of the noble class, should not have sex with other men's wives or his own paternal female relatives, but he did not need marriage or procreation to legitimize sexual relationships with concubines, maids, prostitutes, or female deities.

Records of an Inquest into the Spirit-Realm (Soushen ji; early 4th c.) includes the story of a female deity named Chenggong Zhiqiong, an orphan before ascending to heaven, who was sent by the Supreme God (Tiandi) to marry a man named Xian Chao. The Supreme God, motivated by sympathy for the female deity's difficult childhood, intended this as a comfort for her. The female deity told Xian that because she was a god, she could not bear children for him and yet she also had no jealousy and therefore would not interfere with his real marriage. She stayed with him for several years, even after Xian Chao's parents arranged a marriage for him, and left only after Xian incautiously let others know about their relationship. Five years after her departure, they met again, and from then on the deity regularly descended to Xian on certain days of the year.

A contemporary literatus composed a rhapsodic poem about this deity, in the preface of which he explained that he "questioned those who were close to Xian and knew about [his relationship with the deity]. They say when the female deity comes, they can all smell fragrance and hear her voice. It is thus evident that [this relationship] is not the product of Xian's own excessive [sexual] illusion or fantasy [*yinhuo mengxiang*]. . . . Those who are approached by ghosts and demons all become ill and emaciated. Yet Xian remains hale and hearty to this day. He eats and sleeps with a deity, and his affection and desire are satisfied [*zong qing jian yu*]. Is it not marvelous!"[28] The relationship between Xian Chao and the female deity is benign—and even divine—precisely because it is beyond marriage and procreation. For elite men like Xian Chao and his friends, it seems that marriage and procreation were less important in their sexual relationships with women than who or what the woman was.[29]

Liu's classification criteria more closely resemble those used by today's Protestants and Evangelical Christians than anything used by the people of the Six Dynasties. A false assumption about the relationship among marriage, procreation, and sex leads to reduction of *shengsheng*—a complicated notion in *The Book of Changes* (Yijing) and its commentaries concerning cosmogony and numerology—to an ethic of sex between men and women. Liu's analysis not only imposes modern Protestant values upon historical sources but also neglects the critical role that gender plays in these stories, which several scholars have examined fruitfully.

Literary scholar Mei Chia-ling, for example, has described differences between the narratives about men's encounters with female ghosts and those about women's encounters with male ghosts, and she has observed that tales about elite women tend to be told differently from those about maidservants. Even so, when Mei finds that a story does not fit the gender or class pattern that she has previously observed, she turns to sexual desire as a "primordial force that transcends biological sex, social sex [that is, gender], and class" for an explanation.[30]

A woman could also conceive without having sexual intercourse. One account in *Further Records of an Inquest into the Spirit-Realm* (Soushen houji; late 5th c.) tells of a woman, who while washing clothes by the river, "felt something unusual inside her body and yet was not bothered by it." The woman then became pregnant and gave birth to three babies that all resembled catfish. She raised them in a basin, fed them, and gave them names. The babies quickly grew into aquatic dragons (*jiao*), and departed one day during a thunderstorm. But whenever it rained, they came back to visit their mother. When the woman died, the three dragons returned and wept at her grave for several days.[31]

No sexual intercourse is mentioned or hinted at in this narrative; nor is there any judgment about whether this was a good or bad thing. Nothing particularly good or bad happens to this woman because of the experience. Conception without sex was not a mystery or something supernatural for people of that time. Rather, conception was understood to be a result of the intercourse of *yin* and *yang* (manifested physically as the unification of "blood" and "essence"), which usually—but not exclusively—occurred through intercourse between a male and a female. Pregnancy in the absence of physical intercourse with men was often called "affected pregnancy" (*ganyun*).

Divine affected-pregnancy cases are frequently seen in stories about ancient sages. The chapter on affection and resonance (*ganying*) in *Inquest into the Spirit-Realm* records several such stories: the Yellow Emperor's mother Fubao is "affected" (*gan*) one night when seeing lightning surrounding the Big Dipper and gives birth to the Yellow Emperor after twenty-five months. Emperor Zhuanxu's mother Nüshu is affected and pregnant with Zhuanxu on a night when the star Jasper Brilliance (Alkaid) shines over the moon. Emperor Yao's mother Qingdu is affected by a red dragon that she encounters by the river and becomes pregnant with Yao.[32] The intercourse (*jiao*) between *yin* and *yang*, or the unification (*he*) of blood and essence, was not, then, limited to sexual intercourse, and pregnancy was less closely linked to the moral or sexual conduct of the mother than to the source of *yang* substance or essence.

As in pre-nineteenth-century Europe, there was not even a term in pre-twentieth-century Chinese that specifically and exclusively denoted sex. The terms frequently used in medical and bedchamber texts are *jiao* (intercourse), *he* (conjoin), and their derivatives such as *jiaotong* (communicate), *jiaojie* (contact), *jiaohe* (commingle)—all general terms that could refer to both sexual and nonsexual actions or states. *Jiao* can be rendered as interaction, connection, exchange, or intercourse in its nonsexual sense. *He* means to combine, to integrate, to meet, or to harmonize. The precise meaning depends on the context. Another term, *jiaogou*, tended to mean more specifically sexual intercourse, but was not used exclusively in this sense. The original meaning of *gou* was uxorial marriage (*chonghun*, lit., "double marriage"), a marriage relation built upon an existing marriage relation. In classical Chinese, *gou* can refer to marriage in general, intercourse, and peace-making.

There are also quite a few euphemisms and dysphemisms for sex. But most of them mean only specific forms of sex, and none is used exclusively for its sexual connotation. *Xiani*, for instance, usually indicates that a man and a woman share intimacy beyond a legitimate relationship, but can also describe improperly intimate friendship. *Tongqin* and *tongta*, literally "sharing a bed," can apply to a married couple, a man and a woman, or two (or more) people who simply share a bed. *Jian*, often seen in legal texts, refers to illicit sex. Legal codes of different regimes had different definitions of what *jian* means. It is also used in other texts and everyday language, often meaning illicit sex or describing those who engage in illicit sex, as well as indicating all kinds of other illicit activities and treacherous persons. *Luan* and *yin* are two other terms that can refer to illicit sex, but the sexual meaning is only determined by the context. *Luan* means disorder in general, and *yin* excess. A sentence along the lines of "a man *luan* with a woman" can be understood as saying that the man has illicit sex with the woman, while "General so-and-so *luan*" meant that the general had rebelled. "*Yin* behavior" usually refers to illicit sexual behavior, but a "*yin* shrine" describes an illegitimate or unorthodox shrine.

In other words, in China prior to the twentieth century, things we would now classify as sexual according to our modern standards were not always distinguished in nature from other matters. This is not to say that Chinese people prior to the twentieth century did not draw distinctions between sexual and nonsexual matters. Rather, the alignment and classification of bodily and affective behaviors were different and were subject to change over time. The scientized, naturalized, and apparently neutral and transparent concept of "sex/uality" was not present in either pre-nineteenth-century Europe or pre-twentieth-century China. Apparent references to sex in pre-twentieth-century sources should not be reduced to cultural references to a universal phenomenon or immediately associated with desire and procreation. Instead, one should consider the reference in its original context, examine the matters with which the source associates the activity, and investigate how and to whom it mattered.

HISTORICIZING HETEROSEXUALITY

Heteronormative assumptions still pervade much current scholarship on gender and sexuality in Chinese history, such as taking for granted the link between women's generative and gestational body and their sexual desire, and characterizing medical discussions of women's heterosexual inactivity as discourse about "women's sexual frustration."[33] However, when we no longer assume that premodern Chinese medical authors always considered manless women to be sexually frustrated or that sexual desire was naturally rooted in a reproductive impulse, we are able to see more nuances. Sex–desire–procreation links were in fact peculiar in Chinese medical history, and this peculiarity has to be understood within the context of Song medical culture. Rather than assuming that medical authors discussed female sexuality and desire only in the context of reproductive health, we need to pay attention to when and how women's reproductive bodies were connected to their sexual desire.

Two monographs have been particularly important in advancing the historiography of premodern China by questioning heteronormative assumptions: Matthew Sommer's *Sex, Law, and Society in Late Imperial China* and Tze-lan Sang's *The Emerging Lesbian: Female Same-Sex Desire in Modern China*. Sang uses predominantly literary works. In the first part of her book, while drawing attention to the absence of interest in female sexual desire in premodern Chinese literature, Sang overlooks the development of such interest in medical and religious texts.[34] Sommer examines legal documents and demonstrates how in the High Qing (eighteenth century), sexuality was a product of the legal system and state control.[35] The present study, however, approaches the history of sexuality beyond the legal system and state control and draws attention to the unspeakable, the inexplicable, and the lives that the state neglects. Contrary to the popular assumption that

Confucianism dictated heteronormativity, this book argues that the normalization of heterosexuality—for example, the idea that it is normal for women to desire men—was rare and idiosyncratic in pre-Song and Song sources. It further proposes a different imagination of queer history for women that focuses on expressions of female celibacy and manlessness rather than on same-sex intimacy and desire, for what mattered the most in the historical sources—and perhaps still does in contemporary Chinese-speaking societies—was often not, or not simply, women's desire for one another but their bodies and sexualities without men.

GENDERED IDENTITY, AGENCY, AND SUBJECTIVITY

Scholarship from the past two decades has demonstrated that many female renunciants in Chinese history did not completely give up familial life. Not only did they maintain family ties in various ways, in some cases they also transformed familial relations and redefined the meaning and practice of filial piety. Scholars have also paid much attention to the social, economic, and political contexts of women's renunciation. An emphasis on women's agency has become salient in recent studies on religious women in traditional China.[36] Together these studies form powerful responses to the old narrative that depicts women in traditional China as passive victims of oppressive patriarchal systems—a narrative rooted in a set of progressive and secularist assumptions. We must push the critique of secularist assumptions even further and inquire into the religiosity of female renunciants' agency. We cannot continue to simply depict the exercise of religious women's agency within a modern secularist definition of liberation, success, and achievement. The evidence of women's agency presented in existing scholarship often involves resistance (against whatever we may consider oppressive), choice-making, a career or visibility in the public domain, and the like.

During the Song, "entrance into the monastic life" may have "provided career-minded women an opportunity to achieve fame and publicity," but what if fame and publicity were less important to religious women of that time than to us?[37] What if a woman took on the renunciant life not for fame or publicity but for her advancement on the *bodhi* path? What if she did not consider her action a choice but a response to a divine calling or the marvelous working of karma? Similarly, while it has been argued that some women chose a Daoist life to "escape from marriage," because women within this society had no choice over marriage and married life—whereas a Buddhist nun or a female Daoist could "have access to the topmost tritium of society"—this assumes choice and status in liberal and secular terms to be the priorities of religious women.[38]

This is not to say that social motivations and divine callings do not intertwine or cannot coexist. But does a woman still have agency if her actions cannot be fully explained in secular terms, and if so, how do we understand this kind of agency? The convent could provide women with "a stable life," "social empowerment," a revival of "frustrated intellectual ambitions," a place to recover from the "psychological trauma of losing one's husband," and so on.[39] But to distinguish those "social factors" from the "religious" ones or from "genuine religious calling" veils other possibilities and prevents a more nuanced understanding of the practice of piety.[40] What if a woman's plight in life (including the difficulties of being a woman in her society) was not simply something that she sought to escape, but precisely that through which she came to realize the meaning of suffering and the urgency of practice toward true liberation? What if renunciation as an alternative way of life was not freer than domestic life, and it was precisely the austerity that earned renunciants respect? As the scholar of Daoism Suzanne Cahill has also argued in her study of Tang Daoist women, "Discipline was viewed by Daoists as necessary for liberation from mortality rather than as a hindrance to individual freedom."[41] Without ignoring the social aspects of religious practice, I question what has been left out by a clean cut between the religious and the social in our understanding of celibate women's gendered identity and subjectivity.

A woman's gendered identity (as a "woman" or *nü*) and her subjectivity (that is, her quality of being conscious of her own state and actions) were frequently tied to her sexuality in relation to men in traditional Chinese discourse. A different kind of renunciant identity, one that was gendered but not two-sexed—determined initially by one's sexed body but then open to transformation or transcendence through one's lifestyle, especially a manless lifestyle—is evident in hagiographical collections and the sex transformation motif in both Buddhist and Daoist traditions. A number of different constructions of female sexuality are related to different perceptions of manless women's subjectivity, and are revealed at the intersection between spiritual and sexual possession in women and the conflation of enchanted women, female *wu* (sorcerer; spirit-medium; exorcist), and female *xian* (transcendent; immortal; deity or semi-deity). These intersections and conflations are amply documented in specialist and canonical texts, as well as tales and anecdotes.

PART ONE

RECONFIGURING GENDER, SEXUALITY, AND ILLNESS

CHAPTER ONE

"HUSBANDLESS WOMEN" IN MEDICINE

WOMEN'S HETEROSEXUAL INACTIVITY HAS BEEN EXPLAINED IN some Chinese historical sources as a cause of medical disorder, but it has not always been related to the reproductive body or women's desire for men. In modern China, since the early twentieth century, sex and sexual desire between men and women have been naturalized and linked to the natural laws of human procreation, therefore creating a (hetero)sex–desire–procreation continuum.[1] This continuum is rarely seen in Chinese sources before the twentieth century. Many physicians since the fourteenth century considered women's "excessive thoughts" (about men) to be the causes of illnesses such as "intercourse with ghosts" and "ghost fetus," which tended to occur among widows, nuns, and maidens.[2] But few physicians saw this as related to women's procreative capacity.

Characterizing Song dynasty medical discussions about female sexuality represented by the Southern Song physician Chen Ziming (1190–1270), historian Charlotte Furth observes, "The woman's sexual body was not separated from her generative and gestational body, and desire in both sexes was naturalized as a manifestation of the intentionality of Heaven and Earth rather than psychologized as erotic pleasure. Throughout, however, where woman's fertility was an internal bodily readiness outside of her conscious awareness, the male was assumed to be in charge of timing and in control of the coital event."[3] The phrase "Heaven and Earth," which Song intellectuals frequently used in referring to a moralized cosmological order, was in fact rarely seen in Song medical discussions of female sexuality. If Song physicians considered sexual desire naturally linked to the cosmological force of procreation, was it then unnatural, or even against the principles of Heaven and Earth, for young widows, whose generative and gestational bodies were still robust, to remain chaste?

Chen Ziming worked as a medical instructor (*yiyu*) in a prefectural academy that had close ties with local Neo-Confucian (or Daoxue, "Learning of the Way") scholars. Despite the seeming universality of his claims, Chen was in fact the first medical writer, and the only one during the Song dynasty on record, to make references to Heaven and Earth in the discussion of female sexuality. He was also only the second writer, other than Xu Shuwei (ca. 1080–1154), to make explicit the sex–desire–procreation link in his medical discussions of "husbandless women." Chen and Xu expressly stated that women without sexual contact with men suffered from unfulfilled sexual desire, and that desire was related to the readiness of their reproductive bodies. This view, however, was anomalous in the history of Chinese medicine. Chen's association of desire with Heaven and Earth was symptomatic of the semantic ambiguity of the character *yu* (meaning "desire" or "need" or indicating a future action) in classical Chinese, as well as an intrinsic philosophical conundrum that the Neo-Confucians struggled to resolve.

Were women who had no sexual contact with men considered a medical problem to be solved? If so, what was the cause of the problem? There was little discussion of women's sexual desire in medical texts before the Song. The only textual tradition within medicine prior to the eleventh century that discussed female sexual desire per se was "bedchamber" (*fangzhong*), or sexual cultivation, literature. Up to the Song period, medical approaches to the ailments of manless women focused on either the mechanisms of the reproductive body, making no mention of sexual desire, or, in the case of bedchamber texts, on women's sexual desire with little attention to the generative or gestational body.

In the works of Xu Shuwei and Chen Ziming, however, the two approaches to female sexuality laid out here were haphazardly fused. Xu and Chen represent manlessness as no longer simply a condition of individual female patients, but a category that was defined by women's sexual, rather than marital, status (even though they use the expression "husbandless"). The condition of being husbandless subjected women to certain types of ailments. Xu's and Chen's departure from previous medical discussions of husbandless women is salient when we no longer assume that a discussion of any of the three components—sex, desire, and procreation—necessarily involves the other two. Xu and Chen were also anomalies among their contemporaries in treating procreative capacity and female sexual desire as naturally and necessarily linked.

Let us begin with Chen Ziming and his major medical compilation, *All-Inclusive Good Formulas for Women* (Furen daquan liangfang; *Good Formulas for Women* hereafter), the most substantial handbook of women's medicine of its time. Chen signed his 1237 preface to the volume as "Medical Instructor" at the Mingdao Academy in Jiankang Prefecture (present-day Nanjing). In the preface, Chen tells us that his family had practiced medicine for three generations. His book comprises medical texts collected by his family, tested recipes that his family had used, and recipes Chen himself collected when traveling throughout the southeast. *Good Formulas for Women*, like many other large medical compilations during the Song, takes an all-inclusive and pragmatic approach.[4] It has eight parts: menstrual regulation, various illnesses, seeking progeny, fetal nurturance, pregnancy, the sitting month (i.e., the final month of pregnancy), birth complications, and postpartum care.[5] Each part opens with a general discussion consisting of Chen's own words as well as excerpts from previous medical texts, followed by an array of named medical conditions, each accompanied by another paragraph going into greater depth about the causes and symptoms, and then a list of formulas and treatments that Chen collected from various sources.

Under "Various Illnesses," in the section "*Guafu*'s *Nüe*-like Cold and Heat Disorders: Formulas and Discussions," Chen opens with an ambitious "discussion" (*lun*) on husbandless women:

> On the illnesses of *guafu* [husbandless women], there has been no discussion since antiquity. Only "The Biography of the Director of Granaries" [Chunyu Yi] and Chu Cheng [d. 483] briefly touched upon the matter. By *gua* I mean precisely what Mencius [ca. 372–289 BCE] says: "[Those] without a husband are *gua*," such as Buddhist nuns and widows [*wu fu zhi fu*, "women whose husbands have died"]. They are single *yin* without *yang*; *they want [yu] men and yet cannot have one*, and therefore gradually become sick. *The Book of Changes* says: "As Heaven and Earth mingle, all creatures crystallize [into living beings]. As the essences of male and female mate, all creatures generate." Sole *yang*, single *yin*—can it be so? Since [such women] dwell in the inner quarters, *their desire [yuxin, or "thoughts of yu"] germinates but is not fulfilled*, which results in the *yin* and the *yang* [within their bodies] clashing and intermittent cold and heat,

similar to *nüe* disorders. If prolonged, this will develop into exhaustion [*lao*]. Other symptoms include menstrual blockage, white vaginal discharge, phlegm buildup, headaches, flatulence, belly congestion, facial moles and warts, emaciation—all are the illnesses of *guafu*. In their pulse manifestation, the liver pulse specifically appears stringlike, over the upper wrist and between the thumb and the wrist, caused by abundant blood. The classic says: "When a man's essence [*jing*] is abundant, he thinks of a mate; when a woman's blood is abundant, she conceives children." Observing the essence and the blood is most of the job.[6]

This passage is loaded with intertextual references. "The Biography of the Director of Granaries" refers to that of the famous second-century BCE physician Chunyu Yi, included in *Records of the Grand Historian* (Shiji). The biography records Chunyu's career as a physician and twenty-five of his medical case histories, most from the court of the state of Qi (present-day Shandong).[7]

The second figure Chen mentions, Chu Cheng, was an imperial physician of the Southern Qi dynasty (479–502). None of Chu's works survived into the Song except for the so-called *Chu's Posthumous Work* (Chushi yishu), a text of obscure origin considered by some scholars to be an apocryphal writing of the tenth or twelfth century. Chen's source is most likely Tao Hongjing's (452–536) *Annotated Materia Medica* (Bencaojing jizhu) or the Song texts that quote it, where Tao says, "Chu Cheng treats widows, Buddhist nuns, and monks differently from wives and concubines. This is because he pays astute attention to his patients' characters [*da qi xinghuai*]."[8]

The Book of Changes is one of the five core Confucian classics; it includes a set of divination diagrams and succinct phrases from the Western Zhou period (1046–771 BCE), accompanied by ten parts of commentaries from the Warring States period (403–221 BCE), but was traditionally believed to be authored by Confucius (ca. 551–479 BCE). The quotation is from one of the commentaries, "Xici," a treatise that attempts to tie all divination phrases to an overall philosophy. I have been unable to identify which "classic" Chen is referring to, though the same sentence appears in an earlier text by another Song physician, Xu Shuwei. (Xu does not cite the origin of the sentence.) The very last sentence is seen in *Chu's Posthumous Work*. After this opening paragraph, Chen includes Xu Shuwei's case history of treating a Buddhist nun, Xu's "*dihuang* [*Rehmannia glutinosa*] pill" recipe, and a summary of Xu's "discussion." In fact, despite Chen's claim that no one other than Chunyu Yi and Chu Cheng had ever discussed the illnesses of *guafu*, his discussion borrows heavily from Xu Shuwei, and together Xu and Chen tell us something about a new development in medical discussions of manless women and female sexuality.

Two things are worth pointing out immediately. The first will be obvious to any reader of Chinese: the anomalous use of the word *guafu*. Whether in modern or classical Chinese, literary or colloquial, in medical or other genres, this compound, consisting of *gua* (lack) and *fu* (married women), simply means "widow." It does not include unmarried or divorced women. To use a single term to refer to women positioned in completely different places in relation to the family—widows, maidens, celibate nuns, and such—was unheard of. Chen cites Mencius as the reference for his definition, but he truncates Mencius's original sentence: "[Those who are] old and without a husband are *gua*" (Lao er wu fu yue gua). The original context was Mencius's presentation of his views on "kingly governance" before King Xuan of Qi (r. 319–301 BCE). Mencius specified four kinds of people who were the poorest and needed particular care from the state: the *guan* (old and without a wife), the *gua* (old and without a husband), the *du* (old and without a son), and the *gu* (young and without a father).[9] Here *gua* is among those who are in need of but do not have family support; it is a socioeconomic category defined by age and dependency.

By carefully manipulating the quotation—dropping only two characters from the original sentence, from "old and without a husband" to "without a husband," Chen turns *guafu* into a new medical category defined by sex *and* sexuality. Before, during, and after Chen's time, Chinese lacked a term that semantically encompassed widows, Buddhist nuns, and maidens, whose identities and social statuses were never confused in Song society. In other words, Chen created a term that made the previously insignificant commonality among those women—their heterosexual inactivity—now identifiable and medically meaningful. Chen's linguistic innovation died with him, but this medical category remained, and his passage was incorporated into several later medical books. Although Chen defined *guafu* as women "without a husband," the medical category was defined not by women's marital status but by their sexual relations with men. It included all "single *yin* without *yang*" and did not include courtesans or prostitutes.[10] While Chen assumed that women with husbands by their sides were automatically immune to this problem, his *guafu* category was oddly incongruous with the marriage system in a society where widow chastity and female fidelity were orthodox—regardless of how often widows might have remarried during the Song. If we push Chen's definition just a little further, the result is striking: the countercategory to *guafu* becomes one that includes wives of good families and prostitutes.

The second peculiarity in this passage concerns the two kinds of *yu* in the two italicized phrases. The first phrase comes from the biography of Chunyu Yi, and the second from Xu Shuwei. The original context of the first is one of the twenty-five medical cases that Chunyu Yi recounted in response to an imperial edict inquiring about his experience as a medical practitioner:

> The king of Jibei's maidservant, a woman from Han, suffered pain in her loins and back and intermittent fevers. All the other physicians diagnosed her ailment as [a typical case of intermittent] cold and heat. Your subject Yi read her pulse and said that [her ailment was due to] inner coldness and that she must have menstrual blockage. I then let the medicine enter her body (i.e., medicinal steam or smoke through the vagina). Her menses immediately resumed, and her ailment was cured. Her ailment was caused by her *yu* [wanting, needing] *men and yet being unable to have one.* I knew [the cause of] her ailment because while reading her pulse, I found her kidney pulse slim and disconnected. Slim and disconnected pulses are manifestations of difficult and tough [congestions]. That was why I said she had menstrual blockage. Her liver pulse was stringlike and over the top of the left wrist. That was why I said that she *yu* men and yet was unable to have one.[11]

What does *yu* really mean? In modern Chinese, it means "want" or "desire." But in classical Chinese, in addition to "desire," it is also used to denote "necessity," "tendency," and even near-future events—meanings not always related to one's desire or intention. Its precise meaning largely depends on the context. For example, in medical case records, the author often states that a patient with certain symptoms *yu si*—meaning that the patient is about to or is bound to die, not that she or he wants to die. In another case record of Chunyu Yi's about treating an official's wife who suffered from "*qi* conglomeration lodged in the bladder," he describes that the woman's illness came from "wanting/needing to urinate and yet unable to do so" (*yu ni bu de*).[12] This usage of *yu* is still preserved in Hokkien, a dialect of Taiwan and southern Fujian, pronounced *beh*. In modern Mandarin, the verb *yao* plays a similar role. Three compounds are used to distinguish desire (*xiangyao*) from need/necessity (*xuyao* or *biyao*) and sequential/future events (*jiangyao*). The *yu* in the maidservant's case may still be related to desire, but it is not categorically distinguished from necessity or spontaneity.

This is not to say that classical Chinese writers never distinguished between these senses, but rather that the distinction may not have been as salient as in modern contexts. The semantic ambiguity did not bother Chunyu Yi or Sima Qian (ca. 145–86 BCE), the author of Chunyu's biography. For a physician like Chunyu Yi, what the patient desired was probably less important than what she needed. His case record associates the maidservant's menstrual blockage with her lack of sexual contact with men, but this is not a discussion about sexual desire, at least not the kind of sexual desire that is categorically distinguished from other bodily mechanisms. There is also no interest in either normalizing or pathologizing any specific form of female sexuality in the record, for we are not even told whether "*yu* men and yet being unable to have one" is a shared problem among all (hetero)sexually inactive women or unique to this particular patient.

Whether the woman wanted or needed men, why she wanted or needed men, whether all women or only some women in this circumstance would want/need men—Chunyu Yi's record does not raise or answer any of these questions, perhaps precisely because they were insignificant. Chunyu Yi's treatment deals directly and solely with the problem of menstrual blockage; once the patient's menses resumed, the record says that "her ailment was cured." It is clear from the record that Chunyu Yi considered the patient's illness related to her (hetero)sexual inactivity, but it is not clear whether he thought she was sexually frustrated. Chen Ziming's claim that Chunyu Yi only "briefly touched upon" the illnesses of manless women may have been motivated by this ambiguity.

There is no such ambiguity with the second *yu* in Chen Ziming's passage. Used as a noun in the compound *yuxin* (thoughts of *yu*) and in the phrase "*yuxin* germinates but is not fulfilled," it unambiguously means desire.

From Xu Shuwei to Chen Ziming

Like Chen Ziming, Xu Shuwei was also a scholar-physician. There is no record of Chen ever taking or passing the civil service examination. Xu, on the other hand, earned the *jinshi* degree in 1132, at the age of fifty-two. By then he had spent most of his life studying and practicing medicine. It was said that in the late 1120s, Xu helped the people of his hometown (Zhenzhou, in present-day Jiangsu) survive a serious epidemic.[13] In his *Ninety Treatises on Cold Damage Disorders* (Shanghan jiushi lun), Xu recounts how he treated a Buddhist nun who suffered from fatigue, hot flashes, fast heartbeats, and periodic sweats. Like in other writings of medical case records, Xu makes sure to include the inaccurate diagnoses by other physicians summoned before him and the wrong treatments that had exacerbated the symptom, in juxtaposition with his own success. He determined that the nun's pulse manifestation matched Chunyu Yi's description of the king of Jibei's maidservant and therefore her illness was not a kind of cold damage but one caused by her "*yin* being active without *yang* [to interact with]." Xu then prescribed the medicine that "suppressed the *yin*." The patient recovered after a couple of days.[14] Although Xu identified this case as being of the same kind as Chunyu's record of the maidservant, his treatment was different. The nun was not described as suffering from menstrual blockage, the main symptom of the maidservant that Chunyu Yi treated, either.

This case history is followed by Xu's discussion. In another text that Xu compiled later in his life, *Formulas with Case Histories for General Relief* (Puji benshi fang), he includes the case history and the discussion, and adds the recipe that he prescribed the nun, the *dihuang pill*. Chen Ziming's *guafu* section draws extensively from Xu's *Formulas with Case Histories*—the case history, the discussion, and the recipe alike—but reorganizes and reorders the text. While Xu begins with the case history and the recipe and appends his discussion to the end, Chen starts with the discussion as if it were his own and only mentions "Academician Xu" when quoting his case history and recipe after the discussion. In so doing, Chen turns Xu's less organized text into his theory-based, classified formulary compilation that models Sun Simiao's (581–682) *Invaluable Formulas Worth a Thousand Gold for Emergencies* (Beiji qianjin yaofang; *Invaluable Formulas* hereafter).

Unlike Chen Ziming, Xu emphasizes his agreement with Chunyu Yi and Chu Cheng rather than claiming to have established a new theory. However, Xu did make several groundbreaking points, most of which lie precisely in the sentences that Chen adapted. Xu uses the term *yuxin* (thoughts of *yu*) to interpret Chunyu Yi's case of the maidservant, suggesting that the problem with manless women is their sexual desire and not, or not simply, their other bodily necessities or their readiness for sex with men. Furthermore, in this passage Xu discusses both sexual desire and reproduction and implies a link between them: men's desire for a "mate" is a result of their abundant *jing* ("essence"; semen being one of its manifestations), while women's "ample blood" leads to both *yuxin* and pregnancy. No extant medical text before Xu Shuwei, to my knowledge, ever discussed women's sexual desire and reproductive physiology at the same time as one subject.

About a century later, Chen Ziming, while downplaying Xu Shuwei's contribution, expanded upon Xu's writing in a more systematic direction. As discussed earlier, Chen redefined the term *guafu* to further accentuate heterosexually inactive women as a medical category.[15] He also related more miscellaneous symptoms to this category of illnesses—from menstrual blockage and white leucorrhea to phlegm buildup, headaches, flatulence, belly congestion, facial moles and warts, and meagerness. More importantly, while Xu simply referred to two famous historical physicians, Chen felt the need to quote the Confucian classics to buttress his theory. *The Book of Changes* and its early commentaries have always been part of the five core classics. *Mencius* by this time had also been included in the newly expanded list of thirteen classics—largely out of the Neo-Confucian scholars' effort to elevate Mencius over Xunzi as the orthodox successor of Confucius.

Chen's appeal to the Confucian classics as his source of authority is perhaps indicative of his relationship with his contemporaneous Neo-Confucian scholars and the rising scholar-physicians.[16] It also tells us something about the social status and the plurality of medical knowledge at that time. Historians have noted the gap between the social status of medical practitioners and that of (text-based) medical knowledge in Song times.[17] Even medical knowledge deriving from the scholarly tradition, or texts considered medical canons from ancient times, did not automatically have the power to establish the "truth" about the human body and dictate social norms. For medical writers and practitioners working in a pluralist medical environment, their knowledge constantly required verification and justification.[18] Chen used *The Book of Changes* and *Mencius* as the foundation of his *guafu* theory, in keeping with the contemporary hierarchy that placed Confucian classics above all other sources of knowledge. In other words, medical theory in this case was not used to reinforce Confucian values: on the contrary, Confucian texts were (mis)used to buttress a new medical theory. It was not "one of many ideological tools that men used to discipline and control women," as late imperial *fuke* (women's medicine) has been labeled.[19] Chen's *guafu* theory even potentially contradicted Confucian values with the inadvertent implication that widow chastity was against the "Way of Heaven and Earth" and could jeopardize women's health—although this theoretical contradiction seems not to have challenged the family system in society at large, just as other *fuke* theories did not serve to buttress it.

Yu *and Desire in Neo-Confucian Philosophy*

Chen's *guafu* theory embodied a conundrum about *yu* and human desire in Neo-Confucian philosophy. Chen inherited Xu's link between desire and procreation and, by citing *The Book of Changes*, further associated the link with a higher principle of Heaven and Earth, which many Daoxue scholars of the Song spent their lives comprehending and practicing. One of the most influential Neo-Confucian philosophers, Zhu Xi (1130–1200), painstakingly established the ontological distinction between "Heaven's patterns" (*Tianli*) and "human desires" (*renyu*). To Zhu, human nature (or innate capacity, *xing*), since it belonged to the "Heaven's patterns" category, was fundamentally good; "human desires," however, constantly misled one's moral judgment and had to be extinguished. At the same time, to distance what he considered orthodox Confucianism from asceticism and "heresies," including Buddhist and Daoist teachings, Zhu had to insist that Heaven's patterns and the basic needs of humans were hierarchically arranged rather than mutually exclusive. In many of his writings and recorded conversations, Zhu used *yu* to describe humans' physical needs. He emphasized the distinction between humans' natural tendencies or impulses, which come from the "human heart" (*renxin*), and humans' capacity for moral judgment, which comes from the "heart of the Way" (*Daoxin*). For example, the need (*yu*) for food and drink comes from the human heart, and the judgment of proper and improper behaviors in eating and drinking (*de yinshi zhi zheng zhe*) comes from the heart of the Way.[20] But when it came to the kind of "*yu* between men and women*," Zhu was much more cautious. When a student asked, "[Regarding the distinction between] the human heart and that of the Way, if the desire/need for food and drink and that between men and women are rooted in righteousness [*zheng*], this is the heart of the Way. What then is the difference?" Zhu simply answered, "This is, after all, born out of blood and *qi*" (i.e., the physical realm that is subject to corruption).[21]

To Zhu Xi, the distinction between desire and necessity or spontaneity mattered significantly, and the semantic ambiguity of *yu* bothered him. Commenting on the idiom, "Father and son should/desire to [*yu*] be kin [to each other]" (Fu zi yu qi qin), Zhu stressed, "It is not that they *desire* [*yu*] to be so" but that they are "spontaneously so" (*zihui ruci*). What does such spontaneity entail? Zhu continued his explanation by using an example of physical impulse: "One feels hot and spontaneously [*zihui*] waves a fan; it is not that one desires [*yu*] to wave a fan." And what is not spontaneous? Zhu names the pursuit of favoritism and fame (*neijiao, yaoyu*) as an example.[22] While elsewhere Zhu uses *yu* to describe natural impulses and needs, here he deems *yu* to be (excessive) desires beyond basic needs. The core of the problem is that the word *yu* does not in itself distinguish desire from necessity and spontaneity, but the distinction was crucial for Daoxue scholars like Zhu Xi.

The Mingdao Academy, with which Chen Ziming was affiliated, had close ties with the Daoxue tradition in general and Zhu Xi in particular. Chen Zhi (*jinshi* degree 1214), the principal of the academy in the 1220s, just a decade before Chen Ziming finished compiling *Good Formulas*, was a student of Zhu Xi's.[23] As mentioned earlier, Chen Ziming's quoting from *The Book of Changes* and *Mencius* might have been related to the Daoxue scholars with whom he associated. However, his linkage of women's desire for men with Heaven and Earth would have been problematic in Zhu Xi's eyes because *yuxin*, or the desiring heart, should never automatically belong to the realm of Heaven and Earth. But like the question raised by Zhu's student about the "*yu* between men and women" and Zhu's own inconsistent usage of the word *yu*, Chen's *guafu* theory also embodies the intrinsic tension within Neo-Confucian philosophy—the effort to establish a hierarchical but not mutually antithetical relationship between Heaven's patterns and human needs through naturalizing morality and moralizing nature.

In sum, Chen Ziming departed from Xu most significantly by bringing in the Confucian classics and elevating the sex–desire–procreation link to a higher level. But unlike Zhu Xi or Zhu Zhenheng (a more sophisticated Neo-Confucian scholar-physician of the fourteenth century), Chen seems not to have aspired to establish a moralized natural philosophy or to provide another ideological tool to dictate social norms. It would have been a major failure if he had done so by arguing that chaste widows were prone to sickness.

BEFORE CHEN ZIMING

Before Xu Shuwei and Chen Ziming, medical discussions that mention women's sexual status reveal two separate approaches to what are considered related ailments. One situates women's heterosexual inactivity within the context of reproductive health without discussing desire. The other deems women's desire for men a necessary outcome of celibacy while neglecting women's reproductive body. The link between women's reproductive body and sexual desire was not articulated until the Song.

Pulse Classic: *Diagnostic Aid for Gestational Uncertainty*

Wang Shuhe (3rd c.), the imperial physician of the Western Jin dynasty, in his *Pulse Classic* (Maijing) once refers to treating "court ladies and widows" differently from married women. The difference is not pathological but simply serves as an aid to diagnose pregnancy. In the section on various conditions during gestation, Wang records that a female patient had the pulse manifestation that indicated pregnancy and yet still had intermittent menses (or mense-like discharge). He comments that if she was indeed pregnant, she should "immediately be treated lest her menses resume." No specific recipe is recorded in this entry, but we can learn from the context that the treatment was meant to prevent miscarriage. Immediately following this case record, Wang adds, "If [the patient] is within the palace or is someone without a husband, such as a widow, who has once dreamed of intercourse with malign *qi* at night, in some cases carrying [the malign *qi*] for a long time that develops into *zheng* and *jia* [conglomerates], [she] should immediately be purged and treated with the two [abortifacient] decoctions."[24]

Given the uncertainty of diagnosing pregnancy, Wang took into account the patient's marital status when making his diagnosis.[25] When presenting the same set of symptoms and pulse manifestations, if the patient is a married woman (*furen*), it means that she is pregnant, yet the pregnancy is unstable; if she is a court lady or a widow and has such dreams, it is false pregnancy. To diagnose false pregnancy in this condition, in other words, requires not simply pulse-taking but also knowledge of the woman's marital status and her dreams. There is no direct indication in this passage that court ladies and widows are necessarily more susceptible to "dreaming of intercourse with malign *qi*." Right before this passage is another case record about a pregnant woman who suffered coldness in her abdomen, and Wang prescribed her a "menses/meridian warming decoction" (*wenjing tang*). Wang adds, "If the patient comes with her husband's family, she is pregnant. If she comes with her natal family, [the condition] should be diagnosed as excessive coldness; if the condition lasts, she would not be able to conceive." There is no discussion of desire or any physiological difference in either case. In both cases, the female patient's marital status is only used as an aid to determine whether or not the patient is actually pregnant.

Chu's Posthumous Work: *Reproductive Physiology*

Both Xu Shuwei and Chen Ziming identified Chunyu Yi and Chu Cheng as their predecessors. In fact, neither the record of Chunyu Yi nor Chu's one-sentence remark quoted in Tao Hongjing's *Annotated Materia Medica* constitutes a specific discussion of female sexuality or desire. Chen Ziming probably had also read *Chu's Posthumous Work*, a text said to have been discovered in an old tomb during the Huang Chao Uprising (878–84) and preserved by Xiao Guang and his son Xiao Yuan (10th c.) before being buried with Xiao Guang and unearthed again in 1126 by a Buddhist monk, Yikan. It was printed in 1201 under the title *Chushi yishu*.[26] This text, however, makes no mention of nuns or widows. The sentence quoted by Chen Ziming is from the section "Essence and Blood" (Jing xie), a discussion about the physiology of women's and men's reproductive bodies rather than sexual desire as such. It says,

> Once a woman's menstruation [*tiangui*] begins, it would be disharmonious if she does not have intercourse with men for more than ten years; it would also be disharmonious if she thinks of intercourse with men within less than ten years. Such disharmonies lead to the old blood not being discharged and the new blood circulating deviantly. [The old and new blood] may either permeate into bones or transform into tumors. Even if she later has intercourse [with men], it may be hard for her to produce children. Having intercourse with men too much dries up the fluid and exhausts the woman. Giving birth to too many children and breastfeeding them dries up the blood and kills the mother. *One may comprehend most of the principles by observing the essence and the blood.*[27]

The first sentence can be confusing, for it juxtaposes two disharmonious conditions that seem to describe different things: the former is simply sexual inactivity (*wu nanzi he*) and the latter seems to refer to sexual desire (*si nanzi he*). But the rest of the section contains no further discussion of desire. In fact, it suggests that women should *not* have sexual thoughts about men within the ten years following their first menstruation. Immediately after ten years, however, they simply should begin to have sex with men and bear children, regardless of whether they think of or desire such things. This passage emphasizes the right timing for women to conceive and to give birth, the right and the wrong circulations of blood, and the physical problems emerging when a female body is ready for successful childbirth but the act is deferred, or when the act (or thought) precedes one's readiness. There is also no mention of whether single women *naturally* think of men; it simply says that they will become sick if they do so before a certain age. The passage immediately follows a parallel passage describing the irregular circulation of "essence" in men who have sex with women before their "essence" is not yet fully developed (*jing wei tong*) or after their reproductive organs have ceased to function (*yin yi wei*).

Another section in the same text, "Asking for Progeny" (Wen zi), reiterates that in order to successfully produce children, men and women must consummate their marriage at proper ages: "Nowadays women, before reaching the age of *ji* [proper age to get married, fifteen to twenty] and whose menstruation is just beginning, already are intimate with men. Their *yin* energy leaks prematurely, damaged before fully developed and disturbed before growing solid. Therefore, even if they have intercourse [with men], they will be unable to conceive; even if they conceive, they will be unable to give birth; even if they give birth, their children will be weak and short-lived."[28]

The concern here is, again, reproduction and the physiology of women's reproductive bodies, not sexual desire. Rather than suggesting that young maidens are prone to sickness because of their manlessness, it stresses the opposite: young maidens will be sick if they have sex with men too early. The subject is women's premature sexual activity and not desire or "thoughts." The author's concern is not whether women are sexually frustrated or satisfied but rather that women need to conceive at the proper age and with proper frequency for the well-being of themselves and their children.

Bedchamber Literature: Sex and Desire beyond Procreation

There is almost no medical discussion of women's sexual desire in extant pre-Song sources except in "bedchamber" (*fangzhong*) texts. The concerns of bedchamber works are very different from those of the medical tradition acknowledged by Song physician-writers.[29] Bedchamber literature discusses sexual desire explicitly and extensively, often (though not exclusively) focusing on men. The two main purposes of the bedchamber arts, as seen in early texts, are successful conception (especially the production of sons) and bodily cultivation. At the core of the generally male-centered bedchamber arts was men's power of control—of their own bodies and their female partners.[30] Fragments of bedchamber works from medieval China are preserved in the "Nourishment and Benefit in the Bedchamber" (Fangzhong buyi) section of Sun Simiao's *Invaluable Formulas*, the chapter of "Damages and Benefits of Dominating Women" (Yunü sunyi) in the *Records of Cultivating Nature and Prolonging Life* (Yangxing yanming lu; *Cultivating Nature* hereafter),[31] and Tanba no Yasuyori's (912–995) *Recipes at the Heart of Medicine* (Ishinpō; *Heart of Medicine* hereafter).[32] Scholarly physicians in the Song would likely have studied Sun's works and had access to *Cultivating Nature* and perhaps would still have been able to see some of the texts included in *Heart of Medicine*.[33] But none of them mentioned any bedchamber texts in their own works.

The sexual arts are referred to as the methods of "utilizing/dominating women" (*yunü*). The core concern is to preserve and make optimal use of *jing*, the source of men's life and longevity, as described in *Invaluable Formulas*: "The *jing* moves upward and fortifies the brain, which makes men live long."[34] It warns men of the danger of losing their *jing*: "When a man's *jing* is scarce, he becomes ill. When his *jing* is exhausted, he dies."[35] The opening of the "Dominating Women" section of *Cultivating Nature* echoes this: "The Way is to treasure *jing*. Bestowing it [upon women] generates children; keeping it sustains [one's own] body."[36]

The last passage suggests that the core methods of "generating children" and "sustaining one's own body" are mutually exclusive, even if many of the physical conditions and socio-cosmological taboos involved are similar.[37] The two major principles for men to cultivate their bodies through sexual intercourse, as *Invaluable Formulas* suggests, are to "adopt *qi* [from women]" (*caiqi*) and to minimize the frequency of ejaculation according to one's age and physical strength. Practitioners are advised to "change women frequently" in order to absorb the most *yin qi*, because a woman's *yin qi* weakens as she has intercourse with men. In the meantime, the practitioner should manage to keep his *yang qi* by withholding from ejaculation: "The ability to dominate twelve women without ejaculation keeps men from aging"; "those who can have intercourse with a hundred [women] without ejaculation live long."[38] A passage included in *Cultivating Nature* likewise states, "Once desire emerges, change the partner. Changing partners prolongs life."[39] While the method of "sustaining one's own body" focuses on minimizing the frequency of or even refraining from ejaculation, the key to "generating children" is the timing of ejaculation according to astrological calendars and women's menstrual cycles.[40]

According to some physicians, some of the bedchamber methods for men to cultivate their bodies would damage the reproductive and overall health of their female partners. While *Chu's Posthumous Work* warns that having sex too early damages women's lives and makes it difficult for them to give birth to healthy children or even to conceive, some bedchamber authors advise their (male) readers to find young and even immature maidens.[41] *Secret Instructions of the Jade Chamber* (Yufang mijue; ca. 6th–7th c.; *Secret Instructions* hereafter), for example, advises men to "often [sexually] utilize young girls and not to leak *jing* frequently";[42] *Principles of the Jade Chamber* (Yufang zhiyao; ca. 7th c.) suggests that men "simply need those who are young and plump and have not yet developed breasts."[43]

While the overarching principle for bodily cultivation was to reserve the *jing*, views differed as to whether, and why, one should copulate. Again, most of the discussion concerned men. Men's sexual desire for women was considered to be normal, though not optimal, and to require meticulous self-control. One view held that men had to copulate with women, there being no other way for *yin* and *yang* to circulate, and that as men could not achieve the goal on their own, they had to "move without giving away [*jing*]."[44] Another view held that sexual intercourse was a compromise. Sun Simiao suggested that men above sixty "close up their *jing* and do not let it out." He did not recommend so for most men under sixty because the damage of suppressed *jing* outweighed the benefit. His answer to the question if men below sixty should "close up their *jing*" is:

> No. Men cannot be without women. Women cannot be without men. Without women, [a man's] mind moves. His mind moves and his spirit is fatigued. His spirit is fatigued and his life is shortened. *It would be the best if one's mind is perfectly just with no thoughts.* And yet there is not one such person even among ten thousand. To forcefully withhold and close up the *jing* is difficult to maintain and easy to fail. It causes men to leak *jing* and to have turbid urine, leading to the illness of intercourse with ghosts. The damage out of one such case equals a hundred [regular ejaculations].[45]

The entire passage is about men. The phrase "women cannot be without men" is little more than a rhetorical parallel to "men cannot be without women." While Sun provides the rationale behind the need of men below sixty to have regular ejaculations, there is no explanation of why women must have men. It is not all clear if the statement about those perfect minds with no sexual thoughts is simply another rhetoric or a true ideal. But it is clear that the statement "men cannot be without women" is conditional— for ordinary men below sixty—and a compromise only to prevent greater damage. Another passage in *Cultivating Nature* seems to be more explicit about the ideal of celibate men: "Supreme men separate beds. Mediocre men use a different blanket. Sleeping alone is more beneficial than taking a thousand doses of medicine."[46] Taken together, the bedchamber authors recognized men's celibacy and desireless mind to be ideal and rare; in the meantime, they provided solutions for ordinary and mediocre men who had less control over themselves. For men, the problem is not excessive, absent, or deviant sexual desire; it is desire itself. Desire is not anything beneficial, but something that men are advised to take control of. Even when the texts describe pleasure, men remain solemn observers of both their female partners' and their own physical reactions.[47]

There is little comparable instruction for women and no comment on women's sexual desire or needs in *Invaluable Formulas* and *Cultivating Nature*.[48] The texts preserved in *Heart of Medicine* contain some discussion of women's desire for men, the "benefit" for women in having (properly conducted) sexual intercourse with men, and problems resulting from the lack thereof.[49] In these descriptions, we see not simply a fear of women who devour men ("sexual vampirism," as R. H. van Gulik calls it) but also the fear that women will not desire men.[50] This fear is salient in a passage from the *Secret Instructions* in which Pengzu explains to Cainü, both mythical figures enjoying longevity, that the cause of women's "intercourse with ghosts" (*guijiao*) is "a lack of intercourse between *yin* and *yang*; [the woman's] desire [becomes] deep and severe, and ghosts assume [human] form to have intercourse with her." An explicit link between women's lack of sex with men and their unfulfilled sexual desire is clearly drawn. Pengzu continues: "The way in which ghosts have intercourse with [women] surpasses men. Over time, [the woman] will become enchanted. She will hide it and not disclose it to others, keeping it for herself. Eventually she would die alone, without anyone knowing how."[51]

While *Cultivating Nature* describes men's intercourse with ghosts as resulting in a loss of semen a hundred times worse than usual, here it simply says that the analogous situation for women leads to death, without quite explaining how. The concern here seems less about women's lives and health than about their bodies and sexuality beyond men's surveillance. Three avenues of treatment are recommended: intercourse with men, medicinal smoke from sulfur absorbed through the vagina, and antler powder. The first prescription gives detailed instructions on *how* to conduct the intercourse, instead of simply assuming that sex with men or marriage solves the problem.[52] The medicinal treatments are for "maidens and noble ladies (or court ladies)" without sexual access to men.[53]

But this passage also includes a quasi-experiment, which seems to suggest that heterosexual desire is not all spontaneous but can be contrived. It says, to verify that men and women do dream of intercourse with ghosts, that one can "enter the deep mountains and be surrounded by great lakes in spring or autumn, do nothing but look afar and think intensively only about *yin–yang* intercourse." After three days, one will suddenly begin to have intermittent fevers, disturbed heart, and dazzled eyes. Moreover, men will begin to see women, and women will see men, and simply have intercourse with each other, which is "more enjoyable than with humans and yet will inevitably cause illness that is difficult to cure."[54] In other words, you have to make yourself think hard enough about sexual intercourse before you should see a ghost of the other sex. You can control all the variables and reproduce the effect as you wish, and *only if* you wish.

The "Recipes for Women Wanting Men" section of *Heart of Medicine* consists of a single recipe from *The Classic of Great Purity* (Daqing jing).[55] It is worth quoting in full:

> [This recipe is for] women twenty-seven or twenty-eight, as well as twenty-two or twenty-three years old, with abundant *yin qi*, wanting [*yu*] to have men and unable to control themselves. They find all food and drink tasteless. The hundred vessels stir the body, and the *jing*-awaiting vessel is replete. Fluid excretions soil their clothes. Inside the women's *yin* parts there are worms like horsetails, three *fen* long; the ones with red heads cause irritation, and those with black heads produce froth.
>
> Treatment: Make a jade stem [i.e., phallus] out of dough, length and size free, wrap it with pure rice spirits and two pieces of cotton cloth, and insert it into the *yin*. The worms will attach to it and emerge. Take it out and insert it again. It is as though [the woman is] having a gentleman. There will be between twenty and thirty worms.[56]

The description of this condition and treatment is an intriguing mixture of ambiguities. It implies that such problems affect only women in their twenties, but we do not know whether this is true of most women at this age or only those with abundant (or perhaps excessive) *yin qi*. It is unclear whether abundant *yin qi* and the symptoms described are a natural state or a kind of disorder—or perhaps a natural disorder—for women at this age. It seems to imply that such women are not sexually active with men and their need (or desire) for men is the result of their abundant *yin qi*. But we do not know whether the worms are the cause or the symptom of abundant *yin qi*, or indeed what the worms are. The jade stem, however, seems to (conveniently) serve dual functions—to fish out the worms and to make it "as though [the woman] is having a gentleman." If the problem is caused by an unsatisfied demand for men, or the abundant *yin qi*'s demand for *yang qi*, it is curious that a phallus-shaped lump of dough will suffice to balance the *yin qi* and accomplish the mission.

This recipe seems even more peculiar when compared with other roughly contemporary prescriptions for vaginal worms. The recipe for "vaginal itchiness resembling crawling worms" in *Invaluable Formulas* is to wrap three medicinal ingredients (aluminite, Sichuan lovage rhizome, and cinnabar) with cotton cloth and insert them into the vagina, making "the worms automatically die." This is listed among other kinds of vaginal wounds and discomfort, without any reference to patients' ages or sexuality.[57] *Cui's Important Formulas* (Cuishi zuanyao fang; ca. late 7th–mid-8th c.) contains two recipes, one almost identical to the one cited here and the other using chicken liver.[58] Zhen Quan (541–643) also collected two recipes. One uses ox or pig liver to fish out the worms. Despite treating symptoms including "wanting to have men," the other recipe (processed carp bone and lard wrapped in cotton cloth) is simply to relieve the pain and nothing else.[59] None of these recipes associates vaginal worms with "abundant *yin*" or women of a particular age. *The Classic of Great Purity*, by comparison, reveals a peculiar gaze at young women's bodies and a fantasy about their desire for men. Taken together with the *Secret Instructions* passage about women's intercourse with ghosts, the hidden message seems to be: "It is fine for women not to have men, provided we know *exactly* what is going on."

Dreaming of Intercourse with Ghosts: Two Etiologies

As we have seen in bedchamber literature, intercourse with ghosts (or other malign entities) is considered a symptom of unfulfilled sexual desire and "forcefully refraining" from (hetero)sexual activities; the descriptions of men and women who have the problem are very different. But this etiology is not seen in pre-Song medical texts outside the bedchamber tradition. Other medical texts provide entirely different explanations for dreams, sexual dreams, and intercourse with ghosts—generally a combination of external intrusions (such as malign or deviant *qi*, ghosts, and demonic entities) and internal depletion—that do not take into account patients' desire or sexual status.[60] The bedchamber texts, in contrast, when discussing the cause of women's intercourse with ghosts, never include the preexisting condition of the woman's *qi*, blood, or *zang*- and *fu*-viscera. There seem to have been two parallel etiologies of sexual dreams and intercourse with ghosts—until the Song physician Qi Zhongfu.

In his *One Hundred Questions on Women's Medicine* (Nüke baiwen; 1220), Qi answers the question, "What are the causes of intercourse with ghosts at night?" as follows:

> Humans have the five viscera, in which reside the seven *shen*-spirits. If the viscera-*qi* is abundant, then the *shen*-spirits are strong, and external afflictions [*wai xie*] and ghosts cannot intrude. If [a person's] management and defense [of his or her body] miss the proper measures, and [his or her] blood and *qi* become depleted and weak, ghosts and malign forces will invade and cause damage. This is why many women dream of

intercourse with ghosts. They appear unwilling to see people, talk and laugh on their own as if being with someone, and at times weep sadly. Their pulses come slowly, and some resemble bird pecks. [Some who have such pulses] have no irregular complexion. These are all illnesses caused by malign entities. *It is said that nowadays court ladies, Buddhist nuns, and widows who have dreamed of intercourse with ghosts are affected by the malign* qi. *Over time it becomes* zheng- *and* jia-*conglomerates, and in some cases it develops into ghost fetuses. There are many such cases.*[61]

The first half of the passage, before the italicized sentence, is a paraphrase of Chao Yuanfang's *On the Origins and Symptoms of Various Illnesses* (Zhubing yuanhou lun; 610). The italicized sentence, however, is adapted from *Pulse Classic*. The original sentence is precisely the one discussed earlier.[62] In its original context, the sentence is about using the patient's marital status as an aid for diagnosing pregnancy. Qi Zhongfu rewrote the sentence and fit it into a different context, one about the causes and symptoms of ghost intercourse. It was not simply a textual bricolage. Qi added "Buddhist nuns," a category of people not present in third-century China, to the list of court ladies and widows. He also mentioned the "ghost fetus," a term not seen in *Pulse Classic*.[63] We do not know whether Qi consciously appropriated the sentence or was reading new ideas into old text. Either way, he treats court ladies, Buddhist nuns, and widows as a single class on the basis of their common manlessness and hints at manless women's susceptibility to ghost intercourse. The entire passage, however, is an awkward mixture of two etiologies, one focusing on the bodily mechanism of internal depletion and external intrusion and the other on sexual inactivity. The paragraph is written in a seemingly coherent style with no clear transition of voice. But Qi did not explain why court ladies, Buddhist nuns, and widows would have weaker "viscera-*qi*" and more depleted blood and *qi* than other women, which by Chao Yuanfang's explanation would make such women more susceptible to intercourse with ghosts.

This is another example of multiple textual layers in Song medical writing and of the convention of quoting or paraphrasing earlier texts without always citing the reference. Qi's passage appears less consciously constructed than Chen Ziming's discussion of *guafu*, but may still reveal a continuity between the bedchamber tradition and Song medical texts. Even if Song medical writers consciously excluded bedchamber texts from their compilations, they seem to have inherited to some extent the bedchamber authors' gaze at female sexuality.[64] Qi's explanation of the cause of women's inter-course with ghosts, Xu Shuwei's discussion of Buddhist nuns and widows, and Chen Ziming's *guafu* theory, display a rising interest in manless women and women's sexual desire among Song physicians.[65] But no other medical writers before or during Xu's time drew an explicit link between women's heterosexual inactivity, sexual desire, and reproductive bodies as Xu and Chen did.

Other Song-Jin Opinions

The Northern Song court-sponsored medical compilation *Formulas of Sacred Benevolence Under the Great Peace* (Taiping shenghui fang; compiled 978–92; *Sacred Benevolence* hereafter) quotes, via Tao Hongjing, Chu Cheng's remark on widows and nuns in its sections on swelling (*yongju*) and women's foot-*qi* (*jiaoqi*). In the former, the quote follows a discussion that explains how different lifestyles lead to different degrees of severity of the same illness, such as when upper-class people have worse symptoms than commoners when afflicted with swelling disorders. It then says, "For the same reason, Chu Cheng . . . treats widows, Buddhist nuns, and monks dif-ferently from wives and concubines. *It is because widows, nuns, and monks, although not exhausted by the bedchamber activities, suffer from distressed thoughts.* [Chu] knows deeply [his patients'] characters."[66] The italicized sen-tence, which is not in Tao's original quote, specifies what makes the two kinds of patients different: less bodily exhaustion and more distressed thoughts. Supposedly, both come from sexual inactivity; widows, nuns, and monks, although suffering from distressed thoughts, are not exhausted by the bedchamber activities. In other words, sexual inactivity is not all bad. Bedchamber activities in general, not just excessive ones, are also apparently a source of exhaustion.

Treatment for women's *jiaoqi* differs from men's because of "the damage resulting from gestation and childbirth," and "therefore Chu Cheng treated widows and nuns differently from wives and concubines." This focus on a nonreproductive aspect of a manless female body makes no mention of such women's desire or "thoughts." Notably, it regards pregnancy and childbirth, rather than the lack thereof, as a source of bodily damage. And it puts widows and nuns into the same category with men shared by their nongestative bodies.[67]

Sacred Benevolence was compiled not by a single author but a team under Northern Song imperial patronage. It takes an all-inclusive and pragmatic approach. The two interpretations of Chu Cheng may represent the diverse opinions of multiple authors or may also be one person's viewpoint on widows and nuns that include three aspects—sex (exhaustion from bed-chamber activities), desire (distressed thoughts), and procreation (damage of gestation and childbirth). Either way, this is an early Song example of relating women's celibacy to desire or frustration and to (non)reproduction *separately* rather than together. No link is drawn between women's sexual desire and their reproductive bodies.

Another Northern Song physician, Kou Zongshi, commented on virgin boys' and girls' excessive "thought" when discussing the physical effect of mental activities. The preface to his *Expanded Commentaries of Materia Medica* (Bencao yanyi; 1116) states: "There are virgin boys and maidens who have accumulated thought in their hearts and whose deliberation has transgressed what is appropriate. This often leads to the damage of exhaustion. [If they are] male, then their *shen*-spirits and countenance first disperse. [If they are] female, then their menses first stop. What causes this to be so? Worries and thought damage the heart. If the heart is damaged, the blood becomes reversed and dried up. Because the blood is reversed and dried up, *shen*-spirits and countenance first disperse and menses first stop."[68]

Before this passage, Kou makes reference to both Buddhism and Daoism in stressing the danger of "greed and desire" (*tanyu*) and all kinds of dissipation (*ziqing*). Immediately after this passage, Kou explains how the damage to the heart (corresponding to "fire" in the five phases) affects the spleen (earth), the lungs (metal), the kidneys (water), and the liver (wood)—in this sequence. The "exhaustion of water-*qi*" makes "the four limbs dry" and explains the menstrual blockage. The depletion of wood-*qi* makes one prone to anger. For Kou, this is "the most difficult to treat among all kinds of exhaustion [*lao*]," and the patients can only survive if they "are able to transform their own thought and mind" (*zineng gaiyi xinzhi*) and aid with medicine.

Sexual thoughts may be a major kind of worry for virgin boys and girls, given their shared sexual status. But in the larger picture, Kou does not make a categorical or pathological distinction between sexual and nonsexual thoughts. The heart can be the same damaged by too much thought and worries of other kinds. Moreover, virginity is not the only thing virgin boys and girls have in common—there is also age. This exhaustion problem is age specific and the patient is advised to work on his or her own mind. That means, first, that sexual thoughts are not uncontrollable impulses, and second, at the core of the problem is the person's immature mental capacity rather than sexual or reproductive impulses. There is no mention of the reproductive bodies of virgin boys and girls. It is different from both *Chu's Posthumous Work*, which mainly concerns how the age and frequency of sexual intercourse affect men and women's reproductive and general health, and bedchamber literature, which regards the loss of semen as the major source of damage. Whereas some bedchamber authors speak of women's desire for men as something that the women cannot control, Kou advises both boys and girls to transform their minds. It is also different from Chen Ziming's *guafu*, whose disorders are caused by "ample blood" (*xie sheng*); Kou's virgin boys and maidens suffer from accumulative thoughts and "reversed and dried-up blood" (*xie ni jie*).[69]

AFTER CHEN ZIMING

Xu Shuwei's case history and Chen Ziming's *guafu* discussion appear in a number of late imperial medical compilations. Most of these simply reproduce the passages in their entirety, as large medical compilations generally did when preserving and sometimes reorganizing previous medical texts. But because many of these large compilations aimed at being all-inclusive, it is not always clear what the compilers thought of the texts that they collected. Xue Ji's (1487–1558) *Annotated Good Formulas for Women* (Jiaozhu furen liangfang; 1547), a revision of Chen's *Good Formulas* with substantial commentaries, is an exception. Xue keeps Chen's original organization and section titles, revises the content, and adds his comments. In the *guafu* section, Xue trims Chen's original piece significantly. He removes Chen's claim of originality, the new definition of *guafu*, and the references to *Mencius* and *The Book of Changes*. In other words, Xue removes precisely what makes Chen different from Xu Shuwei, while keeping the medical category of "husbandless women" as well as the sex–desire–procreation link. In his comment, Xue adds five prescriptions, each corresponding to a group of different subsymptoms, and four short case histories. The four cases include one widow, one woman whose husband was away from home, and two maidens.[70] Xue's other book, *Xue's Case Histories* (Xueshi yi'an), in the section on "Buddhist Nuns' and Widows' [Intermittent] Cold and Heat," uses "the natural/spontaneous principle of Heaven and Earth" to describe men and women's bodily readiness for consummation and procreation—after quoting, "When a man's essence [*jing*] is ample, he thinks of a mate; when a woman's blood is ample, she conceives children." Xue does not cite or quote any Confucian classics.[71]

Other physicians offered radically different explanations and treatments. Zhu Zhenheng (1281–1358), a Yuan physician known for his attempt to synthesize Neo-Confucianism and medicine, once diagnosed a betrothed maiden as "thinking [*si*] of men and unable to have one, causing *qi* to congeal in the spleen." The woman's fiancé was away from home for five years, and she had the same pulse manifestation as Chunyu Yi's maidservant. But the association between manless women and "*qi* congealing in the spleen" does not appear in previous records. Instead of medicinal prescriptions, moreover, Zhu's treatment was to trigger the woman's anger, because the anger–liver–wood phase conquered the worry–spleen–earth phase. He went on to use the joy–heart–fire phase to nourish and sustain the spleen.[72] Unlike Xu Shuwei, Chen Ziming, or Xue Ji, Zhu did not discuss the woman's desire or "thought," where it came from, whether or not it was natural, or its relation to the reproductive body. He focused directly on the problem of the spleen. But in addition to working as therapeutic emotional manipulation, his interaction with the woman also seemed to suggest that such "thoughts" were inappropriate—he "reprimanded [the woman] for having thoughts beyond [her inner quarter]." In other words, for Zhu, women did not *necessarily* desire men; they also did not *have to* have men. This is evident in another record, which describes Zhu's treatment of a widow who suffered from *lai*—sores on the skin. Zhu regarded her illness as curable because she was "poor and without appetite for rich food, widowed and without desire" (*gua er wu yu*).[73] The problem is not heterosexual inactivity or reproductive readiness but the failure to manage one's thoughts in manless conditions.

As historian Hsiu-fen Chen notes, quite a few physicians from late imperial times came to identify excessive thoughts as a major cause of celibate women's illnesses, including intercourse with ghosts.[74] This would have been a much less problematic approach to manless women than that proposed by Xu Shuwei or Chen Ziming—because, by implication, it would not automatically render chaste widows less healthy and certainly would not turn female fidelity into something against the principle of Heaven and Earth. Not all celibate women are prone to sickness in this view, only those with excessive thoughts. The fundamental solution, by further implication, is not marriage, sex with men, or medicine but self-discipline. Quite a few authors of popular literature and drama from late imperial times, in contrast, took pleasure in depicting celibate women as spontaneously desiring men and, like the bedchamber authors, indulged in their fantasies about the young female body and sexuality.[75]

Historian Shigehisa Kuriyama notices "a modulation of accent" in the medical attention to emotions after the Song. From the Ming (1368–1644) onward, "anxieties about male dissolution were supplemented by keen attention to female frustrations." A critical development during the transition, as Kuriyama points out, was the emergence of a new vision of "fire" as "at once a vital necessity and a wild menace" as first elaborated by Zhu Zhenheng.[76]

Other possible sources of this new medical interest in desire and women without men include the bedchamber texts' gaze at female sexuality and obsession with women's desire for men, as well as the discussion of *yu* and the distinction between necessity and desire in Neo-Confucianism.

There was thus little medical discussion of female sexual desire in pre-Song sources except in bedchamber texts, which, in treating the ailments of manless women, gazed into women's sexual desire and paid little attention to women's generative or gestational body. Several Song medical texts, while excluding bedchamber texts from orthodox medicine, shared with the bedchamber authors the gaze at female sexual desire. Xu Shuwei and Chen Ziming were the first medical writers, and the only two during the Song period, to make explicit a (hetero)sex–desire–procreation link and to naturalize women's sexual desire for men. This new link, however familiar to a modern audience, was idiosyncratic in twelfth-century China. It was also incongruous with the family ethics of its time and the institution of widow chastity. The case of Chen Ziming, in particular, prompts reconsideration of what constituted medical discourse of the female body—how could one normalize female sexuality by asserting "women without men will become sick" and "young widows should remain chaste" at the same time? Much more medical attention focused on female sexual desire in post-Song times, and yet many Ming-Qing physicians identified "excessive thoughts" rather than the "principle of Heaven and Earth" as the main cause of the illnesses of husbandless women.

CHAPTER TWO

GHOST INTERCOURSE IN MEDICAL AND DAOIST CONTEXTS

DISCUSSIONS OF "GHOST INTERCOURSE" AND "GHOST FETUSES" (*guitai*) in medical and Daoist contexts—the causes, symptoms, diagnosis, and treatments—exceed modern assumptions about the parameters of sexuality and illness. If ghost intercourse was not always considered categorically distinct from other nonsexual dreams or ghost afflictions, we have to adjust the lens through which we look at historical sources, a lens that has been very much shaped by the modern invention of sexuality as a naturalized and universal category.

Ghost intercourse was often, although not always, associated with a ghost fetus. A comparison between records of ghost fetuses in medical texts and those in Song anecdotal accounts reveals the difficulty and dilemma that physicians faced in diagnosing and treating false pregnancies. Such a comparison prompts a reconsideration of the relationship between ghost fetuses and women's sexual status and desire. How were discussions of ghost intercourse gendered? What did it mean when women's manless state was not simply considered a cause but also a symptom of ghost intercourse? Was ghost intercourse a result of the lack or the excess of sexual activity, or simply its very existence? Daoist approaches to ghost intercourse, distinct from those of physicians, further expose the limitation of not simply the modern definition of sexuality but also that of illness. In Daoist manuals of self-cultivation or exorcism, ghost intercourse was often not distinguished in nature from other nonsexual illnesses, and it was even juxtaposed with other bodily functions that physicians did not consider symptomatic. To Daoist adepts, ghost intercourse was simply a contingency of being ordinary.

The Yellow Emperor's Inner Canon: Numinous Pivot (Huangdi neijing lingshu; ca. 2nd–1st c. BCE; *Lingshu* hereafter) identifies the cause of various dreams as external *qi*. As such "excessive and deviated" (*yin xie*) *qi* travels within the human body, it leads to surpluses or insufficiencies of proper *qi* in various viscera and body parts. A surplus or insufficiency in each body part produces a specific kind of dream. The "receding *qi*" (*jue qi*) that "lodges in the *yin* organ [i.e., the genitalia]" leads to "dreams of having intercourse with [consorts in the] inner [quarters]."[1] While the passage does not specify the patient's gender, the wording suggests that the targeted patient is male. This is only one among many dreams and their corresponding conditions on a long list. Sexual dreams were not distinguished categorically from nonsexual ones; nor was dreaming of sexual intercourse singled out as a distinctive type of illness.

Ge Hong's (283–343) *Formulas for Emergencies to Keep at Hand* (Zhouhou fang; *Formulas at Hand* hereafter) mentions ghost intercourse and sexual dreams in two larger categories of illness: "delirium caused by sudden malign shock" and "leaking urine in sleep and leaking *jing* [essence] in dreams." The former includes three recipes for "women who have intercourse with malign entities, speaking and laughing on their own, or in some cases in melancholia and delirium," and one for "men and women who dream frequently and have intercourse with ghosts, which leads to delirium." No specific cause is given. Three recipes are medicinal, using primarily realgar and deer antler; the other uses needles and exorcist ritual.[2] The latter includes five recipes for "men and women dreaming of intercourse with someone and hence leaking *jing*," and the cause is "inner depletion triggered by malign *qi*." Three recipes are medicinal, using primarily leek seed and dragon bone (animal fossils); two others are moxibustion.[3] The two categories represent the two major kinds of illnesses related to ghost intercourse and sexual dreams in medieval Chinese medical discussions.[4] One focuses on mental and behavioral disorders, and the other on the loss of *jing*. Although the former mentions men in one recipe, it is clear that the main subject is women. The latter treats both men and women without explicit emphasis on either. Both men and women can suffer from the loss of *jing* during sexual intercourse. As discussed in chapter 1, however, the bedchamber texts characterized the loss of *jing* as a major crisis for men. The gender separation of the two kinds of ghost intercourse became more salient in several medical texts of later times.

Men's and women's dreaming of intercourse with the other sex can also be a result of "wind affliction" (*fengxie*). A fifth-century text records a "separation powder" (*bieli san*) that "treats men's and women's wind affliction: men dreaming of women; women dreaming of men; chronic exhaustion out of sexual intercourse; sorrow, melancholia, and distress; sudden anger and sudden joy." The recipes use osier mistletoe and atractylode rhizome, among other medicinals. While according to the text this illness happens to both men and women, *Heart of Medicine* (10th c.) lists it under "Recipes for Women's Ghost Intercourse."[5]

Some recipes use large portions of powerful purging medicinals. *Monk Shen's Recipes* (Seng Shen fang; 5th c., preserved in *Heart of Medicine*) records the recipe of a certain "red pill in the jade jar of the Divine Mother of the West," made of realgar, aconite tuber the size of star anise, veratrum rhizome, supreme cinnabar, arsenopyrite, and croton fruit. It uses one "supreme grade" medicinal (cinnabar) as the "lord," one of "middle grade" (realgar) as the "minister," and four other "lower grade" medicinals as the "assisting courier." The lower grade medicinals, according to ancient Chinese materia medica, are "toxic," "expelling malign *qi* and breaking conglomerations."[6] This elixir cures numerous illnesses, including "men's and women's [affliction by] malign *qi*, intercourse with ghosts, singing and crying irregularly, and in some cases a swelling abdomen and the cessation of menses, which resemble [signs of] pregnancy."[7] The *Invaluable Formulas* (7th c.) includes an almost identical recipe that treats the same illnesses, named "pill in the jade jar of the immortals."[8] A "*qi*-freeing pill" (*tongqi wan*) consists of a large portion of Shu pepper (zanthoxylum, lower grade) and a combination of other medicinals (including centipede, lower grade), mixed in malt sugar. In cases of "dreaming of having intercourse and drinking and eating with ghosts," the instruction says, "use all centipede" instead.[9] Another "supreme pill against five *gu*-poisons" (*taishang wugu wan*), an early seventh-century recipe, uses a similar combination of ingredients: one supreme grade, one middle grade, and another eleven lower grade. It treats all kinds of *gu* poisons, including "dreaming of intercourse with ghosts" and "enchantment by fox demons."[10] The names of these recipes hint at their connection to religious exorcisms. Many of these medicinals were also known for their abortifacient effect.[11]

Chao Yuanfang's *On the Origins* (610) incorporates the entire *Lingshu* passage on dreams into the section "Depletion and Exhaustion" (Xulao). Chao emphasizes the preexisting bodily condition that allows external *qi* to intrude: the depletion and exhaustion of a person's *qi*, blood, and *zang*- and *fu*-viscera.[12] Although ghost intercourse and dreams of ghost intercourse supposedly happen to both men and women, they are listed only under "Women's Miscellaneous Disorders." Chao explains not simply the cause but also the method of diagnosis:

> Human's lives are endowed with the refined *qi* of the five phases and nourished by the *qi* of the *shen*-spirits in the five viscera. If [a person's] *yin* and *yang* are harmonious, his or her *zang*- and *fu*-viscera are strong and replete, then wind-affliction and ghosts would not be able to cause harm. If [a person's] management and defense [of his or her body] miss the proper measures, and [his or her] blood and *qi* become depleted and weak, wind-affliction will override the depleted, and ghosts will disturb the proper [condition]. As for women who have intercourse with ghosts, their *zang*- and *fu*-viscera are depleted, their *shen*-spirits' guard weak, and therefore ghost *qi* is capable of affecting them. They appear unwilling to see people, talk and laugh on their own as if being with someone, and at times weep sadly. The pulses come slowly and discreetly, and some resemble bird pecks—these are all [pulse manifestations of] illnesses caused by malign entities. There are also cases where the pulses come subtly and continuously and cannot be counted, and the woman has no irregular complexion—these are also [signs of] illness.[13]

As in his discussion of dreams, Chao identifies the cause of "intercourse with ghosts" as a combination of external intrusions and internal depletion. The external forces are more specifically "ghost *qi*," but the internal condition is very similar—the depletion of the patient's *qi*, blood, and *zang*- and *fu*-viscera. "Intercourse with ghosts" happens to both men and women. From this passage alone it is hard to tell if Chao considered women as more susceptible to such condition. The wording is ambiguous: it could be read as either "for those women who have intercourse with ghosts, their viscera are depleted" or "the reason that women have intercourse with ghosts is that their viscera are depleted." Either way, we do not know whether Chao meant that women in general had more depleted viscera than men or that only women who had ghost intercourse did. Although it was quite likely that Chao deemed women in general weaker than men, he did not seem to be more interested in making generalizations other than in discussing women's individual conditions. There is also no indication of any correlation between the patient's sexual status, desire, and his or her chances of contracting this illness. The symptoms, however, are gendered. In the bedchamber texts, the symptoms of women's ghost intercourse also include withdrawal from personal interactions and seemingly responding to someone invisible. Chao's description of the symptoms lacks anything that we would consider sexual today. Furthermore, Chao expected his readers to observe the patients' behavior and complexion *as well as* their pulses. The inclusion of pulse lore suggests that Chao's intended readers were his fellow practicing physicians and that their specialist skill could accurately pinpoint the problem. Chao's etiology was widely quoted by later medical works and set the basis for medical opinions on this issue throughout the Song.[14]

Formularies and pharmacopeias from the Tang (618–907) recorded several new recipes and medicinals that treated ghost intercourse and specifically fox and spirit enchantment; some medicinals were newly incorporated from areas beyond China's central plain. For instance, *Cui's Important Formulas* (ca. late 7th–mid-8th c.) records a recipe for "treating dreaming of intercourse with ghosts and spirits, enchantment by foxes and goblins, and such." The ingredients include old medicinals, such as realgar and atractylode rhizome, and new ones such as fox's nose, leopard's nose, seal's genital (*wana qi*), and asafetida (*ewei*).[15] Fox and leopard were not in the original *Divine Farmer's Materia Medica* (Shennong bencao jing); Tao Hongjing's *Annotated Materia Medica* mentioned both; but only during the Tang did pharmacologists begin to speak of them as apotropaics and to distinguish the effects of different parts.[16] Seal's genital was imported from Silla (Korea).[17] Asafetida was from Central Asia.[18]

A rather obscure text, *On Ingesting Minerals* (Fushi lun; ca. 8th c., preserved in *Heart of Medicine*), mentions a mysterious "golden fluid floral divine elixir" (*jinyi huashen dan*) that "cures all illnesses," including "men, women, Buddhist monks and nuns, widows, young women [maiden], and the like dreaming of intercourse with ghosts and spirits." It seems to suggest a link between sexual inactivity and ghost intercourse. But this passage was not likely part of an ordinary medical text authored by a physician. Unlike with other drugs in traditional Chinese pharmacology, there is nothing that one needs to avoid or be careful of when taking this miraculous panacea. Furthermore, there is no recipe because it was the secret formula of a certain immortal deity: "The recipe of this drug is not known to the mundane." Perhaps not surprisingly, the symptoms resemble those recounted in bedchamber texts: "[The experience of ghost intercourse] truly resembles that with a living person for the first time; [the patient] will be too ashamed to confess and later simply disclose it altogether. As it prolongs, ghost *qi* is attached to the body and constitutes illness in the abdomen. Cherishing the affection of [or for] the ghost, [the patient] will not turn away from the entanglement of the enchanting ghost and malign *qi* even until death."[19] No cause is given; the patient's desire for the ghost comes *after* the affliction. Other surviving passages of the text mostly concern mineral ingestion, a form of bodily practice for immortality or longevity.[20]

Song medical discussions of the causes of ghost intercourse in general did not exceed *Formulas at Hand* and *On the Origins*. Many Song texts simply quoted or paraphrased *On the Origins* on this subject, such as the court commissioned *Sacred Benevolence* (978–992) and Chen Ziming's *Good Formulas for Women* (1237). Only Qi Zhongfu's *One Hundred Questions on Women's Medicine* (1220), as discussed in the previous chapter, for the first time drew an implicit link between ghost intercourse and women's sexual status. After the Song lost its territory in north China to the Jurchens in 1127, the geopolitical separation between north and south contributed to the development of separate medical traditions. Zhang Congzheng (1156–1228), a physician of the Jin dynasty (1115–1234) in north China had a different opinion. A case history records that he treated a married woman of thirty-three, who, for fifteen years, "dreamed of intercourse with ghosts and deities at night," and in dreams she saw shrines and the underworld, ships and bridges. Rather than conceiving a ghost fetus, the woman was simply unable to become pregnant. Zhang diagnosed her illness as belonging to the "damp type" (*shixing*); what the woman saw in her dreams were all symptoms of an overflow of *yin* and water in her body.[21]

None of these texts treats suppressed or excessive desire as the cause of such illness. Furthermore, no extant Chinese medical text from before the thirteenth century drew an explicit link between heterosexual inactivity and ghost intercourse, except for the bedchamber literature. The first medical writer who clearly explicated a positive correlation between the patient's desire and ghost intercourse was the Yuan physician, Zhu Zhenheng. The bedchamber authors, while encouraging men to take control of their own desire, regarded women's "deep desire [for men]" as an inevitable outcome of their manless state. Zhu, in contrast, asserted that both men and women should and could take control of their desire regardless of their sexual status. The cause of ghost intercourse was not spontaneous but improper desire. Zhu asserted: "Ghosts have no form. They only respond [to humans] and become connected. [Women dream of intercourse with ghosts] because their minds are not upright [*xinnian buzheng*] and therefore attract the ghost. Ghosts attach to the malign *qi* [*xieqi*] to enter the human body and connect to the person's *shen*-spirit. This is why [the patient] frequently sees the ghost in dreams." This concorded with Zhu's rationale of his treatment of an engaged maiden and a widow discussed in the previous chapter. To Zhu, it was not inevitable for women to desire men; additionally, it was not the quantity but the quality, or the propriety, of desire that mattered. While giving an entirely new explanation to the cause of this centuries-old illness—different from both the bedchamber literature and other medical traditions, Zhu did not alter the medicinal recipes for the treatment.[22]

GENDERED SYMPTOMS AND THE IMPERCEPTIBLE WOMEN

Bedchamber literature and other medical texts explained the causes of ghost intercourse in different ways. But the symptoms described in both were gendered. The main concern for men's intercourse with ghosts in the bedchamber texts was preserving or losing *jing*; for women, however, it was about their lack of interest in (real) men, their uncontrollable desire, and inexplicable behavior. In other medical texts, as mentioned earlier, *Formulas at Hand* already implied a gendered distinction between the two kinds of ghost intercourse. *On the Origins* had one section for more general "symptoms of exhaustion and frequent dreams" (*xulao ximeng*), sexual dreams included, and another specifically for "women having intercourse with ghosts." Symptoms such as unwillingness to see people, talking and laughing to oneself, and inexplicable tears only appeared in the women section.[23] The gender difference was still salient in *Sacred Benevolence*, which incorporated a large number of recipes up to its time. Like *On the Origins*, *Sacred Benevolence* discussed intercourse with ghosts chiefly in the two sections: "exhaustion and dreams of intercourse with ghosts" and "women's intercourse with ghosts." The former began with citing *On the Origins'* general discussion of the cause. The symptoms in the subsections indicated that the target patients were men: four out of six subsections included the symptom of leaking or losing *jing*.[24] The rest of the symptoms included feeble and emaciated limbs, depleted and restless heart (*xinshen xufan*), itchy genitals, leaking urine, and pain in the loins and knees.[25] In contrast, women's symptoms, in line with those described in *On the Origins*, were mostly delirious behavior and inexplicable emotional expressions—such as seeing or hearing what others did not see or hear, inconsistent speech, and irregular laughter, tears, or anger.[26] The men's section also included behavioral symptoms, but in comparison, women's symptoms were characterized by a loss of subjectivity and a sense of imperceptibility.

Ghost intercourse also appeared as a symptom in the sections relating to "corpse transmission" (*chuanshi*, a kind of fatal and transmissive disease) and women's "bone fever" (*guzheng*, another name for *chuanshi*).[27] Corpse transmission afflicted all regardless of sex or age. One group of symptoms was similar to those of men's exhaustion—*jing* leaking, pain in the abdomen and genitals, and emaciation. The other was more behavioral, including a disturbed mind as if drunk, hyperbolic and inexplicable words, fright, dreams of ghostly intercourse, and a delirious mind—supposedly, this happened to both men and women. But descriptions of women's bone fever contained some familiar female-specific symptoms side-by-side with ghost intercourse: irregular emotions (now happy, now angry) and an unwillingness to see people.[28]

For some physicians, inconsistent speech and inexplicable emotional expressions could also be symptoms of women's other problems. The *Synopsis Recipes from the Golden Cabinet* (Jinkui yaolüe; by Zhang Ji (145–208); *Golden Cabinet* hereafter) listed two kinds of women's disorders whose symptoms resembled those of ghost affliction: "heat entering the blood chamber" (*re ru xieshi*) and "visceral agitation" (*zangzao*). The former happened when women caught the "cold damage" and were feverish during their menstrual period. During the day their minds were still clear, but at night they talked deliriously "as if seeing a ghost" (*ru jian gui zhuang*). Women with "visceral agitation," in contrast, were "prone to sadness and tears" and yawned frequently; the symptoms "resemble what spirits do [to women]" (*xiang ru shenling suozuo*).[29] Both Wang Shuhe's *Pulse Classic* (3rd c.) and Sun Simiao's *Supplement to Formulas Worth a Thousand* (Qianjin yifang) contain identical passages.

The Bureau for Revising Medical Texts (Jiaozheng Yishu Ju), which the Northern Song court established in 1057, collated fragments of Zhang Ji's works and published them as the *Golden Cabinet* and *Discussion of Cold Damage* (Shanghan lun).[30] The Song editions of Zhang's works became the most widely circulated ones from then on. Xu Shuwei, known for his familiarity with and application of Zhang's works, applied Zhang's diagnoses and treatments for both "heat entering the blood chamber" and "visceral agitation" in his practice. In one case record, Xu recounted how he treated the sister of a local academy official in Piling (in present-day Jiangsu). The patient was already in a coma when Xu arrived. Xu asked her mother about her symptoms before the coma, and her mother said that she "spoke deliriously at night as if seeing a ghost." Xu further asked if she was menstruating when first sick. The mother confirmed and added that there was fever. Xu then came to the conclusion that this patient suffered from what Zhang Ji described as "heat entering the blood chamber," treated her accordingly, and succeeded.[31]

In another account, Xu described how he treated a village woman who "wept ceaselessly for no reason" and yawned frequently. Her family thought it was ghost affliction and had used exorcism, which did not work. Xu "suddenly recalled" the description of "visceral agitation" in the *Golden Cabinet* and successfully cured the woman's illness with a decoction of licorice, wheat, and jujube (*gan mai dazao tang*), as the text prescribed.[32] Chen Ziming also recalled that a pregnant woman, the wife of a local scholar, in his hometown once appeared "woeful at night, shed sad tears, and yawned frequently as if possessed." Another scholar (likely a scholar-physician) recalled that he once learned of a disorder called "visceral agitation and distress" that matched the symptoms; the treatment was the previously mentioned decoction. Chen later incorporated this case and the recipe, along with Xu's record of the village woman, into his *Good Formulas for Women*.[33]

This brief history of women's "heat entering the blood chamber" and "visceral agitation" in Chinese medical discussions tells us a few things. First of all, from as early as the second century to as late as the Southern Song, symptoms such as delirious speech and inexplicable distress, in general understanding, had been associated with women's ghostly enchantment. Physicians, however, developed a separate set of knowledge to make distinctions between actual enchantment disorder and what merely resembled it—based on other contingent symptoms and conditions. But no matter whether these symptoms were regarded as being caused by ghosts or not, to many physicians' eyes, they were *women's* symptoms.

Another symptom unique to women was their "unwillingness to see people" (*bu yu jian ren*). If we read *yu* in a semantically open way as explained in chapter 1, this phrase could simply mean women being unpresentable or inapproachable. The people that women were expected to see and to interact with were most likely their direct family members, including and perhaps especially their husbands. The fact that this "symptom" applied almost exclusively to women tells us something about the expectation of women's sociability and approachability at home as an integral part of their womanhood.

Manlessness was not considered a cause of women's ghost intercourse in most medical texts, but was often a result. One bedchamber text also implied that women's manless status was not simply the cause but also a symptom: the *Secret Instructions* stated that the way of ghostly intercourse "surpasses that of human's" and, if no intervention was taken, the women afflicted would die *alone*.[34] In tales and anecdotes, women's indifference to their husbands and their unapproachability were often signs of enchantment. To consider women's manlessness as a cause means that it should be avoided lest it lead to certain problems. As a symptom, however, it is a problem that needs to be rectified.

The connection between women's ghost intercourse and false pregnancy had been drawn as early as the third-century *Pulse Classic* and fifth-century *Monk Shen's Recipes*, although neither text used the term "ghost fetus" (*guitai*). The term became commonly used in medical literature only after the seventh century. The contexts where such a connection was mentioned in both texts reflected less of the authors' personal insight than a common sense of the time. Both texts spoke of ghost intercourse and false pregnancy to make other points: a condition to aid diagnosing true pregnancy in the *Pulse Classic*, and one among many illnesses that a miraculous elixir cured in *Monk Shen's Recipes*. Neither treated the link between ghost intercourse and false pregnancy as something that required explanation or argument. And neither bothered to explain what caused ghost intercourse.

The fact that no specific term was used in reference to false pregnancies resulting from ghost intercourse probably meant that this kind of false pregnancy was not distinguished categorically from either other kinds of false pregnancy or other kinds of lumps in the belly. Even true pregnancies, as Yi-Li Wu points out in her study of ghost fetuses, were not differentiated from false ones in nature; they were "two points on the same continuum" and formed in processes analogous to each other.[35] True pregnancies were results of the inter-affection (*jiaogan*) between a *yang qi* (usually but not necessarily from a man) and a *yin qi*, after the *yang qi* entered a woman's womb, which usually but not always happened during sexual intercourse. A false pregnancy arose when either the *yang qi* or the *yin qi* was corrupted or replaced with something else.

Cases of anomalous pregnancy and monstrous births were recorded in other types of texts from early medieval China as well, most frequently in tales about "affected pregnancy" (*ganyun*) and records of political omens (*zaiyi*; literally, "catastrophes and anomalies"). The term "affected pregnancy" often referred to pregnancies that were not the result of physical sexual intercourse. Some affected pregnancies produced human babies and others did not, depending on the source of the penetrating *qi*. In the literature of political omen interpretation, monstrous births (among many other kinds of anomalies) were the result of a larger scope of *qi* in the universe being corrupted by political failure; the bodies affected were victims, and the rulers were responsible. This is similar to the emphasis on external pathogens in early medical texts and distinct from the shift in focus on the patient's internal imbalances following *On the Origins*.

On the Origins began to use the term "ghost fetus," emphasized the same internal causes of both ghost intercourse and ghost fetuses, and explicated the mechanism by which ghost fetuses were formed: the *jing* of enchanting demons and ghosts entering the viscera.[36] By identifying the intruding pathogen as the *jing* of demons and ghosts and naming such a condition ghost fetuses, *On the Origins* differentiated this specific form of false pregnancy from others. The term "ghost fetus" or a discussion of false pregnancy, however, was rarely seen in extant Tang sources. Song medical texts, in contrast, generally adopted the etiology and classification of *On the Origins* and frequently used the term "ghost fetus." The Song uses of the term, nonetheless, seemed to include a wider variety of false and malign pregnancies as well as tumors in the womb.

Sacred Benevolence, for instance, under "Recipes for Women with Ghost Fetuses in the Abdomen," first quotes *On the Origins*' etiology and then lists recipes for treating the following conditions:

1. Women's ghost fetuses, acute and piercing pain in the abdomen nonstop day and night.
2. Women's menstrual blockage for one to three months, *qi* tumors in the abdomen, and [pains] arising from both sides of the upper chest and rushing to the heart—these are [symptoms of] ghost fetuses.
3. Pregnancies of ghost fetuses cause frequent discharge of dark blood and pain in the abdomen.
4. Women's ghost fetuses and blood and *qi* [disorders] that are unbearable.
5. Women's menstrual blockage, *zheng*-conglomerates filling the abdomen, and ghost fetuses.
6. Women's depletion and emaciation, ghost fetuses, *zheng*-conglomerates, and menstrual blockage.[37]

Most of the ingredients had been used in previous recipes for ghost intercourse, *gu*-poisons, abdominal tumors, and menstrual blockage since pre-Song times.[38] The compilers of *Sacred Benevolence* aimed at being inclusive and, in most cases, did not comment on the similarities or differences among the recipes. Nor did they elaborate on or revise the old etiology. All recipes, nonetheless, were to "free the blockage" (*tong*), to "discharge" (*xiali*), or to "drop the fetus" (*taixia*). Zhu Duanzhang's *Life-Guarding and Precious Household Handbook for Childbirth* (Weisheng jiabao chanke beiyao; 1184; *Handbook for Childbirth* hereafter) included a different recipe that specifically "drops ghost fetuses"; there was no discussion of the cause.[39] Chen

Ziming's *Good Formulas for Women* simply quoted *On the Origins* and selected four out of the six recipes from *Sacred Benevolence*.[40]

It seemed that for Song medical writers, treatments for ghost fetuses were mainly about removing whatever was stuck in the womb that was hurting the patient or was not going to develop into a child. The etiology did not seem to matter much, even if the term "ghost fetus" was widely used.[41] But perhaps a more difficult task for Song physicians was not to remove a ghost fetus but to diagnose one—especially for married women, considering that a misdiagnosis could mean aborting a true fetus. Diagnoses of ghost fetuses recorded in medical texts were quite different from those in tales or nonspecialist anecdotes. *Sacred Benevolence* did not specify diagnostic methods, but ghost fetuses were always accompanied by other much more obvious symptoms: menstrual blockage, irregular discharges, pain, or other kinds of discomfort. The *Handbook for Childbirth*'s recipe for "dropping ghost fetuses" was to be used when "a woman appears to be pregnant but the child does not come out during long labor, in some cases for three or five days; it is a case of ghost fetus."[42] In other words, in medical treatises and formularies by the thirteenth century, a ghost fetus was only diagnosed when there were noticeable discomforts during pregnancy or complications during labor.

In tales and anecdotes, however, a woman pregnant with a ghost fetus often did not have obvious symptoms. There were few stories about demonic pregnancies before the Song.[43] I found only three stories involving pregnancies caused by spirit intrusion—one from the fifth century and two from the eighth century. Although these instances were not called ghost fetuses, all were results of intercourse with demonic spirits. All were caused by animal spirits, and the women gave birth to the same kinds of animals that had intercourse with them. One woman showed symptoms of spirit enchantment; the others did not. In the fifth-century account the afflicted women were six palace courtesans. In the two eighth-century tales both women were unmarried maidens. Their pregnancies did not appear to be different from ordinary ones until they gave birth to nonhuman babies.[44]

In Song anecdotes, spirit-inflicted pregnancies, like ghost intercourse, also happened to both married and unmarried women regardless of their sexual status. But the ways in which married and unmarried women were found to be carrying a ghost fetus were different. For a married woman, it was often not until she gave birth to a monster or had an unusually prolonged pregnancy that people identified her as a victim of spirit infliction. For unmarried maidens, however, the stories usually began with the parents noticing their daughter's growing belly and the daughter's confession of having intercourse with a ghost, a deity, or an unknown spirit. The demonic fetus would then be purged with the use of medicinals or rituals or a combination of both.[45] The term *guitai*, or ghost fetus, appears in only two accounts in the extant parts of *Record of the Listener*, a twelfth-century collection of contemporary anecdotes about the extraordinary. One is about the demon-deity Wutong, who brought fountains of wealth to a poor peddler in exchange for his entire family's worship and devotion. It was said that "women [in this household] all had intercourse with the spirit [*ganjie*] and some gave birth to ghost fetuses."[46] This is another example of a woman's sexual or marital status being irrelevant to whether or not she was susceptible to ghost intercourse or ghost-afflicted pregnancy.

The other ghost fetus reference in *Record of the Listener* is in an account that records several successful medical treatments by a physician named Yang Daozhen. Yang, once a soldier in Jiankang (present-day Nanjing), was convicted of a certain crime and was tattooed and exiled to Raozhou (in present-day Jiangxi). He called himself a "man of Dao" (*Daoren*, an epithet that could refer to a Buddhist, Daoist, or an eclectic religious practitioner during the Song). Yang "had always been good at medicine and was particularly skilled in acupuncture." He cured two patients of chronic nasal bleeding with needles. He was also summoned to see a rich man's concubine, who was eight-months pregnant, always felt sleepy, and lacked appetite. But she herself "could not quite describe the discomfort." Yang took her pulse and said, "This is not a good pregnancy. I am afraid it is a ghost fetus." The family was very unhappy and challenged his diagnosis. Therefore, Yang did not prescribe anything besides the mild fetal stabilization formula that the pregnant woman had already been taking. He said to the family, "You will know [that I am right] in the future." After two months, the woman gave birth to a small creature that resembled a frog. With hindsight, the record concludes, "her belly had been larger than the ordinary ones since conception . . . not until now did [the family] believe it to be a ghost fetus."[47]

Chao Yuanfang described in his *On the Origins* the pulse manifestations of women who had dreams of ghost intercourse, but there was otherwise no historical record of the actual practice of such pulse diagnosis from Chao's time to the end of the Song. The story here is the only reference before the thirteenth century, to my knowledge, of a physician using pulse diagnosis to determine ghost fetus during a woman's pregnancy. The woman, according to this account, was a "favored concubine" (*chongqie*), in other words, not manless at all. There was no mention of any suspicious behavior or encounters. The fact that Yang diagnosed a ghost fetus simply by taking her pulse highlights his outstanding medical skill in the narrative. This probably also meant that it was very rare for any healer to assert that a married woman had a ghost fetus before she suffered from complications or actually gave birth to a monster (or a simple lump). Such assertion was risky because the treatment for ghost fetuses was basically abortion.[48] Yang was also cautious and did not prescribe abortifacient drugs because the family was already angry with his diagnosis. We do not know exactly what triggered the family's anger—the story was told as though no explanation was needed. It could perhaps be an indication that ghost fetuses were generally associated with ghost intercourse in popular perception. It could also be that a diagnosis of a ghost fetus meant no baby for the family at that time. Either way, in this case the ghost fetus was irrelevant to the woman's sexual status, and whether or not she had the experience of ghost intercourse was not part of the diagnosis. Yang was not an elite physician like most medical writers. The case of the ghost fetus described here was quite different from what we see in concurrent medical texts—the woman had only minor discomfort during pregnancy and did not suffer any complications during labor.

Another account in *Record of the Listener* tells how the physician Pan Jing treated three women who had experienced significantly prolonged pregnancies. Pan was likely an elite physician, or at least made himself appear like one, for he had a styled name in addition to his formal one. His clinical practice was still quite different from what we see in the surviving medical texts. One woman was pregnant for five years, another two years, and the other fourteen months. Pan asserted that these were all "illnesses" (*ji*) and that "mediocre physicians confused them with pregnancy [*youshen*]." He prescribed abortifacient for all three of them. The first woman discharged "more than a hundred lumps of flesh that appeared to have eyebrows and eyes." The second woman dreamed of two boys of dark complexion fleeing in horror. The third gave birth to a giant snake. All three women recovered afterward.[49] Pan did not record these cases as ghost fetuses. But he explicitly declared that these were not pregnancy but illness, and the immediate outcomes of his treatment suggested demonic involvement, although it was not clear whether these involvements were sexual. In Song medical texts and earlier ones that circulated during the Song, the descriptions of ghost fetuses did not include prolonged pregnancy; prolonged pregnancies were associated with underdeveloped (human) fetuses and not ghost fetuses or other kinds of false pregnancy.[50]

In sum, in Song sources, ghost fetuses and monstrous births were not always considered a result of ghost intercourse. Even when they were or seemed to be, they were not correlated with women's sexual status or desire. *On the Origins* regarded ghost fetuses as an outcome of ghost intercourse, and Song medical authors shared this opinion. But with regard to diagnosis and treatment, Song medical texts associated ghost fetuses most closely with obvious symptoms of illness during pregnancy or complications during labor. In anecdotes, however, spirit-inflicted pregnancies often did not come with obvious symptoms. It was usually not until a married woman had given birth to a monstrous baby or an unmarried maiden had confessed to spirit intercourse that the pregnancy was considered one with a ghost fetus.

Yang Daozhen's medical case was a significant exception, which further attested to how tricky it was for a physician to diagnose and treat ghost fetuses. If the medical treatment for ghost fetuses was primarily abortifacient recipes, it was not surprising that a physician would have been more reluctant to make such a claim when treating a married woman than they would with an unmarried or widowed woman. In light of this, if we revisit Qi Zhongfu's statement about "court ladies, Buddhist nuns, and widows who have dreamed of intercourse with ghosts" being "affected by the malign *qi*" that "in some cases developed into ghost fetuses," it might not have been because manless women were more susceptible to conceiving ghost fetuses but because physicians were more willing to diagnose manless women with ghost fetuses.

Descriptions of ghost fetuses in medical treatises since the fourteenth century were distinctively different from those of the Song. Most noticeable was the opinion that ghost fetuses were actually not caused by spirits but by the woman's excessive desire, which led to the congestion of *qi* and blood in the womb.[51] Even for those who still regarded spirits as the intruding external pathogen, more attention was paid to women's desire than before. Certain symptoms and some of the narrative styles, however, were similar to Song anecdotes. For instance, when Hua Shou (1304–1386) diagnosed that the daughter of a temple custodian was pregnant with a ghost fetus, there was no other symptom than the woman's growing belly and her confession (through her mother) about her sexual encounter with a "yellow-robed deity." Hua's case history is preserved in Yu Tuan's (1438–1517) criticism. Yu disagreed with Hua regarding the cause of the woman's "ghost fetus." He asserted that (spirits of) temple statues had no *jing* to form a fetus, and that the case was "not [caused by] the deity's enchantment of the woman but the woman's fascination with the deity." Yu further "speculated that the woman was grown-up and yet had no husband," and her "endless thoughts and desire were not fulfilled."[52]

Lü Fu (14th c.) treated a maiden in a similar fashion. The maiden also did not have obvious symptoms other than menses blockage and a pregnant-like belly. The narrative says that Lü made the diagnosis based on her complexion and pulse manifestation, and the diagnosis was conveniently confirmed by the girl's confession (through an elder maidservant) that she had dreamed of having intercourse with a deity that she saw in a temple. Lü then explained that her now-red, now-pale complexion was an indication of her shame and her now-strong, now-weak pulses were signs of spirt infliction.[53] The complexion and pulse manifestation here were different from what Chao Yuanfang described about ghost intercourse in the seventh century. Both Hua Shou's and Lü Fu's records mention that the deities encountered caused the women's "hearts to stir" (*xindong*).

Fu Shan (1607–1684) in his monograph on women's medicine discussed "[married women's] ghost fetuses" and "[unmarried] maiden's ghost fetuses" back-to-back but separately. The major symptom for married women's ghost fetuses was prolonged pregnancy, "even as long as two or three years." This opinion was not seen in Song medical texts but in Pan Jing's case histories in *Record of the Listener*. Fu further explicated that either "erotic thoughts arising from visiting a temple" or "ideas of affectionate intercourse emerging from sojourning in the mountain woods" could attract spirits. If the woman still had shame, spirits could not stay long, although one intercourse was enough to conceive a ghost fetus. For unmarried maidens, the symptoms were "the sudden pause of menses, the abdomen as large as if pregnant, complexion now red and now pale, and the pulses in the six positions now strong and now weak." These symptoms were identical to those recorded in Lü Fu's case history. Fu commented, "If one keeps oneself upright, various evils would not dare to offend; if oneself is not upright, various evils would naturally offend."[54] Similar to Zhu Zhenheng's theory of ghost intercourse, Fu regarded ghost fetuses as a result of women's excessive and inappropriate desire, which, however, was not a product of manlessness but of individual moral defect.

EXORCISM AND THE DAOIST REMEDIES
FOR THE ORDINARY

Descriptions about "intercourse with ghosts," or ghost and demon afflictions in general, appeared in two types of Daoist texts: those about immortality cultivation for the Daoist adepts themselves, and those about exorcisms that the Daoist ritual masters perform for others. Both insisted on "separating human from ghost" (*qubie* or *fenbie ren gui*).[55] Unlike most medical texts, these Daoist texts were written for specialists only. The exorcist manuals focused on various ritual treatments (mostly talismans) and did not always mention the cause, whereas the cultivation texts often elaborated on the causes—usually the practitioner's lack of caution or discipline.[56] The cultivation texts usually did not explicitly specify the gender of the practitioner, although in some cases we can imply that the intended readers were male. In the exorcism manuals, on the other hand, some talismans and rituals treated specifically "women's ghostly intercourse" and some descriptions resonated with those in Song anecdotes and medical texts. Several Song medical compilations incorporated a variety of treatment methods beyond medicinal recipes, including Daoist talismans, although medicinal recipes were predominantly the majority in Song formularies.[57]

Wang Xichao, a Southern Song Daoist priest, in his 1205 annotation of an early Lingbao scripture, described the "eight leaks" that practitioners should avoid during their thousand-day-long fast: "Tears leak the liver. Nasal mucus leaks the lungs. Saliva leaks the kidneys. Sweat leaks the heart. Night sweat leaks the small intestines. Drooling during sleep leaks the brain. Dreaming of intercourse with ghosts leaks the *shen*-spirit. Lust [*yinyu*] leaks bodily substance."[58] All eight actions were considered harmful to the body even if most of them seem to be ordinary bodily functions to us. To a Daoist practitioner, it was precisely the accumulation of such ordinary bodily functions that led to aging and death. In other words, "dreaming of intercourse with ghosts" in this particular context was less an "illness" to be cured than a bodily reaction as ordinary as having tears, nasal mucus, saliva, and sweat.

The Ming Celestial Master (Tianshi), Zhang Yuchu (1361–1410), described the *hun*-spirits' intercourse with ghosts as a more serious problem that was deviant and excessive. If, on one's birthday, when one's *hun*-spirits descend onto the body, one indulges oneself in activities such as drinking and sex that pollute the body, the *hun*-spirits would then fail to join the body and the *po*-spirits therein.[59] As a result, the person's "*yang* declines and *yin* flourishes, the *hun*-spirits have intercourse with *yin* ghosts," which leads to "wandering among various evils in dreams," hypersomnia, delirium, and all kinds of illness.[60] In this context, the cause of ghostly intercourse was not the lack of sexual intercourse or unfulfilled desire but precisely the opposite— having sex in the times when the practitioners should be abstinent. The text refers to its readers as the "gentlemen of supreme learning" (*shangxue zhi shi*).[61] When speaking of "indulgence in drinking and sex," it most likely meant indulgence by the practitioners' standards, not those of ordinary people. In other words, such indulgence should have referred not to addiction to alcohol or sex but to the practitioners' failure to observe a fast. The result of such a failure, however, was physical and mechanical. The mechanism of illnesses and the movements of *hun* and *po* applied to everyone and not just the practitioners. In this respect, ghostly intercourse could still be deemed an ordinary condition, just like drinking and having sex on one's birthday. Ordinary men and women got sick; Daoist practitioners aimed for the extraordinary.

The Daoist traditions provided other services for ordinary men and women who got sick, such as exorcism, which flourished since the twelfth century. The "new therapeutic movements" and the emergence of a class of exorcists called "ritual masters" (*fashi*) in the twelfth century coincided with the burgeoning of new Daoist lineages in south and southeast China that specialized in various exorcist "methods" (*fa*).[62] The centuries-old Daoist tradition, Orthodox Unity (Zhengyi), also assimilated the new therapeutic movements, and their priests, the Celestial Masters, came to be portrayed almost exclusively as exorcists. When incorporating the new therapeutic movements, the Celestial Masters returned to the concerns of their Han dynasty predecessors—therapeutic ritual. What differed, however, was that during the Song, the Celestial Masters, like other Daoist and non-Daoist ritual masters, provided their exorcist-therapeutic service not to "self-conscious religious communities" but to a "secularized society." As a result, in the exorcist ritual manuals that gave instructions to combat demons, illness was dissociated from morality and no longer (or not simply) the result of sin.[63] In this sense, illness was also a contingency of being ordinary.

The treatments in the Daoist ritual manuals mostly differed from those in medical texts, but the classification and terms of illnesses resembled what we see in Song medicine. The Daoist exorcist manuals' adoption of medical terms and categories, nonetheless, reflected a conscious selection that intended to distinguish the Daoist ritual masters' specialty from the physicians'. For instance, *The Golden Book of Salvation According to the Lingbao Tradition* (Lingbao lingjiao jidu jinshu; compiled ca. 13th–14th c.) included a series of talismans and incantations to be used in the Welfare-Aiding Retreat (Zifu Zhai), a rite specifically for the relief of various illnesses. The ritual masters used these talismans and incantations to summon the "celestial physicians" (*tianyi*) of thirteen subjects: wind; formulas and pulses for adults; eyes; childbirth; children; external medicine; ears and nose; mouth, teeth, and throat; fractures; military wounds; lances and heating; ulcers and tumors; incantations.[64]

The thirteen subjects generally corresponded to those in the Song Imperial Medical Academy. The subjects were for the imperial medical exams and posts and not entirely reflective of medical practice in Song society at large. The "celestial physicians" thus corresponded not to physicians of various specialties in Song society but to the medical offices in the imperial bureaucracy. The ritual masters' job was to accurately produce the talismans and incantations and to use them properly. The celestial physicians would in turn conduct the treatment. In addition, there were 204 talismans and incantations for specific disorders, organized into the thirteen subjects, supposedly to tell the celestial physicians summoned what the patients suffered from. That did not mean that the ritual master would have to conduct a preliminary diagnosis to determine which talisman to use. The listed items were mostly obvious symptoms or the kind of commonly known illnesses that ordinary people could easily identify, for instance, pain in heart and spleen, *qi* congestion, *nüe* disorders, red and white diarrhea, and so on. In case the ritual master encountered an unknown illness, there were talismans for "unclear and anomalous symptoms," "miscellaneous disorders," "all kinds of women's anomalous illnesses," "all unpredictable illnesses on the body," and such.[65]

"[Dreaming of] intercourse with ghosts" was not listed in the manuals for the Welfare-Aiding Retreat ritual, perhaps because in those cases the ritual masters would more likely summon celestial officers and soldiers to battle against the demon or ghost. Based on what we see in Song anecdotes, Daoist ritual masters performed exorcist rituals much more often than summoning celestial physicians.[66] But ritual masters could potentially use a combination of talismans and incantations for "unclear and anomalous symptoms," "all kinds of women's anomalous illnesses" if the patient was female, and those for "convulsion, now singing now laughing, and insomnia" if the patient had such symptoms. The Commanding and Summoning Rites of the Purple Magnificent Numinous Script (Ziying Lingshu Shezhao Fa; rites mainly to pacify wandering ghosts, also included in *The Golden Book of Salvation*) included a diagram indicating the sections of the hand, each of which targeted a specific kind of affliction. The ritual master conducted the therapy by pressing the corresponding section of his or her own hand and chanting a secret incantation to summon the gods. The tip of the middle finger was the section for "nightmares," including "dreaming of evils at night, dreaming of intercourse with ghosts, and ghost fetuses."[67]

Some treatments of demonic dreams and ghostly intercourse in the Daoist scriptures did not specify the patient's gender, while others targeted women. In a scripture dated in the Southern Song or after, the depiction of the demonic spirit Wutong resonated with the stories about the demon-deity Wutong (with a different character for *tong*) in Song anecdotes and the medical discussions of women's enchantment disorders: "Some women today say that there are other men sleeping with them. These women laugh and cry in strange ways, now appear dead and now alive, smile on their own, and talk unexpectedly as if in front of someone else. Those who cannot be sent away, enchant people, and bring stolen goods to aid the household are [Wutong]."

A Daoist ritual master might perform such a ritual to expel Wutong:

> Write the Talisman of Celestial Thearch's True Form in red on a piece of yellow paper of five *cun* [7.2 in] long. Burn it into ashes and mix with scented water. Make the woman swallow the mixture. Hold the Celestial Thearch's Supreme Lord Seal in front of the Celestial Gate, recite the Celestial Thearch's Incantation three times. Take three breaths to infuse the incantation into the seal. Write the name Wutong on a piece of white paper. Apply cinnabar to the seal and imprint on the paper. Place the sealed paper in a red pocket and make the woman wear it on the top of her head.[68]

A ritual manual transmitted by the Southern Song Daoist priest Ning Quanzhen (1101–1181), *Great Lingbao Rites of the Shangqing Heaven* (Shangqing lingbao dafa), included two talismans that treated "dreaming of intercourse with ghosts"; neither specified the gender of the afflicted. One of them was listed among other talismans that treated "Wutong and the mountain goblins (*shanxiao*)," "nightmares," "possession by the mountain goblin," "dark magic affliction (*shen ya xie*)," "ghostly *qi* affliction (*guiqi lin shen*)" and "screaming in fright while dreaming at night."[69]

A set of *Hun*-Spirit Retrieving Rites (Zhuihun Fa) preserved in the *Uncollected Pearls from the Ocean of Rituals* (Fahai yizhu; compiled ca. 14th–15th c.) explicated four kinds of *hun* lost and the rituals to retrieve them. The fourth kind was "ghosts obtaining [one's] *hun*"; "[the afflicted] women often have strange dreams and intercourse with ghosts." If not treated, the text warned, the woman would die in three days. The healing method was to make a Supreme Oneness *Hun*-Guiding Banner (Taiyi Yinhun Fan)—made of yellow silk or paper; length according to the patient's height; and inscribed with the patient's name, birthday, birth year, and address, along with other divine marks—and have the patient lay down, and then burn the banner beside the bed.[70]

One exorcist text from between the late thirteenth and early fifteenth centuries, the *Great Exorcist Rites of Tianpeng of the Supreme Purity* (Shangqing tianpeng fumo dafa), included six talismans for treating dreams of intercourse with ghosts. One was to be written on a stone and placed behind the bed. Two were to be attached to the right and the left corners of the bed near the feet. Two were to be written on the pillow. And the other was for the patient to swallow. All talismans were to be infused with the "killing force" (*shaqi*) by breathing the Tianpeng incantations into them.[71] The locations implied that both the affliction and the treatment took place in the domestic setting. The patient could be either man or woman, but it was less likely that this set of talismans would have been used for the kind of erotic encounters between men and female ghosts in the wild that we frequently see in literary tales.

Another text of the Tianpeng exorcist tradition, the *Dark Book of the Divine Thearch* (Zichen xuanshu; prefaced 1344), also had a talisman treating ghostly intercourse, which dealt with the following conditions: a dead husband seeking the wife and a dead wife seeking the husband in dreams, intercourse with (the spirits) of buried corpses, and all kinds of demonic dreams. The method was similar to the ones described earlier: to infuse the talisman with the Tianpeng incantations and to attach it to the end of the bed near the floor. If the patient wanted to be rid of such problems for good, the ritual master could use iron to make the talismans and nail them on the end of the bed.[72]

None of these exorcist texts offered details about the cause of ghostly intercourse on the patient's end—for instance, what the patient did wrong or what preconditions the patient had to make him or her susceptible to a demonic affliction—except for *The Dark Book of the Divine Thearch*. In its preface, the author Zhang Shunlie, who called himself the fifth-generation successor of the Tianpeng tradition, explicated the causes and symptoms of the major human suffering, the *laozhai* (literally, "exhaustion plague"), and claimed that his lineage received a special divine revelation to cure it. The pathogen was the "three deathbringers and nine worms" (*sanshi jiuchong*), known in many Daoist texts as a major source of human illness and bodily decay. Everyone was born with the three deathbringers and nine worms; they resided inside the body and did not come from the outside. The disease broke out under five conditions: "drinking exhaustion, sexual exhaustion, damage exhaustion, *qi* exhaustion, and contagious exhaustion." The symptoms included "dreaming of evils at night" and "dreaming of intercourse with ghosts." The other accompanying symptoms were quite different from those in the medical texts concerning ghostly dreams but similar to pneumonic plague—intermittent fevers, pain in bones, dizziness, coughing, phlegm, vomiting blood, shortness of breath, and so on. Men and women were equally susceptible and both had the same symptoms. As the symptoms continued, men would suffer from incontinence of their semen (*yang jing*) and women from incontinence of their vaginal fluid (*yin shui*).

Most notably, this preface emphasized two things: that only the properly transmitted and conducted method within their lineage worked, and that the patient had to actively cooperate in the treatment process. It stated that *laozhai* was something that "no physician [*yi*] or [charlatan] ritualist [*wu*] in the world can cure."[73] A true ritualist must have a gentle and pure mind and be approved by the master in order to practice the rite. If anyone learned and conducted the rite without legitimate authorization, they, and their ancestors of nine generations, risked severe punishment. The patient, meanwhile, had to be honest with the ritual master in describing the symptoms, the timeline of such symptoms, and the causes—including what he or she saw and experienced in dreams. In other words, patients would have to report whether they had been drinking, had sexual activities, or had any of the five conditions. Based on the patient's description, the ritualist first used corresponding talismans to test the worms and to summon divine soldiers to catch the ghosts, and then used another talisman to expel the deathbringers and worms. After the worms were cleaned, the ritualist used drugs to determine which viscera were damaged and repaired them with the "fortification talisman." Finally, the patient had to carefully recuperate "as if a woman after childbirth"—"ease the heart, cultivate the mind, avoid exhaustion," and refrain from sexual activities.[74]

Intercourse with ghosts as a symptom of *laozhai*, according to this text, was not caused by unfulfilled or suppressed sexual desire. Quite the contrary, it was caused by exhaustion due to various activities and conditions, including sex. The text did not specify whether it was excessive sexual activities or simply ordinary ones that could lead to the outbreak of *laozhai*. After being healed, the patient had to refrain from *all* sexual activities. Since everyone was born with the three deathbringers and nine worms, the illness could also be deemed a result of being ordinary.

The patriarch of this lineage, Master Fang, was said to have been afflicted with *laozhai* himself and cured by an eminent Song dynasty Divine Empyrean (Shenxiao) Daoist priest, Lu Yanghao, who conducted the ritual according to a text that three mysterious Daoists granted Fang.[75] Furthermore, this text, written from the perspective of a specific Daoist lineage, asserted the orthodoxy of its own methods. Its demand on the patient's honesty could be seen as an effort to assert the ritualist's authority. It meant that the patient was partly responsible for the efficacy of his or her own treatment. It also meant that no one, not even a powerful ritualist, knew someone else's dreams unless that person spoke up, and that the content of the dream mattered for the diagnosis and treatment. Similar to the ritualists of this tradition, authors of Song tales and anecdotes seemed to be more interested in what the patient or the possessed had to say than earlier writers. What we can learn from these anecdotal writings is not simply a change in the literary world of elite men.

PART TWO

INCONVENIENT FEMALE SEXUALITY AND MULTIVOCAL NARRATIVES

CHAPTER THREE

ENCHANTMENT DISORDER AND PRE-SONG TALES

WOMEN'S INTERCOURSE WITH GHOSTS OR DEMONS WAS DESCRIBED
as an illness—a ghostly or demonic "enchantment" (*mei*)—in folk and literary tales from the third century onward. Tales of women's enchantment
bore certain similarities to descriptions of ghost intercourse in medical texts,
but differed in the causes and treatments reported. A story included in two
early fifth-century collections of "anomaly accounts" (*zhiguai*) records a
woman's dramatic behavior on her wedding day:[1]

> During the Yongchu reign [420–423] of the first [Liu] Song
> emperor, when Zhang Chun was the governor of Wuchang, a
> certain household was marrying their daughter. Before ascend-
> ing to the carriage, the bride suddenly lost her temper. She exited
> the house gate and beat people, saying that she was no longer
> willing to marry an ordinary man. An exorcist [*wu*] said that this
> was a case of demonic enchantment [*xiemei*].[2] S/he brought the
> woman to the riverbank, beat a drum, and treated her with an
> exorcist ritual. The governor, believing the exorcist to be a fraud,
> imposed upon him/her a deadline to subjugate the demon. The
> next day, a green snake came to the exorcist's place, and s/he
> pierced its head with a large nail. The same day at noon, a
> tortoise left the river and prostrated itself before the exorcist,
> who wrote a talisman in red ink on the tortoise's shell and sent it
> back into the river. At dusk, a giant alligator emerged from the
> river, bobbing up and down in the water as the tortoise pushed it
> forward. Knowing that its time had come, the alligator rushed in
> through the curtains and bade its farewell to the woman, who
> wept bitterly at the loss of her mate but gradually recovered.

Someone asked the exorcist what the three creatures were. S/he responded that the snake was the messenger, the tortoise the matchmaker, and the alligator the mate.[3] The exorcist presented all three creatures to the governor, who then recognized his/her efficacy.[4]

This story was told from a position sympathetic to the ritual specialist, who proved his or her efficacy to a nonbeliever. In contrast to the medical tradition, which focused on explaining and treating the internal causes of illnesses (be they depletion or desire), this narrative was interested only in the external cause—the demonic intruders.[5] We do not learn why this woman was afflicted in the first place; we may infer that her condition might have had something to do with her maidenhood, but we know nothing beyond her unmarried status, likely because other details about the woman were irrelevant given that the exorcist's treatment dealt only with the demonic intruder. Her manlessness in this narrative, however, was the outcome rather than the cause of her demonic enchantment—it made her "no longer willing to marry an ordinary man," and her transgressive behavior would have rendered her unmarriageable. Compared to stories about men's encounters with female ghosts and demons, this story conforms to the gendered pattern that many scholars have observed in literary tales from early to late imperial China: men were often depicted as active sexual transgressors, women as passive, possessed objects of desire. In ghost enchantment narratives in pre-Song anomaly accounts and Tang "tales of the marvelous" (*chuanqi*), a gendered pattern is evident, but there are also exceptions to the pattern, particularly in the new elements and interests found in Tang tales. At the root of "enchantment disorder," a category in both literary tales and popular perception, lay aspects of female sexuality that were inconvenient to the patriarchal family.

Sources from the seventh century onward described the enchanted women's symptoms in greater detail. These symptoms are significant as indicators of what kind of conditions or behaviors on the part of women were deemed so problematic or unfathomable as to require explanation. In many tales, the family and neighbors already believe, or at least suspect, the woman to be enchanted before a specialist arrives. From the Tang onward, literary tales also began to show more interest in women's experiences of enchantment. The narratives often let women talk about their own experiences or allow men to somehow "see" women's experiences. This bespeaks not simply a desire to know women who seem to have secrets but also the limitation of what can be known—we cannot know unless they tell.

What was "enchantment" (*mei*)? In my sources, *mei* was defined primarily by what it did to victims. The agents of *mei* could be the ghosts of the deceased (*gui*), the essences (*jing*) of monstrous creatures (*guai*), a demonic creature or anomalous beauty (*yao*), a deity or powerful spirit (*shen*), or simply an animated old object (such as a broom or a pillow). They were called *mei* only if they enchanted people, sexually or otherwise.[6] "Demon" or "demonic" are generally used to translate *yao*. As in the case of *mei*, however, *yao* were considered evil or demonic more for what they did than for who they were. A minor deity guilty of some transgression could still be called a *yao*.[7] All the spirits we see in the sources—ghosts, deities, demons, and so on—have physical forms, albeit forms that are oftentimes more malleable or transformable than those of humans and other mortal creatures. "Spirit" here is an expedient translation of *shen*, or the most refined parts within the human body, which can sometimes transcend the constraints of the body to travel to the heavens, the netherworld, or simply to somewhere else on earth.

GENDERED PATTERNS IN EARLY ACCOUNTS

In early tales what determines the nature of a man's relationship with a female other and the result of that encounter is often the identity of the other. A goddess of high status brings not simply affection and content but also material benefits and sometimes promotion in officialdom. An animal spirit or a low-ranking deity often causes harm. The ghost of a deceased woman can bring either weal or woe, depending on her identity and intentions.[8] Women's encounters with otherworldly beings follow a similar principle, though stories about women's intimate relationship with gods are extremely rare. The "other" in such stories tends to be an animal spirit—snake, alligator, dog, turtle, monkey, fox, or rooster, for instance—and is often referred to as a *mei*, or enchanting demon.

Scholarship on the differences between men's and women's encounters with ghosts and demons has observed that many of the female ghosts that men encounter in stories from the Six Dynasties are daughters of prominent families, and that the relationships often help men climb the social ladder. A good ending requires that the ghost woman come back to life, which she does by obtaining the man's "breath in bed" (*qinxi*). In one study, only three of eighteen stories are about encounters between women and male ghosts (or wild spirits), and in all three cases the women are maidservants. There is also a body of stories about dead wives or husbands who return to their spouses. If the ghost is the wife, the purpose is often to leave the husband a son. If the dead husband's ghost comes back, however, it is usually just for sex.[9]

In addition to encounters with ghosts, quite a few concurrent stories describe women who are enchanted, harassed, or (sexually) possessed by demonic or mysterious spirits. These women range from wives and daughters of noble families to commoners. In a survey of forty-one stories about *jing-mei* (nonhuman monstrous creatures or goblins that do harm to humans) from the second to the sixth centuries, eleven concern men's erotic encounters with *jingmei* who assume female forms, and nine concern women's erotic encounters with mostly male (and sometimes simply monstrous) creatures. The men are generally unharmed by the encounters.[10] The women, in contrast, either die or tend to be described as suffering from an illness and in need of treatment.[11] For instance, Cao Pi's (187–226) *Arrayed Marvels* (Lieyi zhuan) records that the young daughter of a Chu king "suffered from [or 'was ill due to'] [demonic] enchantment" (*wei mei suo bing*);[12] another account in the same collection uses the same language to describe a married woman enchanted by a snake.[13] Liu Jingshu's (fl. early 5th c.) *A Garden of Marvels* (Yiyuan) includes a story about a woman possessed by an otter spirit. A healer who was able to "cure demonic afflictions" (*liaoxie*) treated her with just one needle, and her "illness [*ji*] was cured."[14]

A difference in narrative patterns between men's and women's sexual encounters with the "alien kind" is also evident in Tang tales. As in pre-Tang accounts, women are often portrayed as passive victims of demonic intruders, awaiting rescue by men. Men, meanwhile, are usually active agents, and "the focus of their anxiety lies in the level of danger of the female demons (*yao*)."[15] This pattern resonates with that in Pu Songling's (1640–1715) *Liaozhai*: although there are cases of a female ghost tempting a man and of a male ghost molesting a woman, whenever a female ghost approaches a man and is restored to life, "it is almost always in an erotic context," while a woman molested by a male ghost is "almost always [depicted] in the context of illness" and is treated by medical or exorcist means.[16] Similarly in seventeenth- to eighteenth-century fox stories, when a man encounters a vixen, the focus is on how he deals with his sexual desire and self-control; whereas when a woman is molested and sometimes possessed by a male fox, she oftentimes loses consciousness and needs an outside force for help.[17]

A woman's social and marital status determined the way in which her story was told. In some, women's sexual encounters with demonic beings occur in two ways: either she is unconsciously possessed or consciously deceived.[18] A closer look at these stories reveals that the former is usually the case for maidens, while the latter is more common for married women.

Maidens' enchantment disorders often render them unmarriageable, and marriage thus marks their recovery. For instance, Ge Hong's (283–343) *Traditions of Divine Transcendents* (Shenxian zhuan) tells that an unmarried daughter of a noble family was enchanted. Her family visited Dong Feng, a famous Daoist healer of the third century, and promised to marry their daughter to him if he could cure her. Dong successfully expelled the demon, and the woman became Dong's wife.[19]

The latter case—wives tricked into sex—constitutes a type of tale that has been told and retold since the fourth century, and is heavily informed by anxiety over unguarded female sexuality. In such stories, the husband is away—on official business or for other reasons—and the ghost or demon assumes his form in order to trick the wife into sex. Gan Bao's (fl. ca. 317) *Records of an Inquest into the Spirit-Realm* (Soushen ji) tells of a case in which a man observing the mourning period for his mother suddenly entered his wife's room and forced himself upon her. On his next visit to her chamber, his wife rebuked him for violating the norms of mourning practice, and the man realized that it must have been an enchanting demon (*mei*) that forced itself upon her. That night, he saw a white dog stealing his mourning clothes and turning into a human. He followed the man and killed it as it was about to climb up into his wife's bed. His wife then "was ashamed, became ill, and died."[20]

Liu Yiqing's (403–444) *Records of the Hidden and the Visible Worlds* (Youming lu; *The Hidden and the Visible* hereafter) contains a very similar story, except that the wife does not fall ill or die of shame.[21] *Further Records of an Inquest into the Spirit-Realm* (Soushen houji; late 5th c.) also has a story in which a yellow dog takes a man's form and sleeps with his wife. After the deceit is exposed, the wife also "was extremely ashamed, fell ill, and died." In addition to a dramatic confrontation between the man and his doppelgänger, the latter story differs in describing the wife as "young and beautiful"; her husband is sixty years old and often spends his nights out of the house. For this reason the wife is "deeply unhappy" (*shen wu xin*).[22] This story, then, is not simply about women's sexual status but shares with the bedchamber literature the gaze at the young female body and the fantasy about desire for men—rarities among pre-Song anomaly records and anecdotes. Notably, too, the woman falls ill not from a lack of sex with men or from sex with ghosts or demons, but from shame.

Women's responses to enchanting spirits also have much to do with their socio-familial identity. Another story in *Further Records* relates that six palace courtesans in the Eastern Jin (317–420) were all enchanted by a monkey demon in the guise of a handsome young man. All the women became pregnant and gave birth to monstrous monkey babies. When the king killed the monkey and all the monkey babies, the women did not become sick or die from shame but instead cried out to lament their loss.[23] One story from *A Garden of Marvels* portrays two maids who seem to live happily with some wild ghosts, as does another in *The Hidden and the Visible.* Both accounts describe the encounter very differently from other possession and enchantment stories. The women are not tricked or forced; nor are they ill, unconscious, or ashamed. The account in *A Garden of Marvels* tells that sometime between 454 and 457, someone in Luling (present-day Ji'an, Jiangxi) claiming to be a "mountain spirit" (*shanling*) came to "have intercourse with" (*tong*) a maid named Caiwei, who was "young and beautiful." This being appeared "like a naked man," tall, with yellow hair on his chest and arms and is also described as having "clean and regular skin and features" and "speaking in perfect tone and accent." The maid responded that she was "willing to serve you as if you were a person [*yi shi ru ren*]," after which the being paid her frequent visits. It had no constant form and could transform into many things, such as smoke, stone, a small ghost, or a woman. According to the story, it "played and laughed with the maid just like a person."[24]

The Hidden and the Visible story offers no physical depiction of its maiden or ghostly protagonists. It says that a ghost, or an unknown spirit, approached a maid, that they "exchanged greetings" (*xiang wenxun*) and then the two "exchanged affection" (*gong tong qing*). The ghost came home with the maid and they feasted and sang together. Others could hear the ghost's voice, but he was visible only to the woman, whose daily work as a maid seems not to have been affected. Rather than summoning an exorcist or a healer, her master simply "made her leave the house at night lest [the ghost] cause problems."[25] Also interestingly, both accounts characterize the relationship using the term *tong* (intercourse; communication) rather than *mei* or *sui* (ghostly or demonic affliction), both frequently used in other possession or enchantment stories. A maid's sexuality, unlike that of wives and wives-to-be, was inconvenient to no one. They may have become even more socially marginalized (as with the maid who was no longer permitted to stay in the house at night) and would likely not have been considered suitable for marriage—but they did not need medical or exorcist interventions perhaps because there was no problem in which to intervene.

In sources up to the sixth century we already see several patterns forming, many of which were still present in Tang and Song stories. In addition to the asymmetrical narratives of men's and women's encounters, in most cases a woman's social status and her position in relation to the marriage system determined how her behavior was understood and treated. The crux of women's enchantment disorders was women's inconvenient sexuality—inconvenient, that is, to their husbands or husbands-to-be. Anxieties about unmarried young women and unattended wives persisted. But in most anomaly accounts and tales, unlike in bedchamber literature, no explicit link was drawn between ghostly enchantment and the woman's sexual status or desire. (Quite a few stories nonetheless shared the bedchamber gaze at young and alluring female bodies.) Before the Song, and outside medical texts, there were few records of women's ghostly intercourse or pregnancy being treated with medicine. Narratives before the eighth century generally focused on details of the exorcisms or the demon's deception, with little description of the woman in the situation beyond "she was enchanted," "she lost her mind," or "she was young and beautiful." The stories of the two maids were anomalies. We began to see more variation and narrative innovation in stories from the eighth to the ninth centuries, many of which reflected elite men's responses to popular beliefs and reworkings of folktales.

TANG TALES: FOLK PRACTICE AND ELITE RESPONSE

The gendered patterns seen in pre-Tang stories persisted in many Tang tales, most notably anxieties about women who were unguarded by men and fantasies about young female bodies.[26] To be sure, not all enchanted women were manless, nor do all accounts mention the women's age or appearance. In many cases, we simply do not know why the woman in an account was chosen by the demon. Stories about widows and unattended women persisted, as did descriptions of such women's alluring appearance and sometimes lewd character. Tang writers also inherited the category of "enchantment disorder" in describing women's uncontrollable and inconvenient sexuality. Enchantment disorder was a previously existing category grounded in longstanding folk beliefs and practices, rather than an invention of elite writers, many of whose accounts departed from simple folklore and religious tales, while short folk tales and anecdotes in simpler forms continued to be recorded.[27] Descriptions of women's enchantment disorder grew more varied and elaborate. Tang tales reflected a strong interest in women's behavior and experience, especially the kind of mystic experience that would be unknowable unless related by the woman herself.

Though written by elite men, many stories from the Six Dynasties and the Tang had their origins in oral tales.[28] Sarah Allen proposes that Tang tales should be situated "in the context of the exchange of stories among elite men." Their writings were largely based on hearsay rather than being pure fiction, on the one hand, and were highly crafted narratives on the other.

As Allen puts it, "the diversity of forms that a single item of hearsay may take within a cluster of tales that all develop from the same topic attests to the fact that, for many writers, close fidelity to the source per se was neither a goal nor a value; rather, the source was a starting point from which the writer developed his own tale."[29] All the stories discussed in this section reflect, in one way or another, Tang elite men's responses to popular beliefs and the ways such stories had been told. They offer a window onto how non-specialists in the Tang described what they saw, how they made judgments, and what actions they took or thought should have been taken. But the more fundamental question is what initially made people believe or suspect, often even before a specialist was consulted, that a woman had been enchanted or sexually possessed by a spirit. What conditions and behavior were deemed so problematic or unfathomable that they required explanation?

Symptoms and Treatment

What made a woman's family and neighbors think of enchantment disorders? Some Tang tales offer no answer to these questions, while in others, the answers vary. One account in Dai Fu's (fl. mid–late 8th c.) *Wide-Ranging Records of the Strange* (Guangyi ji) tells of a girl who, as soon as a fox demon entered her room and called itself the son-in-law of the family, became "delirious" (*hunkuang*) and began to "weep in sorrow" and "speak nonsense."[30] Chen Shao's *Records of Penetrating the Mysterious* (Tongyou ji; 8th c.) recounts that a village girl "was afflicted by demonic enchantment and went violently mad [*huanmei fakuang*], at times harming herself by stepping in fire or throwing herself into water. And her belly grew large, as if she were pregnant."[31]

Xue Yongruo's *Records of Strange Things Collected* (Jiyi ji; early 9th c.) records that the daughter of an elite family in Runan (in present-day Henan) who had "elegant comportment and beautiful looks" had been enchanted by some ghostly beings for quite some time; one night a family guest saw someone in white enter the daughter's room and "heard delightful chatting and laughter inside."[32] Another story in the same collection tells that a woman in Xiapi (in present-day Jiangsu), known for her beauty in the community, had an affair with a mysterious young man while her husband was traveling away from home. Upon his return, her husband was struck by her indifference toward him—"the bond [between husband and wife] was estranged" (*enyi shuge*). At dusk, she put on adornments and makeup, and disappeared when it became completely dark. The young man turned out to be a fox. After the fox was killed, the story ends with the remark that "the wife no longer wore makeup and adornments."[33]

Amusing Records during Huichang (841–846) (Huichang jieyi lu; 9th c.) describes a clerk's daughter, "enchanted by a demonic being" (*wei yaowu suo mei*), who "wore heavy makeup and fine clothes" when the demon came and "chatted and laughed in her room as if someone were there with her." When it left, she "cried out madly nonstop."[34]

Duan Chengshi (d. 863) in his *Youyang Morsels* (Youyang zazu) recounts that the two daughters of a local official, after fishing up two monstrous creatures and bringing them home, became delirious (*jingshen huanghu*) and often did needlework late into the night. Later their family discovered that they were enchanted by the two creatures, who called themselves the family's daughters-in-law.[35] Finally, Jing Huan's *Leisure Tales of a Humble Man* (Yeren xianhua; finished in 965) records that a commoner girl was "enchanted by a monstrous spirit" (*wei jingguai suo huo*). She often put on fresh makeup when night fell and afterward would talk and laugh delightfully as if receiving a guest.[36]

The most frequently seen symptoms include delirium, wearing adornments and makeup (especially in the evening or at night), talking and laughing on one's own, and inexplicable emotional expressions. We see almost identical descriptions in contemporary medical texts. The telltale signs of "women having intercourse with ghosts" listed in *On the Origins and Symptoms* (610) include: reclusiveness, talking and smiling on one's own, and weeping.[37] *Invaluable Formulas* (651) has a recipe, the "pill in the immortal's jade jar," that treats "men and women having intercourse with ghosts, singing and crying intermittently, or having a swollen belly and paused menses as if pregnant."[38] Many Song anecdotes also contain these symptoms. The similarities in descriptions in texts across genres and by many different authors suggest origins in a shared popular belief. The problem of women's enchantment disorder was a real issue in the popular conception, and there was a specific group of symptoms and behavioral patterns associated with it.

The seventh-century medical treatise *On the Origins* recognized ghosts (or "ghostly *qi*") as an external cause, while its treatments focused on fortifying the *qi* (or sometimes more specifically the *yang qi*) in the patient's body to defend against malign external forces.[39] It further provided a description of such patients' pulse manifestations in order to help physicians diagnose them. In other words, it suggested that physicians pinpoint the problem through both observation of the women's behavior (or relying on her family's description) and pulse diagnosis. In many tales and anecdotes, however, the family was already convinced that their woman was enchanted before a specialist appeared, and the focus of treatment was almost always the demon or ghost, and usually involved an exorcist specialist.[40] The exorcist in pre-Song accounts could be a *wu* (shaman, spirit-medium, or sorcerer), an immortality practitioner, an occultist (*shushi*), a Daoist priest or lay Daoist practitioner (*Daoshi*), a Buddhist monk, or simply someone known to have certain exorcist-healing skills.

In anomaly accounts and anecdotes before the Song, we rarely see physicians (*yi* or *yizhe*), for whom pulse diagnosis and medicinal recipes played a role in treating enchantment disorders. This could mean that, prior to the Song, practicing physicians who specialized in pulse diagnosis and medicinal prescriptions did not really perform exorcisms, even though many medical compilations include exorcist recipes, or at least that their contemporaries did not consider them to be as skilled at such practices. It could also mean that the storytellers, collectors, writers and readers found pulse diagnosis and medicinal recipes less dramatically compelling than physical battles with demons.[41]

Despite their different emphases in treatment, both medical writers and ritual exorcists identified malign intruders as the major external causes of disorders, and neither drew an explicit causal connection between ghost enchantment and women's heterosexual inactivity or desire. In comparison, the description of women's enchantment disorder in *Secret Instructions of the Jade Chamber*, a bedchamber text discussed in chapter 1, was peculiar: the cause was "lack of intercourse between *yin* and *yang*" and women's "deep and severe desire" for the same, and the first treatment (out of three listed) was to "let the woman have intercourse with a man without [the man] ejaculating."[42] Although there was one tale describing the woman as unhappy about her husband's absence—the story from *Further Records* about a dog demon's deception discussed earlier—the process of exorcism in pre-Song and Song anecdotes never took women's sexual desire into account.

Women's indifference to men (or unwillingness to marry) was also a recurrent "symptom." The fifth-century anecdote about a woman in Wuchang, translated at the beginning of this chapter, recounts that she "suddenly lost her temper" and "claimed that she no longer wanted to marry an ordinary man" when she was possessed by an alligator demon on her wedding day.[43] In the story about the woman in Xiapi, mentioned earlier, the woman's failure to warmly welcome her husband home from his long travels is the husband's only grounds for suspicion until he discovers that she disappears at night. This story differs from the former in its disclosure of the woman's secret—the details of her encounter with the demon (a fox in this case), supposedly known only to her: "One day, a grand looking young man appeared. He looked at Wang [the woman] and said, 'What a pity for such a beauty to waste her whole life [living alone].' Listening to such words, Wang fell in love with the man and started a relationship with him [*yu zhi jie hao*]."

This kind of narrative detail can be seen as characteristic of literary reworkings by elite men. The description of the woman's condition hews closely to the bedchamber formula: a fine young woman lives alone, a ghost or demon comes to entice her, the woman secretly enjoys it and no longer wants an ordinary man. In this story, however, the woman's life and health are in no danger, despite her secret paramour. This account makes no mention of how the woman feels about her husband's absence before the young man appears. The bulk of the account, in fact, is devoted to narrating how the husband pretends to be his wife, finds out where the fox demons have their lair, and kills them.[44] Unlike the bedchamber authors, who assume that manless women must be sexually frustrated and that this frustration attracts demonic predators, the husband in this story blames and deals with only the demonic intruder. Common between this account and bedchamber texts, however, is the need to explain a woman's lack of interest in her husband—or, put another way, the resistance to viewing indifferent wives (or unwilling brides-to-be) as ordinary. For such women there could be many explanations. Enchantment disorder was only one of the multiple frameworks through which women uninterested in marriage or their husbands could be understood.

There is an interesting peculiarity among the symptoms associated with enchanted women listed here. One story tells of a village girl who disfigured herself rather than putting on makeup and fine clothes like the women in many other stories. Of course, a village girl probably would not have had cosmetics or fine clothes. Women's self-disfiguration, however, was not simply a meaningless or crazy act but often meant a deliberate disruption of her sexual accessibility to men. This is seen in many accounts of Buddhist nuns as well as chaste widows: for one widow, a Madam Li (to be discussed later), self-disfiguration is a conscious response to harassment by a ghost. The factor uniting the apparently contradictory symptoms of dressing up (for someone other than the husband) and disfiguration is that the women's gendered and sexual bodies are expressed in ways inconvenient to their husbands or husbands-to-be. What happens to a self-disfiguring woman—whether she is enchanted by spirits, defending herself (sexually), or responding to a religious calling—depends on how her story is told.

Another "symptom" that blurs the boundary between the demonic and the divine is women's unexpected literacy. In two accounts, one in Chen Shao's *Records of Penetrating the Mysterious* and the other in *Amusing Records during Huichang*, the enchanted women, previously illiterate, become capable of writing or reciting poetry, and their poems are recorded. Their literacy arrives with the spirit possession and goes away after the exorcism. On the one hand, this is indicative of elite male authorship; only a person of letters would be capable of (and interested in) recording the poems in their entirety. On the other hand, unexpected talent and precocity are common elements in stories of female transcendents and religious women, and sometimes female spirit mediums.[45]

Women's Secrets

Zhang Zhuo (ca. 650–730), an early Tang official and a renowned writer of his day, tells such a story in his *Complete Record of Court and Country* (Chaoye qianzai):

> The wife of Deng Lian in Gonggao, Cangzhou [in present-day southeast Hebei], née Li, was widowed less than a year after marrying Deng. Li took a fidelity oath at the age of seventeen. She set up a mourning table and presented offerings and wept in front of it three times a day. For six or seven years she lived a frugal life, wearing cotton clothes and eating a vegetarian diet. One night, she dreamed of a man, elegant in appearance and demeanor, who asked her to be his mate. Li rejected him in the dream. From then on, she saw him in her dreams every night but never consented to his request. Li considered the man an enchanting being [*jingmei*] and tried written talismans and exorcist spells, but none could stop [him reappearing]. Li sighed and said [to herself], "I swore to maintain my fidelity and yet am harassed by this thing. It must be because my looks have not left me yet." She then cut her hair, wore unwashed linen clothes, left her hair disheveled, and smeared her face and body with grime. The ghost then apologized to her, saying "Madame's integrity is as unbreaking as bamboo, as enduring as cypress trees." From then on, Li dreamed of the man no more. The magistrate conferred honors on her household. Today the place is still called the Village of the Faithful Wife.[46]

Zhang seems to have told this story specifically in response to popular belief in regarding demonic possession and the way women's enchantment stories were told. The story begins with the rather familiar trope of a male ghost appearing to tempt a young and attractive widow. As in some of the stories mentioned earlier, the ghost comes to visit her in dreams because of her youth, attractiveness, and absent husband; it has nothing to do with either her desire or her "blood and *qi*." Unlike in most other tales, however, the woman does not fall for his tricks or lose consciousness—not even in her dreams. She first appeals to exorcist rituals, but none work. The antagonist in this account is still a ghost or demon, but the protagonist is not a powerful exorcist but the woman herself. The ghost is unable to possess her without her consent, and she defeats the ghost simply by rendering herself less attractive to him. This story, in a nutshell, is like an exemplary tale disguised as a story of ghost enchantment; the focus is the woman's incorruptible virtue and impenetrable sexual body. The woman, meanwhile, is not a passive victim or patient but an active defender of herself. Exemplary tales are a double-edged sword: in order for women to be moral subjects, like men they have to think rationally, make moral judgments, act according to their own will, and take responsibility for their own actions. This is particularly salient if we compare this account with contemporary and earlier stories of men and women enchanted by ghosts.

In another story recorded by Dou Weiwu (or Weixian; fl. late 7th–early 8th c.) the women literally strike back.[47] The story tells that during Kaihuang reign (581–601) of the Sui emperor Wendi, "someone frequently came to the consorts' quarters to seduce the palace women." The managing eunuchs reported this to the emperor. Confident in the security of his palace guard, the emperor concluded that the "someone" in question must not have been human, and ordered the women to attack it when it appeared. Later one night, the "man" climbed into the bed of one palace woman and she stabbed it with a knife. It ran, and the woman followed it to a pond. The next day the emperor ordered the pond drained and found a large turtle with knife marks on its back. They killed the turtle and the problem stopped.[48] As in the previous story, the women remain conscious and play the key role in expelling the demon. Although the story says that the demon came to seduce the palace women, nobody is said to be enchanted. The emperor gives orders, and the women are expected to act accordingly. Unlike the faithful widow in the previous story, who fights back with her moral force, here the palace lady does so physically.

Zhang's narrative of the faithful widow, furthermore, displays a hitherto unseen interest in women's own experiences during ghostly encounters, reflected in the narrative's reliance upon what Li herself sees and feels, rather than on her behavior as witnessed by others or her symptoms as identified by a specialist. Zhang's account is most likely putting words into the woman's mouth, rather than recording what she actually or allegedly said, but this is more than just a voyeuristic fantasy. In order to moralize women in ghostly encounters, the author has to reveal women's otherwise unknown experiences—what she dreams of, what she sees and experiences on her own—so that her actions and their consequences can be evaluated. This, too, is a double-edged sword and opens the door for disruptive and unstable voices.

Some stories include a section in which the woman recounts her enchanted experience as a narrative device, and the woman always says what fits the narrative, generally confirming rather than confounding readers' expectations. For instance, the story in *Amusing Records during Huichang* ends with the recovering woman recounting how and where she encountered the fox demon.[49] In real life, women could also have been expected to recount their experiences—demonic or divine—and even to take actions. What if women talked in ways that were unexpected or incomprehensible? What if they did not talk at all? In Song anecdotes, especially those in *Record of the Listener*, we see many more instances in which women recount and interpret their own dreams or other mystical experiences themselves, rather than through a ritualist, a physician, or a family member. Unlike the highly crafted tales from the Tang, Song anecdote collections preserve more incongruent voices and inconsistent narratives.

Another type of story in which woman's secrets are uncovered tells us more about elite men's fantasies and their literary creativity in reusing old motifs to tell new stories. There are two cases in which the husband of the enchanted woman sees with his own eyes—incidentally in one case, deliberately in the other—what his wife has been doing behind his back.

One is in *Wide-Ranging Records of the Strange*, which relates to the reader the enchanted woman's nighttime adventures as seen through the eyes of her husband, a clerk during the Kaiyuan period (713–741) who discovers his wife's secret outings at night. The narrative begins by telling the reader that the wife "had a fine appearance and was afflicted with an enchantment disorder [*meiji*], and yet [the clerk] could not tell." At first, the clerk noticed only that their well-fed horse was growing leaner and leaner. From their neighbor, a Central Asian occultist, the husband subsequently learned that his wife went out at night whenever he was on duty. One night he snuck back home and saw his wife, wearing fine makeup, riding their horse into the sky, with her maid following on a broomstick. Frightened, the clerk asked the neighbor for advice, and the latter simply told him to observe for another night. The next night he hid in a large jar, which the maid—who had burned her broomstick to use as a torch—rode without noticing him inside. They arrived at a wooded mountaintop, where the clerk witnessed an orgy; when the wife and maid flew back, he was left stranded and was forced to walk for more than a month before reaching home. The neighbor helped him exorcize the demon, which turned out to be a grey crane. Immediately after they burned the crane to death, "the wife's illness was cured," and the story ends.[50]

The other story is the one mentioned earlier about the Xiapi woman. In this story, the husband, made suspicious by his wife's indifference to him, hides and watches. Close to midnight, he sees her transported out of the window and through the air in a cage. The following night, he locks his wife in another room, dresses up as a woman, hides a knife in his sleeve, sits in the cage, and waits. At the same hour as the previous night, the cage flies out and brings him to a villa in the mountains, where he kills three young men, who prove to be the old foxes that have been enchanting his wife.[51] In both stories, the woman, although described as being "enchanted" or afflicted with "enchantment disorder," does not lose consciousness or show obvious symptoms; she simply appears to have a secret. The narratives reveal not only men's desire to know, but also the difficulty of knowing even their wives: to see what the women see requires them to take such extraordinary journeys. The failure of knowing and the sense of uncertainty were salient in Song anecdotes. Constructions of enchanted women during the Song continued and developed themes from these earlier narratives.

CHAPTER FOUR

ENCHANTED WOMEN IN SONG ANECDOTES

AN ELEVENTH-CENTURY LITERATUS, LIU FU, TOLD THE FOLLOWING
story about spirit possession and exorcism that he witnessed as a child:

> When I was little, I saw the wife of a peasant family being
> enchanted by something [*wei wu suo huo*]. [During the day] she
> wore makeup and adornments, talking and smiling with an easy
> bearing. At night she did not share bed with her husband but
> slept alone, whispering as if speaking to someone. If not allowed
> to dress up and wear adornments, she would be suicidal and
> weep nonstop. Her family summoned a senior exorcist [*wu*] to
> treat her.[1] The exorcist came and said, "This is due to enchant-
> ment by a fox, and the neighbor's dog was the matchmaker." [The
> exorcist] used a willow strip to expel the dog, and the dog was
> confined in a designated place. S/he then set up an altar [*tan*, or a
> designated ritual space] to treat the woman. In a short while, a
> fox barked from the back of the house. The exorcist made a fire
> wheel and sat on it. S/he spun the wheel. The woman and the dog
> ran in horror and stopped only after a hundred steps.[2]

This story should seem rather familiar to us by now. A similar set of
symptoms affected enchanted women in both medical literature and mid-
to late-Tang literary tales, symptoms including the woman's indifference to
her husband, talking when secluded in a separate room, and other inexplicable behaviors and emotional expressions. We have also seen in earlier
sources ritual healers who played a similar role to that of the exorcist in Liu's
recollection. These elements continue in many other Song stories. In addition to the continuities, new developments related to women who were

thought to be enchanted by spirits concerned a construction of female sexuality, the specialization of healers and healing practices in Song society, the role that medicine and physicians played in cases of spirit possession, and the interchangeable identities of varieties of manless women.

Another new development was the abundance of anecdotal writings and the diverse voices preserved in them. This story is the epilogue of a much longer and elaborate account of a romantic otherworldly encounter from Liu's *Elevated Discussions from the Eminent Households* (Qingsuo gaoyi), a collection of tales about the fantastic.[3] The styles and contents of the two narratives are distinctively different. The contrast between the main story and the epilogue tells us something about their difference in genre and the significance of narrative styles for our historical analysis.

The main story is a highly crafted narrative about a young man of letters and a beautiful fox lady. It follows the arc of their relationship, from their first encounter and early companionship to the fox lady's assistance with the man's career, followed by her affection and jealousy, the man's betrayal, and his eventual downfall. It is a long, elaborate account that runs seven to eight pages in modern print editions.[4] In many respects it resembles the mature Tang tales of the eighth and the ninth centuries. Its subject belongs to that of "a lone man's encounter with a stranger with a secret" that are frequently seen in Tang and earlier tales.[5] Its prologue verse alludes to the famous "Tale of Ms. Ren" (Ren shi zhuan). Like the "Tale of Ms. Ren" and quite a few other mid-to-late Tang tales, it "question[s] the assumptions about the separation between human and other," to use literary scholar Sarah Allen's words.[6] Also like many Tang authors, Liu attaches his comments to the end of the story: "Ghosts and the alien kind live side by side with us in this world, and people are simply not aware of them. What is it so strange about this story of a [fox] lady?" But instead of making more opinionated statements, Liu simply recounts the first short episode and concludes, "Although there are such things, only what happened between the young man and the fox lady was the extreme."

This concluding remark hints at the difference between the two narratives. The difference here is not simply a matter of gender—men's romantic encounters with fox ladies versus women's enchantment afflictions by fox demons—but also one of genre. The short childhood episode is in no way comparable to the main story except for the presence of a fox. It has no complicated plot or romance between human and the alien kind. The purpose of recounting the episode is simply to support authenticity of the main story. Liu does not seem to consider the childhood story itself so marvelous that it deserves to be told in its own right. The main story, in contrast, conforms to historian of religion Edward Davis's characterization of the *zhiguai* literature, in which "homodiegetic techniques ('I saw this,' 'I heard this from . . .') serve the largely heterodiegetic end of sheer storytelling," as opposed to accounts included in *Record of the Listener*, in which "the homodiegetic aim of telling what happened is, on occasion, shaped by heterodiegetic forms."[7]

There are at least two similarities between Liu's childhood anecdote and many (but not all) accounts in *Record of the Listener*. First, there is no omniscient narrator; nothing in these accounts is beyond what Liu and other witnesses could possibly have known. Second, these anecdotes reflect nonspecialist and not particularly elite perspectives. Despite being a literatus and likely also a member of the Song elite, Liu described the peasant woman's symptoms and the exorcist's rituals as a bystander with little critical or moral engagement.[8] This is particularly true if we compare the depiction of the exorcist—the *wu*—in Liu's account and in other Song sources. While many physicians, Buddhist and Daoist ritualists, and scholar-officials of the Song used *wu* as a pejorative term in reference to what they considered unorthodox healers, in Liu's story the *wu* was a legitimate exorcist-healer, who was not supremely powerful but knew what s/he was doing.

The mixture of narrative styles and the blurred boundaries between elite and nonelite voices are also present in other Song anecdote collections. In many respects Song men of letters shared the worldview of others in their time. This is not to say that Song elite men were not interested in distinguishing themselves either from the commoners or from other literati when they wrote, but there were circumstances where social distinction was not their main concern. This is also not to say that we can discover authentic nonelite or female voices or certain raw experience in Song anecdotes. But the identity of the author alone is not sufficient to determine how we should read their texts. A story often conveys more than what the author or the narrator intended to say. It sometimes also reveals what the narrators struggled to make sense of and the voices that they inadvertently carried along. Moreover, when new narratives appear in a number of stories that circulated beyond a small elite men's circle, they offer us a glimpse into the society that would otherwise be obscure without comparison against earlier stories. Both literary and historical analyses, with attention to narrative styles (not simply what but *how* stories were told) and new social developments, are mutually illuminative.

RECORD OF THE LISTENER AND SONG ANECDOTAL WRITINGS

Hong Mai's *Record of the Listener* was a product of the unprecedented social, economic, and technological developments of the Southern Song. It comprised at least thirty-two installments compiled and published over the last forty years of Hong's life. Hong began to work on the first installment in 1142 or 1143, likely after receiving a substantial number of stories that his father Hong Hao brought back from the Jurchen occupied north, and completed it between 1159 and 1161. Initially, the first installment most likely only circulated in manuscripts among Hong's literati friends. After 1162 it was published in many major cities. Hong had not anticipated that it would become a best seller and that he would continue collecting stories and publishing them for the rest of his life. After the publication of the first installment, Hong compiled and published the second installment over a period of five years, from 1162 to 1166. The last known date of completion was 1198 for the twenty-ninth installment, but Hong had continued compiling at least three more installments before his death in 1202.[9] During the Southern Song, print copies of these installments were circulated (most likely separately) in major cities throughout the country and probably crossed the northern border to the Jin. More than half of the installments are now lost. In addition to the surviving fourteen, some fragments are preserved in later texts such as *Great Compendium of the Yongle Period* (Yongle dadian) and *Comprehensive Record of Strange Hearsay* (Yiwen zonglu) as well as in local gazetteers.[10]

Stories recorded in *Record of the Listener* were considered unusual and marvelous to Hong's contemporaries; many but not all of them involve ghosts, deities, spirits, and the like.[11] For this reason the text has traditionally been associated with the *zhiguai* literature. However, in the preface to the second installment, Hong already distinguishes his work from earlier *zhiguai* works in two respects: his sources are all contemporary hearsay and the stories are not meant to be allegorical (*yuyan*; literally "lodged words"). He claims that all of the stories of his collection took place "within a cycle of no more than sixty years, passed down through ears and eyes, and all most distinctively have reliable sources."[12] This is not a completely groundless claim. We know at least from the surviving editions of first four installments that Hong specifically identifies his informants for more than half of the accounts, and these informants were mostly Hong's family, relatives, friends, and acquaintances—most of them Hong's fellow literati.[13]

In the third installment's preface, Hong mentions his effort to resolve some of the discrepancies and to correct certain errors in his previous accounts. He apologizes for errors that are the result of careless oral transmission—"either due to the fault of the tellers, or due to [his] lack of judgment as a listener"—and stresses that he did not mean to "slander the good [people]."[14] This preface implies that Hong must have received criticism about the accuracy, if not factuality, of his accounts, and the preface was his response. The two prefaces expose an intrinsic problem in Hong's project: hearsay was not fact; it was practically impossible for Hong to verify all his accounts; and no matter how much Hong himself trusted his informants, that sense of trust cannot be transmitted to his readers who might not have known those people as Hong did. Hong Mai's attitude changed beginning with the third installment. Probably affected by criticism, Hong became less assertive of the accuracy of his accounts.[15] When Hong compiled the first several installments, he had not yet made a strategic distinction between hearsay and facts. On the one hand, it seemed sufficient to him to empha-size that he had contemporary and reliable references—his fellow literati who had either witnessed or heard directly from those who witnessed the events—and, on the other, to show his effort to make corrections where necessary. He developed a new strategy in his later installments.

In the preface to the fourth installment, using the voice of his critics, Hong "admits" to the diversity of his informant pool. He states that the proj-ect has been criticized for being "not necessarily based on [the words of] worthies and scholar-officials of our time," and that Hong "all too eagerly accepted whatever strange story was to be had from the down and out, unregistered monks, mountain dwellers, Daoists, blind sorcerers, common women, minor officials, and itinerant soldiers. What then is the purpose for us to do research in search of truth?"[16] The critics, if there were any and if their criticisms were not simply Hong's rhetorical disclaimer, must have made the comment based on the content and the style of Hong's accounts because, as mentioned earlier, Hong cites his references for more than half of the surviving accounts and the named informants are predominantly lite-rati. Unlike in the preface to the previous installment, Hong no longer apol-ogizes for getting the facts wrong but claims that his methodology is modeled on that of the Grand Historian, Sima Qian, who faithfully recorded what he heard regardless of the unusualness, inconsistency, or inferior sources of the accounts.[17] More and more Hong came to characterize himself as a faithful recorder of hearsay rather than an investigator of facts, although he never completely gave up the pursuit of facts.[18]

In the preface to the fourteenth installment, Hong points out a few doubt-ful accounts—some with factual discrepancies; others whose logic Hong simply considers false. But instead of eliminating these accounts or editing them for better coherency, he keeps them as they are and leaves his doubt in the notes. He makes another association between his work and canoni-cal historiography: like the three commentaries to *The Annals of Spring and Autumn*, Hong claims that he also keeps whatever he has received regardless of whether the accounts are reliable or doubtful—"transmitting the reliable as the reliable; transmitting the doubtful as the doubtful." In this preface Hong most explicitly lays out his method of faithful recording: "All accounts in *Record of the Listener* come from hearsay. When a story is passed to me, I simply receive it. I know it myself that [such accounts tend to be] awkward to read and self-contradictory."[19] In a still later preface, Hong describes how obsessed he is with recording exactly in accordance with what he is told: "I record the stories of guests whenever I hear them. If we are busy drinking and there is insufficient time, I will write them down the following day and show the teller as soon as I can. I do not cease until there are no discrepancies from the beginning to the end."[20]

In line with Hong's previous claim to preserve discrepancies and the doubtful in his accounts, I read what Hong means by "discrepancies" (*chali*) here as those between Hong's record and his source, rather than those within the details in each account. Hong certainly did not transcribe what he heard word by word, since he wrote mostly in literary Chinese.[21] Yet the literary Chinese in *Record of the Listener* is sometimes mediocre, if not "awkward," as (allegedly) criticized by Hong's contemporaneous literati. Hong also always converted the narration into his voice even if he received the stories in writing. But *Record of the Listener* is not written in a uniform style.

Two questions remain unanswered: to what extent did Hong faithfully record? And to what extent does *Record of the Listener* contain voices beyond the circle of elite men? Hong's own prefaces and the identity of his named informants are not enough for us to answer these questions. We cannot uncritically accept Hong's own claims; we also should not completely reject them simply because many of the named informants were scholar-officials. Simply because a story was passed to Hong by a literatus does not mean that the story did not have other origins and had not been circulating within a wider population. Just as we cannot assume Hong or his elite informants transmitted folklore without any mediation, we also cannot assume that elite men's worldview is the only thing preserved in their accounts. This is particularly true in those accounts with inconsistent, fragmentary, and open-ended narratives. Furthermore, there is still a substantial number of accounts for which Hong Mai did not identify his sources.[22] Could it be that some of his informants were simply too humble to be named?

Close analyses of the narratives and comparisons with pre-Song tales that scholars have produced in the past two decades are illuminating in revealing the text's multivocality. Some propose that the distinction between *Record of the Listener* and earlier *zhiguai* literature lies in different purposes: the latter is "sheer storytelling" even though the narratives are often framed as what people see or hear, whereas the former aims at recording what people see or hear even though the stories are often fun to tell.[23] This quality makes many accounts in *Record of the Listener* different from *zhiguai* works either before or after its time, although some may argue that the distinction between the two is not as clear-cut. Fun-to-tell stories must have been a crucial selection criterion for Hong as well. But Hong and his fellow Song literati indeed were much more interested in others' experiences, including and perhaps especially those beyond their own circles. The stories about the lawlessness in the Southern Song capital Lin'an, for instance, provide "a valuable perspective on the social and mental worlds of the capital's residents."[24]

Two almost identical stories—one in the fourth-century *Records of an Inquest into the Spirit-Realm* (Soushen ji) and the other in *Record of the Listener*—differ in the style of narration, which in *Record of the Listener* reveals unprecedented concerns for pretense and verification in the world of gods and spirits. In *Record of the Listener*'s version, the narrative stands out by its "deferral of truth"—the true identity of the fox spirit and its gruesome trick are not revealed until the very end of the story.[25] Such concerns and anxiety must not have simply belonged to elite men. Interestingly, there are also stories in *Record of the Listener* for which truth is not simply deferred but fully unknown. No one in the story knows what actually happens, and the narrator (be it Hong or his informant) does not end the suspense.[26] Such permanent deferral of truth reveals a sense of uncertainty and bewilderment in face of the unknowable, a sentiment that was not exclusive to elite men.

Also, through comparing *Record of the Listener* with pre-Song *zhiguai* accounts, critics have pointed out two kinds of narratological ambiguity in the *Listener*: the meta-anomaly and the *fantastique*. Meta-anomaly denotes "one whose nature differs from initial expectations," something frequently seen in pre-Song and Song anomaly records.[27] The *fantastique*, in contrast, is extremely rare before *Record of the Listener*. There is no omnipresent narrator in a *fantastique*, and the truth of the anomalous incident (or whether or not it is indeed an anomalous incident at all) remains unknown.[28] These characteristics conform to Hong's claim that his stories came from hearsay and he tried to preserve them as they were passed on to him. The presence of an omniscient narrator would not be logical in hearsay since everyone can only offer what he or she hears or sees. We can still hear conflicting voices in some of the accounts that probably came from different witnesses, community gossip, and oral transmission.[29]

We can conclude that *Record of the Listener* is a unique text that has both strong authorship and diverse voices—the two features contributed to each other. Hong's strategic self-depiction as a faithful recorder was generated in defending himself against the criticisms about the inconsistency of his stories and awkwardness of the writing style; such a strategy had indeed influenced his work. Hong did care about the factuality and accuracy of his accounts, but he most likely did not edit them willfully simply to make his stories seem coherent. *Record of the Listener* was not a project for him to express his creativity or elegant writing. Nevertheless, it is not a monolithic text. It is a voluminous collection and, precisely because of Hong's compiling methods, can hardly be generalized. Some voices can be heard only through careful reading and close analysis of each account.

CONTINUITIES AND DEVELOPMENTS

There is a continuity across time and genre—in tales, anecdotes, and medical texts from the Tang to the Song—regarding the description of women who were believed to have suffered from enchantment disorders. Zhang Shizheng's (b. 1017) *Collection of Anomaly Accounts* (Kuoyi zhi; compiled between 1070s and 1090s) records a story about an elite family's daughter who was possessed by a ghost.[30] The young woman was the niece of Fu Wenxiu, vice commissioner of the Foreign Relations Office (Libin Fushi). It happened when the Fu family had moved away from the capital, Kaifeng, and were on their way back to their hometown, Fengxiang (in modern-day Shaanxi). The woman, still a maiden, began to "wear fine makeup and beautiful clothes at dusk, staying behind the curtains of her bedroom and whispering as if talking to someone." Her family asked her about it, but she did not answer.

The condition lasted for half a year until Fu summoned a certain Luo Jin, or "Luo the Interdictor," known for his spiritual interdiction and exorcism skills, from a neighboring county. Responding to Luo's interrogation, the ghost who possessed the woman confessed that he was the son of Han Qi (1008–1075), a prominent Northern Song official; he had died of illness at their lodging in Chang'an when accompanying his father, who was stationed in this area. When the Fu family passed by, he "loved the daughter's beauty and hence took her as a wife." Luo continued to question him, and he finally agreed to leave. A few nights later, however, the ghost cried and demanded that she give him his son back. He made her drink some medicine, and she "discharged lumps of flesh in the shape of fists." The ghost never came back.[31] The exorcist in this account was not associated with any specific religious tradition, nor was he called a *wu*. He was simply someone known for, and very likely who earned his living by, conducting exorcisms for people in the area.

The description of the enchanted young woman is stunningly similar to that in Liu Fu's account, except that she was not said to be "unwilling to share the bed with her husband," for she was not yet married. In this and many accounts of women's enchantment disorder, the woman withdraws from communication, frustrating those who try to understand her behavior. The silence in this story is rationalized by the later confirmed fact that the woman was possessed.

In another story, "The Fangs' Daughter," however, the woman's intentional silence resonates with the anxiety of not knowing and the fear of women's indifference to men that we have seen in the bedchamber literature. This story, in the third installment of *Record of the Listener* (1171), tells about a daughter of the Fang family who was "bewitched by an enchanting [spirit]" (*wei mei suo huo*) before being married. "Every afternoon, she dressed up and wore flowers before going to bed. When she woke up after more than four hours of sleep, she always appeared tipsy and filled with joy." Her elder brother asked her why, and she simply said, "I cannot say [*bu ke yan*; or, 'It is beyond words']. There is no such pleasure in this world."

The family asked several (alleged) Daoist priests for help, but all were defeated and humiliated. Hearing about this, none of the exorcists in the neighboring counties dared to come. The problem was finally solved after the family submitted a document of complaint (*sudie*) against the demon to Celestial Master Zhang (the legitimate successor of the Orthodox Unity Daoist tradition) at Dragon-Tiger Mountain (in present-day Jiangxi).[32] Once the document arrived, the woman's soul was brought to the court of the deity of Mount Tai, while her body remained home and she appeared in a coma. The narrative proceeds with the details of the woman's spiritual journey that only she herself could have known: the deity, in official attire and sitting in a judge's seat, told the woman that she was harassed by the "mountain goblins" (*shanxiao*) and demanded that she confess all she knew about the perpetrators. She gave all the details about the chief demon and others who drank and partied with her but hid one thing—that the one who first brought the demons to her, the "matchmaker," was in fact her deceased uncle. More than sixty demons (or minor deities) were punished for this, and the woman was sent back home. Since then, the story says, "The woman was fine as usual. Next year when married, she was still a virgin."[33]

The Fangs' daughter appeared to be conscious the whole time. She first kept her relationship with the demons a secret from her family and then avoided mentioning her uncle in her testimony in front of the divine judge. Eventually both secrets were revealed with the intervention of the powerful

Celestial Master. The exorcism—through the divine judicial system—restored not just her behavior and mental status but also her virginity.

Like earlier accounts, Song anecdotes include many enchantment stories about maidens and married women whose husbands are away. Also, like in earlier accounts, such women's sexual status is sometimes relevant to their affliction. But marriage is never automatically a cure. Meanwhile, Song accounts also include just as many enchantment stories about both elite and common women whose husbands are by their side. In early accounts, we see a pattern of correlation between the way women's ghostly enchantment is described and their social and marital status. Some Song anecdotes conform to the old pattern, while others do not. Some women are conscious during the process and others are not; some are cured and others are not—no matter whether they are commoners or from elite families.

The lack of coherent patterns is a result of social change as well as the heterogeneity of Song anecdotal writings, especially those included in *Record of the Listener*. Economic uncertainty contributed to the rise of the Wutong cult. Stories about the demon-deity, Wutong (variously called Wulang, Wumu, and Muke in the sources), as a sexual predator and capricious source of fortune flourished during the Southern Song.[34]

One account, "Sir Wulang," tells of Ms. Zheng, the wife of a shopkeeper, who had an affair with this demon-deity. The relationship began when her husband, Liu Xiang, was unable to make ends meet. Spending his day drinking, he left Zheng hungry, lonely, and resentful. Zheng suddenly came down with a fever and fell into a coma. She later recovered but afterward simply "sat alone in a room without uttering a word." Whenever she saw her husband, she "scowled and sneered at him." Liu then left home altogether. Zheng enclosed herself in a room and "purified herself" (*jieshen*)—a term often used in reference to the bodily preparations one makes to serve gods. People in her household would hear her talk, but when they looked in at her, they saw nothing.

After a long while, Liu returned home and saw the room filled with money and valuable goods. Zheng confessed that a young man who called himself Wulang ("Fifth Lad") had been visiting and sleeping with her for months; all the money and goods had been given to her by this young man. Liu, still in poverty and in need of money, did not blame his wife despite bitter feelings. Wulang further forbade Liu to sleep with Zheng and found him another wife. Liu did as he was told and even asked for Wulang's help to have a son. In response to Liu's prayer, Wulang stole the local governor's son. The governor found out the whereabouts of his son and threw both Liu and Zheng into prison. Wulang then broke them out of jail. The next day the governor arrested them again. Wulang once again rescued them back and then set fire to the governor's compound. The governor eventually gave in and allowed Liu and Zheng to continue serving Wulang. The story ends, "Sir Wulang in the end kept possession of Ms. Zheng."[35]

In this story we see a familiar image of an indifferent, even hostile, wife and the family's curiosity about her secluded room. We also see at least four things that were either new or only became common in Song stories. The first is the connection between women's spiritual or sexual possession and the acquisition of wealth. Material benefits that came along with mating with spirits were not new. But the connection, not specific to women, appeared more dangerous and morally ambiguous during the Song. Stories had been told before and during the Song about men, especially literati, encountering female deities who aided the men's career, wealth, and even progeny.[36] As in the Tang, it was still important in many Song stories for men to accurately identify whether the alluring female was a human, ghost, demon, or deity. Sometimes it was good judgment of this kind, rather than moral strength or self-control in general, that saved a man from fatal seductions.[37] Song stories, however, rarely praised men's relationships with female deities. The only account in Record of the Listener that expressly praised a man's relationship with a female deity was one where no physical intercourse took place. The man, named Chen Daoguang, a retired official, himself recorded the encounter in writing along with the ten poems that he composed in the deity's abode. Hong Mai commented in the end, "The woman and Chen drank together fondly the whole night and yet never transgressed the principle [buji luan]. This is not one with whom those immortals recorded in the petty accounts from the Tang dynasty could compare. Perhaps she was a true divine lady?"[38]

There are also stories about benign relationships between women and male deities, although far fewer than those between men and female deities. One example is in Further Records (late 5th c.). A young woman named Wu Wangzi met a young noble, who was later identified as the Marquis Su, a deity worshiped in the Yangzi Delta during the Southern Dynasties (420–589). The two developed a relationship. Whatever Wu wanted, the deity materialized it out of thin air. Wu's miraculous power was known to the neighboring villages, and the entire region worshiped her. But after three years, she "suddenly had other thoughts, and the deity no longer came."[39]

This story is told in a much more positive tone than "Sir Wulang." The young woman was not ill, possessed, or coerced. She remained in full control of her relationship with the deity. When she was no longer interested in him (or no longer fully committed to him; the wording is not clear), the deity simply left. Song stories about women receiving money or valuable goods from their spirit-lovers ranged from extremely dangerous to seemingly benign. The spirits included deities, demonic deities, animal spirits, and ghosts of the deceased. In all cases that I found in *Record of the Listener*, however, the women who received valuable gifts from spirits were all conscious and voluntary decision-making subjects.[40] Ms. Zheng was the only one who lost consciousness for a short period of time. The spirit Wulang in this account was particularly powerful and vile.[41] Other spirits were less so. One deity—the son of the Thearch of the North who lived with the winery administrator's daughter mentioned earlier—was a rare and intriguing combination of powerful and benign.[42]

The second thing that we rarely see in pre-Song enchantment and exorcism stories is absolute failure. Failure is oftentimes a narrative device that paves the way for the eventual success. We see it frequently in medical case histories and stories about various kinds of healing. This kind of narrative formula is emblematic of the development of storytelling skills as well as the availability of multiple healers or healing methods and the competition among them.[43] These certainly characterize many Song anecdotes. But in "Sir Wulang," all solutions fail. Similar to the failure of treatment is the failure of knowing. In "Sir Wulang" we at least know the perpetrator was called Wulang. Several stories end with such a remark, "no one knows what caused the problem," or the like.[44] The "deferral of truth" is permanent in several *Record of the Listener* accounts. The mystery is never solved, no treatment ends up working, and the truth is simply unknowable. In "Sir Wulang" specifically, there was a strong sense of helplessness in facing economic failure and hence men's control over their wives. Across the Song stories of failure in general, there was a spectrum of more diverse perspectives, including those of the patients and nonspecialists, men and women, and elite and commoners, who did not feel confident about the various forms of treatment or the healers of any tradition. There was often a sense of doubt, uncertainty, and powerlessness. Hong Mai and many of his sources expressed and transmitted that sense of uncertainly and powerlessness.

The third new element is a commonality between Ms. Zheng's symptoms and what the two Song physicians, Xu Shuwei and Chen Ziming, described as afflicting manless women: fever. Fever is a typical symptom of illnesses of the "cold damage" category. Both Xu and Chen noted that manless women's symptoms resembled *nüe,* a contagious cold damage disease. The story of Wulang and Ms. Zheng was the first anecdotal account, to my knowledge, that recorded fever as the initial symptom of an enchanted woman. It was still very different from Xu's and Chen's medical writings. No physician or medicinal treatment was present in Ms. Zheng's story, and neither Xu nor Chen associated manless women's illness with ghostly enchantment. Nevertheless, in Song anecdotes we begin to see more medical involvement in diagnosing and treating enchantment disorders, although it rarely works.

The final new element is that female characters can speak in their own voices. Ms. Zheng's confession is crucial for the narrative to proceed. Two Tang tales have the enchanted (or harassed) women talk. One (about Ms. Li in *Complete Record of Court and Country*) accentuates the woman's moral resistance against ghost enchantment.[45] The other (about a clerk's daughter in *Amusing Records during Huichang*) relies on the woman's own account to reveal her enchanted experience.[46] Many Song anecdotes belong to the latter kind. To count on women to reveal their own experiences could either be a narrative device that makes the story seem like hearsay or the trace of actual hearsay. Or perhaps a mixture of both.

ENCHANTED WOMEN, TRANSCENDENTS, AND *WU*

The overlap of Wutong lore and stories about women's enchantment disorder is emblematic of a certain construction of female sexuality and the porous identities of manless women. In a rather unusual account included in the fourth installment of *Record of the Listener*, titled "The Tree Lodgers in Jiangnan [the lower Yangzi region]," Hong Mai draws a link between enchanted women, female transcendents, and female *wu*. "Tree lodger" (Muke) is another name for Wutong, according to Hong. This account appears more similar to an encyclopedic entry than most other accounts in *Record of the Listener*. Hong (or the person from whom Hong received this account) assumes the role of a researcher or ethnographer, and selects and draws connections among a variety of folklore and textual references, telling the reader who exactly this demon is and what it does.[47] In other words, this entry not only collects and presents raw materials (hearsay) but also expressly turns raw materials into knowledge. According to the narrator, a number of demonic deities and goblins south of the Yangzi River were all the same kind of creature; they were simply called by different names in different regions. The narrator continues to describe their encounter with women in detail:

> They are particularly lascivious. Some disguise themselves as handsome gentlemen; some assume the form that the beholder

desires; some simply show their true forms, the worst of which resemble apes, dogs, or toads. They vary in shape but all are robust and can move at great speed. Their touch is as cold as ice and iron, and their penises are enormous. Women afflicted by such creatures are all in unbearable pain, emaciated and pale, losing all their energy. Some turn to be *wu*, and people regard them as transcendents [*xian*] and call their condition "transcendent illness" [*xianbing*]. Some fall into a coma for three, five, or even ten days as if dead; after waking up, they speak of having been transported to splendid houses and sharing sensuous pleasure with noblemen. Some are kidnapped and do not return until days later. Still some, as soon as they encounter these creatures, immediately descend into madness from which they never recover. Those who are [sexually] possessed by these creatures are not all good women. The [demonic] deities [approach women by] saying they have predestined contact; otherwise, they could not have approached the women. After the intercourse, they leave *jing* [i.e., semen] like black ink. Many women who are afflicted become pregnant. Such bizarre enchantment takes many forms.

This is followed by the record of fourteen incidents that the narrator believes to be the doings of Wutong, or the tree lodgers. Among the fourteen cases, five of the women ended up dead, one's whereabouts was unknown, and one went insane. Eight of them gave birth to monsters or deformed lumps. But only in seven cases does the narrative explicitly state that the woman had a sexual relationship with a demon or deity. Among the other six, one woman (a concubine "with fine appearance") was found hung from the roof beam by her hair bun;[48] one was pregnant before she was married and later gave birth to a "lump of flesh resembling cloth wrapped in purple silk"; one wife gave birth to a son who "resembled a human but was extremely ugly" and was not susceptible to cold or hot weather when becoming an adult; two wives gave birth to sons that resembled pigs with long fur; one concubine gave birth to four sons who all resembled monkeys with tiny hands and feet, but who all lived up to fifty or sixty years old; one wife was pregnant for ten years and gave birth to a monkey as red as blood.[49]

Although each case tells quite a different story, Hong Mai (or the original narrator) lists all of them under the umbrella of Wutong. And among all the doings of Wutong in its diverse and heterogeneous folklore, he picks only those related to its intrusion of female sexuality and draws a parallel between fox spirits in the north and Wutong in the south. But as we know, fox spirits affect both men and women.[50] Wutong, as characterized in this account, victimizes only women. The way it describes the Wutong's violation of female sexuality is intriguingly inconsistent with regards to whether the afflicted women are agents or objects of desire, and whether or not they are responsible for what happens to them. We have seen something very similar in the bedchamber texts' description of women who have intercourse with ghosts, as discussed in chapter one: the ghosts, like Wutong, are lascivious and hyper-sexual; women are attracted to them in the beginning but they will suffer and eventually die. The knowledge that is constructed here is not just about Wutong but also or perhaps particularly about female sexuality. It is as if only through describing and classifying such possessions and violations can female sexuality be defined—female sexuality as a palpable entity that can be possessed and violated.

As mentioned earlier, this entry is a rather anomalous one in *Record of the Listener* for its obvious effort to produce knowledge out of raw materials through selecting and generalizing folklore. Some cases that are included in this account match the conventional description of women's enchantment disorders (*mei*); others do not. In numerous other accounts about women's ghost enchantment and anomalous births, the causes vary significantly. There is no doubt that the Wutong cult was popular in this region during the Southern Song or that associations were drawn among Wutong, enchanted women, monstrous births, and female *wu*. But popular perceptions and practices were messier than what is presented in this one account, and the association between female *wu* and enchanted women seemed new and still unstable during the Song.

Who was a *wu* and who was a female *wu*? A challenge in studying *wu* is that when the source refers to someone or a certain kind of people as *wu*, we rarely know if that was also how those people identified themselves, especially after *wu* became a general and sometimes derogatory term in popular use.[51] In the Tang, those who were called *wu* often were involved in practices including healing, divination, *yasheng* (conquering the enemy with occult means), and rain conjuring. But in contrast to those who were also healers—physicians (*yi*), physiognomists (*xiangzhe*), occultists (*fangshi*), Daoist priests, and Buddhist monks—*wu* were distinctive in their capability of making gods descend into their bodies and speak through their mouths.[52]

In studying spirit possession and exorcism in the Song, Edward Davis accentuates the difference between a shaman and a spirit-medium. The former, in the case of the Tungus shaman, is "master of the spirits in his journey to the underworld"; "the subject of trance—the shaman—coexists with the guardian spirits." A spirit-medium's possession, in contrast, "is a trance of identification in which the persona of the divinity is substituted for, and does not coexist with, that of the subject. The possessed subject does not converse with or imitate the divinity; he (or she) is the divinity!" In light of this distinction, *wu* can be thought of as spirit-mediums.[53] Indeed many of them were. Nonetheless, in Song (as well as pre-Song) sources the meaning of *wu* often depends on the context. Song physicians used *wu* as "a general derogatory term for any healer they considered heterodox or illegitimate." There was no clear or uniformed definition. In the eyes of the Song government, *wu* were not those who practiced any specific kind of "witchcraft" but those who did not conform to the imperial order.[54] Officials and other literati used *wu* as a negative epithet for those ritual masters whom they looked down upon.[55]

There are also plenty of nonderogatory references to *wu* in Song sources. Liu Fu's account is an example where the senior *wu* was an efficacious ritual healer. One account in *Record of the Listener* tells of an old female *wu* (*wu'ao*) who could see and communicate with the souls of the deceased. Through communicating with a magistrate's deceased wife and having the magistrate write her a formal divorce letter, this *wu* cured the mysterious illness of the magistrate's current wife. But there is no mention of her being possessed by the ghost that she communicated with or that she served any particular deity.[56] In another story, a female *wu*, the Divine Seventh Lady, helped an official who fled south during the Jurchen invasion to find his lost family. She did so as a spirit-medium of a deity of the South Peak. The record says that the official was deeply grateful and brought a large amount of money to her; she accepted nothing but scented candles and flowers.[57] In sum, the use of the term *wu* varied during the Song. Those who were called *wu* were usually involved with some kind of sorcery, sometimes but not always related to spirit possession. *Wu* was often distinguished from those healers who used mainly medicinal recipes (such people and their medicine were called *yi*). A Daoist master would distinguish himself from a *wu* but he could not prevent everyone else from calling him one. Someone who was called a *wu* did not necessarily deem him or herself so; those who called themselves *wu* did not always do the same thing.

Many sources do not specify whether the *wu* was a man or a woman. In most Song cases where we know it was a woman, she did not do things particularly different from a male *wu*, except that in two *Record of the Listener* accounts, the female *wu* was described as sexually involved with the deity or demon. One is the "Tree Lodgers" cited earlier. The other is "Chen the

Female *Wu*," which tells of a woman, née Chen, who was brought up in a hereditary *wu* family and offered to serve their god as a *wu* before married. We do not know why the plan changed, but Chen later married into a local elite family and left the *wu* business. But the god continued to visit her after she was married. The record describes what happened to Chen just like an enchantment disorder case—she dressed up and met the god in a trance. The family that she married into also dealt with the problem as if it were an enchantment disorder—summoning a Daoist priest (or a popular ritualist who claimed to be a Daoist priest) for help. After submitting a divine petition, the Daoist priest successfully extinguished the god's interest in the woman. But the family was still scared and decided to send the woman back to her natal home. The woman then went back and became a *wu* again.[58]

Both accounts draw a connection between female *wu* and women's enchantment disorder. But in the latter case, Chen became a *wu* not because she was enchanted but because she inherited this profession from her family. The god kept visiting her despite the fact that she had married and quit being a *wu*. She only went back to being a *wu* because her husband's family was still scared, even though her god had promised to stop visiting her. A hereditary *wu* family like Chen's probably did call themselves *wu*. In many nonderogatory stories *wu* were depicted as legitimate healers and exorcists who helped their enchanted patient-clients with their specialist knowledge and power, just like the *wu* described in Liu Fu's account mentioned at the beginning of this chapter.

On the one hand, it seemed unlikely that a professional healer who was able to cure enchanted women would have deemed herself to be in a similar category as her patient-clients. On the other hand, "Tree Lodgers" and "Chen the Female *Wu*" show that if a woman was considered incurable from enchantment disorder and therefore unfit for a conventional marriage, she could perhaps go along with popular perception and become a *wu* by trade. What the two accounts also tell us is the conflation in some Song people's perception of a female *wu*'s ability to conjure up spirits and a woman's sexual relationship with the spirits. Such a conflation downplays a female *wu*'s subjectivity, talent, and professional skill; but at the same time, it reflects a particular construct of female sexuality and subjectivity that was related to the social presence of women's economic independence.[59]

Hagiographies, however, never confuse a female transcendent with a *wu* or an enchanted woman. Nakamura Jihē in his study on Chinese shamanism associates the "illness of transcendents" mentioned in "Tree Lodgers" with a Tang account that depicts a woman who became connected to deities after a period of illness. Nakamura further links both cases to what

Akiba Takashi terms the "shamanic disease" in Korea that occurs in the process of becoming a shaman.[60] However, the woman in the Tang account (a maid named Miaonü) was not called a *wu* but a *xian* (transcendent, or deity, in this context). Her symptoms (heart attack, coma, vomitoria, and diarrhea) resemble those of spirit possession, but she was not said to have a sexual relationship with any spirit. The account tells that she was originally a *xian* and was exiled to the human world for her wrongdoings. During the coma her soul was sent to heaven to meet her divine family and her true identity was discovered.[61] The conflation of *wu, xian*, and enchanted women is unique in Song accounts.

NARRATIVES OF TREATMENT

Quite a number of stories in *Record of the Listener* are adapted in the fiction and drama of later times. In Ming-Qing literary fiction, men usually do not lose consciousness when involved in a relationship with a vixen spirit or female ghost, and it depends on men's moral strength to rid themselves of the danger. Women who are molested by male spirits, meanwhile, are often depicted as possessed and in need of external intervention such as medicine and exorcism.[62] In Song anecdotes, however, people often appeal to professional healers as long as they believe some kind of spirit is involved, no matter whether the afflicted is a man or a woman. Even when a man meets a female deity who makes him look healthier than before, his father still summons all kinds of exorcists and tries every recipe to "cure" him— probably because no one is completely certain who the woman really is.[63] The gender of the patient and whether or not the relationship is sexual still affects the ways stories are told—for example, the symptoms of men and women are not all the same; the patient's marital status sometimes matters for women but almost never does for men; enchanted women are considered unfit for marriage, but such men are not. The postexorcism treatments also seem to be gendered in some cases: there are more stories of men than of women who need replenishment of their essence and blood, whereas purgatory therapies, including aborting a ghost fetus, are usually given to women.[64] But the methods of exorcism did not seem to vary according to gender or sex. In other words, like in medical treatises and Daoist ritual manuals, and unlike bedchamber literature, treatments for men's and women's sexual involvement with spirits as described in Song anecdotes were not distinguished in nature from those for nonsexual contacts.

Despite plenty of recipes for ghost intercourse recorded in Song and pre-Song medical texts, there is no mention of using medicine or physicians (*yi*) or recipes seen in medical texts to treat such problems in pre-Song tales.[65] Only during the Song do we begin to see anecdotal records of using medicinal recipes or summoning physicians in dealing with ghost intercourse or enchantment disorder. But medicine was usually not the first nor the only resort; it was mostly applied after the spirit had been expelled. The use of medicine or medicinal recipes was not a privilege of physicians either.

For example, the daughter of a family became pregnant before marriage. Questioned by her parents, she confessed that a man in yellow came to rape her every night and that was how she became pregnant. Her family prepared an ambush outside her room that night and saw the man coming. They stabbed the man, who turned out to be the neighbor's old yellow dog. They then "use medicinals [*yao*] to remove the fetus," which appeared to be a "strange baby animal."[66] The story does not mention any involvement of a specialist. The nieces of Fu Wenxiu mentioned earlier also took a medical decoction after the ghost left. The decoction was provided by either the ghost or the exorcist, Luo the Interdictor, who was called a "ghostbuster" (*shan zhigui zhe*; literally, "one who is skilled in subjugating ghosts") rather than a physician.[67] In two stories about men's erotic encounters with female spirits, "Clay Fetus" and "Lady by the West Lake," medicine was used to replenish their lost essence and blood. One man had a relationship with a clay woman in a Buddhist temple. The abbot discovered their relationship and shattered the clay woman with a stick. A clay fetus appeared among the broken pieces. The abbot told the man to "grind it and take with medicine."[68] The other man lived with a woman for half a year before the woman confessed to him that she was a ghost. She predicted that the man would soon have acute diarrhea due to the six months of their contact; "[my] *yin qi* penetrated you deeply," she said. That was the reason they had to part. She further instructed the man to take the "stomach soothing powder," a recipe recorded in the *Formulary of the Medical Bureau* (Taiping huimin hejiju fang; 1109–1110), to "replenish and stabilize essence and blood."[69]

A variety of healers appeared in Song exorcism stories, and they were called by various titles: occultist (*fangshi, shushi*), *wu*, healer-*wu* (*yiwu*), physician (*yi*), ritual master (*fashi*), ritualist (*faren*), person of Dao (*Daoren*), Buddhist monk (*seng*), Daoist priest (*Daoshi*), et cetera.[70] Some were simply called by what they did, such as "the ghostbuster," "Liu the Ghost-Capturer," "the one who knows the skills," "the practitioner of the Celestial Heart [or other traditions of exorcist rituals]," or "the talisman-water peddler." By the titles we can tell that some of them were professional healers, while others were practitioners of certain rituals or healing methods but not necessarily by trade. There were also secular but quite advanced practitioners such as the "scholar-official Zhang" who recited *The Book of Changes* to expel the spirit of a lion statue, "Uncle Yu the noodle peddler" who could perform the Daoist ritual "Steps of Yu" and write talismans (*fu*), and "Guardian Liu the frankincense eater" who also knew the Steps of Yu.[71]

Exorcist rituals dealt with the external intruders—the spirits—while medicine usually focused on fortifying the body from within, although there was sometimes no clear-cut line between the two. In Song times, the specialization among various healers seems to have increased. When Song people suspected that spirits were the cause of any affliction, their first reaction was often to find a way to expel them; in many cases, they hired professional ritualists.[72] The twenty-eighth installment of *Record of the Listener* includes a case history of Xiong Bangjun, who was a physician from a physicians' family. In 1189 Xiong was afflicted with a feverish illness, so his father found a colleague of his to treat him. This colleague took Xiong's pulse and prescribed medicine with heat properties, which simply exacerbated the symptoms. Another physician came in and prescribed a cooling medicine. Xiong felt slightly better but relapsed in less than a day and began to see visions, compose metered poetry, and recite songs and scriptures that he never knew before. Xiong's father finally came to realize that it was a case of malign spirit possession (*sui pingfu*) and invited Ritual Master Long over for treatment. Long applied a ritual stamp on Xiong's palms and tied his hands together. Xiong finally came back to himself but needed another half month to fully recover.[73]

Another man was not as lucky. Chen was a residential scholar for Pan, the magistrate of Puqi (in present-day southeast Hubei), in 1192. Pan and Chen often drank in front of a yard of luxuriant plantain trees and jokingly invited Lady Plantain Tree to accompany them. After a year, a beautiful woman in green began to visit Chen regularly and slept with him. After a hundred days or so, Chen looked pallid. Pan did not know about the woman and thought Chen was simply sick. He summoned physicians to treat Chen but did not see much effect. As Chen grew extremely sick, he finally confessed to Pan that there was a Lady Plantain Tree who had been visiting him. Pan immediately made someone cut the trees down. But it was too late to save Chen's life.[74]

The two stories deliver a similar message: the demon has to be killed or expelled before anything else can work. It was not necessarily because ritualists were considered more powerful than physicians—the first story was told by a physician about his own experience; in the second story, a special ritual was not needed to kill Lady Plantain Tree. Rather than a matter of perceived efficacy, what the two stories tell us is the specialization of healers or healing methods and the sequence of treatment in popular practice.[75] Medicine was usually effective and sometimes necessary *after* the spirit was timely removed. "Clay Fetus" and "Lady by the West Lake" are both examples. In two other stories the men, after a short period of relationship with a female spirit, left the haunted place and went to see a physician. Both recovered.[76] In none of the four cases did the man use medicine or go to see a physician because a *wu* or an exorcist ritual did not work. They did so because the spirits had gone and now it was medicine's turn to take care of the rest.

In the meantime, many Song people did go from one healer or method to another until someone or something finally worked, if they were lucky enough. A kind of efficacious narrative occurs frequently in *Record of the Listener*: The spirit defeats or scares away one ritualist after another until the most powerful and upright master arrives. "The Fangs' Daughter" is an example, where the powerful exorcist is the famous Celestial Master Zhang from Dragon-Tiger Mountain.[77] In another story, the exorcist was an aloof and obscure "Daoist kind" (*Daoliu*), who was called "Master Spirit-Killer." The daughter of a local official, when turning eighteen in 1190, was suddenly "afflicted with an illness and often whispered as if intimately talking to someone." Before Master Spirit-Killer came, "neither physicians/medicine or sorcerers could treat [her]" (*yi wu buneng zhi*). The master at first was also unable to defeat the demon simply by using ritual sword and exorcist water. Then he sent his spirit away and met with a divine messenger, who told him which spell to use, after which he succeeded. The demon confessed that he was in fact the deity of a temple nearby. When the woman's father was still poor, he once asked for the deity's help and in return promised to offer his daughter as the deity's wife. After he became rich, however, he broke his promise. The master, instead of killing or punishing the deity, negotiated with him and proposed to make a statue of the woman beside him, and let her spirit come home. The deity agreed. The daughter then recovered and later took a husband at her natal home.[78]

It was said that the granddaughter-in-law of the infamous Northern Song prime minister Cai Jing (1047–1126) also had an enchantment experience. In 1120, she began to dress up in the evening and sit outside as if waiting for someone. After returning to her room, she whispered as if talking to someone and laughed joyfully for the whole night. The next day she often slept deeply, ignored her close family members, and did not eat. Cai first summoned the Daoist priests from the Abbey of the Precious Registers (constructed under Emperor Huizong's commission, finished in 1116) and subsequently various famous ritualists in the capital. All were defeated and insulted by the demon. At the time Zhang Xujing (the thirtieth Celestial

Master in the Orthodox Unity lineage) happened to be in the capital. Cai secretly called him over. The moment Zhang entered the hall, the demon roared over the roof to intimidate him. Zhang told Cai that this demon was unusually powerful and that he could try but not guarantee success. If he could not expel it, no one else could. Zhang spent two days preparing for the ritual and, on the third day, successfully defended himself against the demon's attacks and subjugated it. But the demon could not be killed because it "has connection to heaven and killing it will result in great misfortune." Zhang sent the demon into exile, and the granddaughter-in-law immediately recovered.[79]

There are several similar stories in *Record of the Listener.* A Daoist priest from Quanzhou healed a local official's daughter after physicians and *wu* failed.[80] Lu Dangke, an exorcist who featured in several *Record of the Listener*'s stories, defeated the son of a tutelary deity after a number of ritualists failed.[81] A Buddhist monk who practiced the Rites of Three Altars saved a young woman from an alligator spirit when none of the *wu* were able to do so.[82] The Yongs' daughter was taken as a wife by the son of a powerful deity. Neither Daoist priests nor Buddhist monks who practiced the Rites of Impure Traces (Huiji Fa; the Rites of Ucchuṣma) could help. A "man of Dao," Yang Gaoshang, finally sent the deity away.[83] The famous Daoist leader of the early Southern Song, Ning Quanzhen (1101–1181), saved a physician's daughter from a monkey spirit after ineffective rituals performed by *wu*.[84] By documenting failure, such efficacious narratives emphasize the efficacy of the true healer and at the same time accentuate the power of the spirits and the severity of the problem. The abundance of such narratives was also emblematic of the competitive healing market in Southern Song society and people's experiences with mediocre healers. Furthermore, in efficacious narratives the final successor was often a Daoist ritualist, even though across all *Record of the Listener* stories all kinds of healers had their moments of success as well as moments of failure. It was likely that there was a collective effort for the Daoist ritualists and those who were in favor of them actively engaged in such efficacious narratives—both through writing and oral transmission.

Another kind of narrative—I call it the amateur's narrative—similarly documents unsuccessful treatment attempts, but there is no powerful and true healer in the end. All the professional healers fail, and some self-improvised method invented out of desperation or on a whim solves the problem. We already saw in pre-Song stories several cases where nonspecialists successfully killed or expelled demons, and in one Tang story the upright widow herself fought back by disfiguring herself.[85] But in many Song stories, the afflicted or their families would first go to specialists and only manage to devise something on their own when the specialists fail. "Sir Candlenut of Xincheng" tells of the daughter of a local magistrate. One day when she climbed up a tower in the magistrate's compound and looked outside, she suddenly began to talk and laugh on her own in front of an old candlenut tree. From then on, she wore makeup and climbed up to the building every day, rain or shine. Her father "summoned a *wu* and looked for medicine to treat her," but the condition continued. The problem only ended after her family cut down the tree whose spirit was believed to have enchanted their daughter. As the tree was chopped, the girl cried out "Sir Candlenut!" in despair. But afterward, she remembered nothing.[86]

"Chen's Wife" tells about a woman in Xingan (in present-day Jiangxi) who had been enchanted by a certain spirit for several years beginning in 1163. She was a commoner's wife living with her husband and mother-in-law in a village. The spirit seemed to have bothered the entire household and was not a secret. The woman did not show symptoms of enchantment disorder, nor did she lose herself. She seemed simply as annoyed as the rest of her family. The story makes no mention of how the family discovered the enchantment, but focuses on the coordination in dealing with the problem. After "a hundred methods of exorcism all failed," the husband asked the wife what she had been seeing and what they looked like. The wife said, "At first, a man in white forced me to sleep with him. Now whenever I weave linen, an old woman always comes to weave together and brings two girls to help cook. It happens every day." The mother-in-law was also annoyed and asked the wife to inform her next time the demon came. The wife did, and the mother-in-law carried a knife in and stabbed the old woman. The old woman revealed the gold in her pocket and said, "I am here to enrich your family. How can you kill me!" The mother-in-law was stunned, and the old woman disappeared in the blink of an eye. The husband said, "This demon is easy to deal with." He passed a knife to the wife and told her to attack the man in white. The wife did and hit the man's shoulder. The old woman came again, talked to the wife about the injured man (who turned out to be her son), and tried to invoke the wife's feelings. The wife, however, spared no sympathy for the man or the old woman and tried to stab the old woman again. The old woman ran away and exposed a fox tail behind her skirt. Soon the two girls came crying, accusing the wife of hurting and betraying their husband and mother-in-law. The wife stabbed them too, and both girls turned into stone. From that time on, the spirits never came back.[87]

These two stories contain two sets of almost opposite elements: an unmarried maiden from an elite family and a commoner's wife with her husband at her side; lost subjectivity versus remaining consciousness during the enchantment; the father cutting down the tree and saving the daughter versus the wife working with the rest of the family and physically attacking the spirits on her own.

Hong Mai's collection also contains more complicated amateur's narratives such as the two that follow. The source of both accounts was a scholar-official named Zhu Conglong.[88] One tells that in 1180 a group of spirits haunted a scholar's house in Yongfeng Prefecture (in present-day east Jiangxi) and played all kinds of tricks. The scholar, named Guan, was extremely disturbed. He "summoned *wu*-masters to exorcise [the spirits]—not effective; he commissioned Daoist priests to hold a *jiao* rite to purify [the house] and also invited those who practiced [exorcist] rituals. All tried their best to chase [the spirits] and investigate [the problem]. Even if [the spirit] temporarily became quiet the day [when the ritualists came], all went back the same after they left." Guan continued to gather more of "the Daoist kind" and perform all kinds of rituals. The spirits showed no fear and proclaimed, "You hicks just grab your money and go! We're not scared of you!" The situation continued for a long time. One of the spirits assumed the form of a beautiful woman and visited a servant's bedroom at night. The servant knew she was not human and yet still slept with her. They spent several nights together, and the servant began to worry about the consequences. One night he hid a knife and chopped off her head. The woman turned back into a large raccoon dog. The servant took the head out and announced to the Guan family, "I've killed the ghost!"[89]

On the one hand, the contrast between the failure of the specialists and the success of a lowly servant creates enough tension for a good story. On the other hand, the distrust of the professionals and the disrespect for profit-making ritualists might have been part of the popular sentiment during this time. Still, this is a twist on the moralized discourse on ritual and healing practices. In many Daoist scriptures and popular anecdotes from the Southern Song, we see the emphasis on the correlation between efficacy and the purity of the ritualist's personality and practice.[90] It is perhaps part of this larger narrative that the spirits scorn the ritualists for begging for money. But the ending turns it all around: a petty and lustful servant simply kills the ghost.

The other story tells of a spirit that forced a rich merchant's young and beautiful wife into a relationship when the husband was away for business. The wife first saw the spirit disguised as a handsome young man in her backyard; when the young man flirted with her, she solemnly reprimanded him. Later that night the young man went straight to the woman's bed, and she was unable to resist even with the help of all her maidservants. From that time on he always came at night and left in the morning. Whatever she wanted appeared in front of her immediately and without her request. And yet she still missed her husband and did not give up seeking help. She informed her family, who summoned a "Daoist priest to perform the Five Thunder Rites and to hold a *jiao* rite" and "twenty Buddhist monks to set up a yoga altar." But all were defeated by the spirit.

After several months when the husband was about to come home, the spirit threatened the wife to keep their relationship a secret. But she confessed and asked her husband to punish her by death. The husband vowed to kill the spirit and succeeded by ambushing it and stabbing it in the back. The spirit was gone, and, the story says, the couple treated each other like newlyweds.[91] What the narrative depicts in most detail is the wife's resistance and honesty throughout. In contrast to stories like "Sir Wulang," the husband in this story is affluent and the wife always loves him; the spirit only seems powerful until the husband comes home. It presents an interesting viewpoint on morality and conjugal relations: the wife is resistant against the intruder, but she does not have to defend herself to the point of death; the husband is forgiving and fights for his wife. The wife, nonetheless, is still supposed to confess. Honesty and the conjugal bond are key to their success.

We know from other stories by Zhu Conglong that he did not distrust all ritual specialists—the Daoist priest Dong Zhongfu and the recluse Ritual Master Huang were both efficacious in two other stories.[92] All four amateur narratives discussed here were transmitted to Hong Mai by literati, but they present a mixture of perspectives and voices. They shared the sentiment that an enchanting spirit should still be expelled, but they did not seem to particularly favor one method over another. In addition to the failure of multiple ritual specialists, the collaboration between the enchanted woman and her husband and other family members is something that we rarely see in pre-Song stories.

FAILURES AND UNCERTAINTIES

There are also narratives of complete failure, where no one is able to expel the spirit and people just have to live with the fact that their women have been taken and nothing can be done. Some narratives of this kind are fragmentary and incoherent; others are polished and cohesive. "Sir Wulang" is an example of the latter. Afflictions by powerful and capricious spirits were not unique to men in poverty and women in solitude like Liu and Ms. Zheng.

A Rao family in Fuzhou (in present-day Jiangxi) was haunted by a spirit precisely because they were rich. The Raos lived in a village called Shupo, which was surrounded by luxuriant forests. One day during the Rao family's outing, the daughter-in-law saw a fallen willow tree with clear water inside like a mirror. She looked into the water and immediately became ill. When she returned home, she could no longer recognize anyone and only stayed in bed. The family started to hear voices from the air interacting with people, discussing poetry and music with them, and taunting them for their errors in prosody. But no one saw anything. The spirit also snitched on everyone in the family, and all were annoyed. For several years, the Raos tried every method of exorcism, but none worked. The Raos then prayed to the spirit and promised to build a shrine for it. For a few days the spirit became quiet. The Raos thought the spirit had accepted the deal and commissioned a beautiful shrine to be built and made sacrifices to it every day. Five days after the shrine was built, the spirit came again and played tricks as before. The head of the family, Mr. Rao, was vexed and accused the spirit of breaking the agreement. The spirit laughed and said, "Am I so stupid as to give up such a grand mansion for a tiny shrine?" The Raos became more and more frustrated and fearful. The spirit only left after the daughter-in-law died, and the Rao family went into decline.[93]

While Wutong was the reason for Liu and Zheng's acquisition of wealth, this unknown spirit caused the Rao family's downfall. Like the Wutong cult, this story also vividly embodies the Song society's anxiety about the sudden rise and fall of personal fortunes in the emergence of a monetary economy.[94] Unlike many other enchantment stories, this narrative does not give much detail about the afflicted woman—she only appears at the beginning and the end. More focus is placed on the mysterious spirit's caprice and the family's struggle to send it away. The story was told after the Rao family had gone downhill but perhaps still maintained some local influence—judging by the fact that there was no erotic depiction of their late daughter-in-law—and the shrine they built was probably still there. It was unfortunate for the Raos but perhaps somewhat comforting for the rest of the village who did not have a grand mansion to worry about.

Another story is much shorter but more unsettling. It also took place in Fuzhou. Lan Xianqing, a scholar-official from Jinxi, Fuzhou, and his wife were caught in a thunderstorm on their way to the wife's natal home. During the rain, a beautiful red leaf fell gently into the wife's arms. She loved it and kept fondling it. That night in her sleep, she felt as though someone climbed up on her bed and had intercourse with her. She told her husband the next day and soon became crazy, talking nonsense and walking around with loosened hair and bare feet. Lan was extremely disturbed, but "no physician or exorcist was able to wield their power," and "no one knew what was causing the evil."[95] In many Song stories the knowledge of the enchantment situation is very much dependent upon the woman's self-disclosure—either during the enchantment or after the woman recovers. But if the woman remains unconscious or unable (or unwilling) to communicate, like Lan's wife, the situation often falls into a mystery. This account is titled "Red Leaf in the Arms," but the connection between the red leaf and the woman's condition is no more than a speculation. Nothing further was said about the mysterious red leaf, perhaps because, unlike the fox spirits, the snakes, the mountain goblins, and the like, there was not a lore about red leaves. There was no available epistemic framework more specific than enchantment disorder in general through which this woman's condition could be understood.

In two other stories, the women's conditions were more readily associated with the types of spirits that people were familiar with. But uncertainties and speculations linger in the narratives. One account is titled "Snake Anomaly in the Yu Family":

> Yu Liuqilang of Leping [in present-day Jiangxi] married the Cheng's daughter for just a year. Once Cheng was about to ascend the bed during the day and saw a snake coiled on it. The snake was only somewhat over a *zhang* [twelve feet] long and three *cun* [4.3 inches] wide. Cheng was terrified and called people in the household to drive it away with sticks. The snake leapt off the bed, exited the room, and disappeared. People say in the village that there are the so-called fortune gods in the mountains, the *xiao*-goblin type, who can show bizarre things to people in order to request offerings. And yet such goblins are not particularly powerful. Even village exorcists and local ghost-seers can cast them away. Some of the worst ones assume the form of human or snake to molest women. Yu was therefore suspicious. Cheng appeared bewildered and somewhat different from usual. But no one knew if she was afflicted by a spirit or not. She died after a month. When her body was about to be buried, a snake that resembled the previous one exactly came again and coiled on top of her belly. People brought sticks over, and the snake quickly ran away. No one knew where it went. This snake

was named "Piglet." It was the second month of the first year during the Qingyuan reign [1195].[96]

The story seemed to be a result of the attempt to reconstruct the woman's experience in order to explain her sudden death. No healer was summoned to diagnose or treat her—perhaps because she died too quickly and her symptoms were minor—and therefore a specialist's perspective is lacking. The family drew from local folklore, the tales about the fortune gods, to help understand the woman's seemingly unusual behavior. Or, perhaps conversely, local folklore about the mountain goblins caused the Yu family to understand the minor discomfort suffered by this woman through the language of spirit enchantment. But they could only suspect; they could not know. Furthermore, there was a discrepancy between the local knowledge of the mountain goblins and what happened to the woman: The mountain goblins as described in this region were "not particularly powerful," and yet the woman died suddenly. Compared with "Sir Wulang," there is more perplexity than fear in this story. Perhaps the naming of the mysterious snake in the end could also be seen as the expression of a desire to know by the action of naming?

The other story tells that in 1195, the wife of a man in Zhuji (in present-day Zhejiang) was pregnant and two months overdue. One night the wife felt pain in her belly, and the husband accompanied her and slept by her side. He woke up in the middle of the night and found that his wife had disappeared, and yet the door was closed as if never opened. He carried a lantern and gathered the neighbors to search for her. Past midnight, they heard voices from the lake and saw under the moonlight that the wife was in the lake. As they brought her home, they discovered she had lost the baby. She recalled that a group of people came to her room earlier that night and brought her to a small chamber set up as a delivery room. There she delivered the baby and heard people surrounding her congratulating her for having a boy. But the baby boy soon disappeared before she was able to see him. She said, "Now as I recall it, I must have been close to death and was simply fortunate to have survived." The next day she felt fully recovered and no lingering pain. The story describes the lake as not big but connected to a river. People (or the narrator) "suspected that when the woman conceived the fetus, she must have dreamed of having intercourse with an aquatic dragon or the like although she was unwilling to speak of it."[97]

The body of this story is made of both what others saw and what the woman said. But the narrator (and perhaps the people in the village as well) was not content with what the woman had said. What she said was then supplemented with popular knowledge. Although this account does not cite or explain the references that it draws upon, unlike the previous story, we know from earlier tales that women living by the rivers pregnant with aquatic dragon babies was a familiar trope; such stories had been told since the fifth century.[98] In earlier stories women did not need to have sexual intercourse (or dream of such) with aquatic dragons to be pregnant. The narrator(s) of this story, however, asserted that the woman in Zhuji must have done so and that she was simply reluctant to say. This resonates with discussions of ghost fetuses, ghost intercourse, and enchantment disorders in both Song medical texts and popular anecdotes. It also shows how the knowledge of enchanted women was shaped not simply by medical or religious specialists but also by the processes of storytelling, gossiping, and information exchange in local communities.

There is yet another kind of failure—the failure to be happy. Several stories in *Record of the Listener* challenge what is considered successful treatment. The "successful" removal of the spirit does not always seem to be a good thing. The best example is perhaps "Yong's Daughter." Yong was the administrator of the prefectural winery in Jiankang (present-day Nanjing). The story states that his daughter encountered an elegant young man when she and her mother visited a temple of Zhenwu (the Perfected Warrior, a major Daoist god). The man followed her from the east wing to the west wing. The mother scolded him and quickly brought the daughter home. However, that night when the daughter was about to go to sleep, the young man was already in the bed, telling her that he was of noble birth and that she deserved better than her family's status. They then spent the night together. The next morning the mother knew and was worried. After ten days, the young man formally greeted the woman's parents as his parents-in-law, behaving like a scholar-official.

Another day, he said to the woman that he would like to contribute to the household and told her to look into the rice when cooking. In the rice she found several pearls, and this became a daily routine. The family soon became rich and built a new house and a separate multistoried building as the man and woman's residence. Anything the family needed came upon request. During their family banquets, furniture and utensils always came down from the steps as if someone was carrying them. This continued for several years until someone said to the father, "Are you really willing to sacrifice such a daughter to an evil ghost? Besides, all the fortune you received may not be real. There must be misfortune in the future if this continues." The father was never happy about the situation; hearing this, he began to summon exorcists, from Daoist priests to Buddhist monks, but all were defeated. Someone taught the father to expel the "ghost" by arranging a marriage for the daughter. The young man played tricks on the wedding day and made the groom fall off the bed multiple times. The groom was scared and ran away. The Yong family did not dare to mention any plans of exorcism again. The young man treated the woman the same way as before but told her that he would bring misfortune on her parents for their betrayal, even though he had prayed to the bureau of the netherworld to elongate the woman's previously destined short life.

Some time later, the Yong family invited over a "man of Dao" named Yang Gaoshang, who was known for the efficacy of his rituals. The young man foresaw this and told the woman that the coming one was a "true ritual master" and so he would soon have to leave. Before he was able to escape, Yang the ritual master had arrived and captured him in the "net of heavenly power." The Yong family could all see him standing in a cage. Yang reprimanded him, "The paths of humans and gods differ. How could you violate heaven's law on purpose? Now if I punish you by the degree you deserve, I am afraid that it would bring trouble to your honorable father. If you do not comply with my command, I will submit a memorial to the bureau of heaven and let you be punished by exile to the hell of eternal suffering." The young man repented and apologized in tears. Yang held his hand and sent him off. Yong asked Yang about the identity of this god. Yang answered that he was "the son of the Thearch of the North." The young man never came back. The woman stayed home, and no one dared to propose to her. After her parents died, she sold wine on her own. "Whenever thinking of the happiness she once shared with the young man, she shed tears." The story ends by pointing out that the temple of the Thearch of the North was located under Mount Yin, ten *li* (about 3.5 miles) from the south gate of Jiankang.[99]

We do not know from whom Hong Mai received this story. Many details correspond to what we know about Song society—the popularity of the Zhenwu temple in the Jiankang area, the specific exorcist rituals mentioned in the account, and the abundance of stories about sudden wealth and spirit enchantment. The relatively long and cohesive narrative, compared with other accounts, suggests that at least some editing had taken place. And yet it is not readily clear what the narrator's message was, if there was any. The spirit was the son of a legitimate god instead of a minor deity, an animal spirit, or a goblin. There was a strict prohibition of god-human relationships in heaven's law as Master Yang pronounced, and it seemed that the law should apply to all deities, male or female, high or low. This was different from the rich tradition of human-divinity romance in earlier times and resonated with the caution seen in Song stories.

Like the dubious "god" Wutong, the young man in this story also brought significant wealth to the family. But unlike Wutong, he treated the woman's parents as his in-laws and did not do any harm—he cursed the parents only after the father betrayed him. What drove the father to seek an exorcist was not real harm but the words of others, which magnified his own fear. The damage, if any, was that "no one dared to propose a marriage to her anymore." But the readers are left wondering if the woman's loneliness was the fault of the deity, the parents who allowed her to visit temples in the first place, or the successful exorcism. Perhaps it would not have been such a bad thing to keep the deity in the family even though it was against the "heaven's law." But there is no way to tell. Maybe the reason that it is so difficult to extrapolate a clear message from this narrative is because the narrator(s) also was not quite sure what to make of it. The sense of uncertainty—over a family's future, the world of spirits and divinities, and women's enchantment experiences—seemed to have been shared by the narrator(s), the readers and listeners, and the Yong family.

This account is the only Song story I have seen that mentions marriage as a potential cure to women's spirit enchantment, even though it failed. In other women's enchantment stories, marriage was only occasionally mentioned as the outcome of successful exorcism and the woman's full recovery. In this story, however, the woman was unable to marry after the powerful ritual master's successful exorcism, and she resented her deity-husband being sent away. The woman's emotions and desire were not pertinent to the narrative until the very end. What the woman liked or disliked did not seem to have affected what the parents or the young man did. The progression of the narrative depends much on what the young man said to the woman, and those words could only be known to others through the woman herself. But the narrator does not let her talk about her own feelings until the very end. We also know that she was not spiritually possessed or unconscious, because she could recall the events. The woman's desire and feelings surface in the end of the narrative seemingly in order to shatter any potential comfort or sense of security that the audience might find in the success of the exorcism.

PART THREE

GENDERED IDENTITIES AND FEMALE CELIBACY

CHAPTER FIVE

GENDERED PRACTICE AND RENUNCIANT IDENTITY

IS A FEMALE RENUNCIANT A WOMAN FIRST OR A RENUNCIANT? IS A Buddhist nun closer to a laywoman or to a Buddhist monk? These seem like unfair questions because identities intersect. She is perhaps also a daughter, a mother, a (former) wife, and a subject of the state. The ways and meanings of these intersections, however, vary in different times and places, and from person to person. Monastic codes and the social institutions of gender often set female renunciants apart from their male counterparts. A female renunciant, however, does not always identify herself—nor is she necessarily identified by others—as a woman. Many scholars have questioned the liberal and feminist category of women.[1] Buddhist nuns in Chinese society, past and present, do not share the same womanhood with laywomen. Under the hegemony of Confucian family system, Buddhist nuns are degendered in the sense that they do not identify themselves as nuns in contrast to monks; instead, nuns and monks together identify themselves as Buddhists.[2] The scholar of religion Nirmala Salgado recounts an intriguing conversation with a senior Sri Lankan *bhikkhunī* (fully-ordained Buddhist nun) who was engaged in a program that prepared nuns for the *upasampada* (higher ordination), which has been considered a feminist cause by the local media and the global feminist Buddhist community:

> I interviewed her shortly after her own *upasampada*. She had spent most of her life as a *dasa sil mātā/dasa sil mäṇiyō* (Ten [Training] Precept Mother) rather than a *bhikkhuni*. I ask her if she thought that the attempts to institute the *bhikkhuni upasampada* in Sri Lanka could be considered feminist (*strīvādī*, literally "woman-ism"). Her immediate response was, "We are not women (*strī*); we are renunciant[s] (*pävidi*)." . . . I have often pondered

what she meant. The monastic code of conduct (*Vinaya*) stipu-
lates that a female ordinand must affirm her sexuality as a
woman by responding to a series of questions; she must have
what is considered a normatively female body and a clear-cut
sexual identity as a woman in order to enter the community of
bhikkhunis. Well versed in these *vinaya* codes, this senior
bhikkhuni appeared to reject her womanhood.[3]

Rejecting the identity of women does not mean that this senior *bhikkhuni* was unaware of her gender difference from monks or that her life and
practice were not gendered; rather, as Salgado aptly puts it, "Like other nuns
I have known, [she] did not see herself as having a gendered identity in the
way that one might expect. A nun is first and foremost a *celibate* renunciant."
Salgado comes to the realization that it was "the conflation of gendered identity with gendered practice" that explains her surprise at the *bhikkhuni*'s
denial of a "woman" identity. It is the same conflation, Salgado argues, that
"has likely led scholars to position nuns, despite their renunciation of what we
generally understand as gender, in feminist frameworks of interpretation—
frameworks that . . . are often misplaced."[4]

Focus on the liberal and feminist assumption of a universal womanhood prioritizes the perceived similarity in women's experiences of patriarchal oppression. Another aspect that we should consider when trying
to understand renunciants' gendered identity is that the two-sexed model
rooted in modern biology is not universal. Gender analysis that begins
with the assumption of two fundamental and opposing sexes is also insufficient and sometimes misleading. Few sources from pre-twentieth
century China deployed an all-encompassing, strictly biological category
of women that transcended one's age, marital status, and position in the
family.[5]

In 972, the first emperor of the Song, Taizu (r. 960–976), issued an edict
to segregate the ordination of Buddhist nuns from that of the monks. The
Buddhist monastic code prescribes that *bhikṣuṇī* should be ordained with
the presence of both an assembly of monk masters and one of nun masters—
it is called the "dual *bhikṣuṇī* ordination." Monks' ordination, in contrast,
does not require the presence of nun masters. The "dual *bhikṣuṇī* ordination" has been observed, or at least considered orthodox by the Buddhist
clergy, in China since around 433, when a "second ordination ceremony" for
nuns took place with the arrival of a sufficient number of Sinhalese nuns.[6]
Taizu's edict, however, states, "'There are distinctions between men and
women' [*nan nü you bie*]—this is noted in *The Book of Rites*. That there is no

segregation between Buddhist monks and nuns truly disturbs the [ortho-dox] teaching."[7]

The Book of Rites is a collection of treatises on ancient ceremonial rites and political philosophy that was written by multiple (mostly anonymous) authors from about the fifth to the first centuries BCE; it was canonized as one of the five Confucian Classics during the Tang. The phrase "There are distinctions between men and women" appears several times in the text, and the context is always a discussion of the meanings of marriage and the relationship between husband and wife. In other words, the "distinctions between men and women" in the original context refer specifically to those between a husband and a wife, the roles that Buddhist monks and nuns renounce in the first place. This edict was not meant to force Buddhist monks and nuns to resume what they renounced but to assert that Song imperial authority surpassed Buddhist monastic precepts. For Taizu, Buddhist monks and nuns were first and foremost subjects of the state; as subjects of the state, monks and nuns were first and foremost *nan* (men) and *nü* (women) in the family-state continuum. This edict reflected how closely family and marriage relations were tied to the gender identities of *nan* and *nü* in traditional China.

The "Buddhism" section in *History of the Great Jin* (Da Jin guozhi; ca. late 13th c.) provides another example of the fact that marriage and familial roles served as the basis for the references of *nan* and *nü* in traditional Chinese discourse. The text states, "[As a result of] the Buddhist teaching, many people, even from aristocratic families and prominent clans, renounced manhood and womanhood and became [Buddhist] monks and nuns [*she nan nü, wei seng ni*]."[8] Manhood and womanhood were closely tied to roles in marriage. Those who were neither wife nor husband found themselves outside the institutional boundaries of manhood and womanhood. In this way, discussions of the gender of celibate men and women should not be con-strained by a two-gender model. Buddhist nuns certainly belonged to a dif-ferent gender from monks both institutionally and in actual practice. But what did it mean to "renounce womanhood"?

Three single-author hagiographies—Baochang's *Lives of the Nuns* (Biqiuni zhuan), Ma Shu's *Students of the Dao* (Daoxue zhuan), and Du Guangting's *Records of the Assembled Transcendents of the Fortified Walled City* (Yongcheng jixian lu)—are useful for exploring this question. The sub-jects of the first are Buddhist nuns; the subjects of the latter two are female Daoist transcendents.[9] The three collections are very different in nature. Although all three authors asserted the veracity of their accounts and they all intended to present ideal images for both practitioners and other elite readers, Du Guangting's work, which incorporates both mythical and historical figures, clearly contains much more adaptation of his own and less faithful record of female Daoists' lives. All three works are nonetheless narratives. Of interest here is the (trans)gendered identity presented in the narratives, as well as the meanings of gender differences that go beyond the distinction between men and women.

LIVES OF THE NUNS

Lives of the Nuns (Biqiuni zhuan) is the earliest extant collection of Buddhist nuns' biographies in China, compiled in or around 516. *Biqiuni* is the Chinese transliteration of *bhikṣuṇī* (Sanskrit) or *bhikkhunī* (Pali). The author, Baochang (ca. 466–?), a Buddhist monk, compiled both *Lives of the Nuns* and a collection of monks' biographies, *Lives of the Eminent Monks* (Mingseng zhuan).[10] In the Buddhist tradition, the Assembly of Monks and the Assembly of Nuns were differentiated from the beginning. Nuns were subject to monks and were required to observe an additional monastic code over and above the one shared by monks and nuns.[11] *Lives of the Nuns* may also have been inspired by the indigenous Chinese collections of exemplary women's biographies such as *Biographies of Exemplary Women* (Lienü zhuan; 1st c. BCE). However, *Lives of the Nuns* places little emphasis on the hierarchical distinction between the monks' order and the nuns' order. Nor does this collection seem to be an attempt to establish a separate set of female virtues or to accentuate qualities that were usually associated with women during that time. The author was, however, attentive to the specific societal *conditions* that women faced in adopting and practicing renunciation. The author, Baochang, may have aimed not at reinforcing gender difference but at consolidating a Buddhist renunciant identity that transcended perceived gender or sex differences while recognizing the distinct realities that female renunciants faced.

Baochang's preface states that his purpose in compiling this book was to preserve a written record for the nuns' lineage and to provide "those who seek liberation"—prospective nuns, supposedly—materials for emulation. His intentions might have also included depicting the Buddhist faith and monastic lives to his contemporaries, both Buddhists and non-Buddhists. Aside from the reference to the first *bhikṣuṇī*, Mahāprajāpatī, however, there is nothing particularly gendered, nor is there any mention of the difference between nuns and monks in this preface. Baochang expresses the urgency of leaving a record of the nuns and lists their outstanding virtues: Jingjian as the founder of a thriving tradition of the nuns, Shanmiao and Jinggui's extremely arduous practice, Fabian and Sengguo's excellence in *dhyāna* (meditation) contemplation, Sengduan and Sengji's unwavering resolution, and Miaoxiang and Faquan's wide spread of the Dharma.[12] None of these virtues was considered specifically feminine (or masculine) during that time.

Baochang's *Lives of the Eminent Monks* divides the monks' biographies into seven categories: Dharma masters, Vinaya masters, Chan masters, possessors of miraculous power, arduous practitioners, mentors, and *sūtra* masters.[13] *Lives of the Nuns* is organized chronologically, but the seven kinds of achievements are all seen throughout the collection.[14] The quality that most often qualifies a person's Buddhist renunciant identity in both the nuns' and the monks' accounts is arduous practice, especially with regard to observation of the monastic precepts. It is often described as "assiduous, meticulous, and arduous practice" (*lijing kuxing*), "meticulous and assiduous practice of the precepts" (*jingqin jiexing*), and the like. The nuns' achievements and virtues are often not described in specifically female terms in *Lives of the Nuns.* However, in multiple accounts we see Baochang's awareness of the distinct social conditions that the women faced and therefore the gendered actions they took in order to live a renunciant life that transcends such limitations.

One distinct social condition that many female renunciants faced was marriage. Both monks and nuns refrained from marriage, but marriage meant something different for men than for women. The biography of An Lingshou (4th c.) recounts that, like many other female renunciants, she began to practice Buddhism in childhood and encountered the issue of marriage during her teenage years. As she expressed to her father the wish to become a Buddhist nun, Baochang records,

> The father said, "You should belong to another family [*waishu*: to marry to another family]. How is it that you can do so?"
>
> [An Ling shou] responded, "I focus my mind on the workings of *karma* and refrain from thoughts of the mundane matters. [Worldly] blame and praise have no influence on me. I am content with purity and uprightness. [If I can do so,] why must the "three belongings" [to one's father, husband, and son] be considered the only noble norm [*li*]?"
>
> Her father further asked, "You want to benefit only one person—yourself. How can you aid your father and mother at the same time?"
>
> She answered, "I set myself to practice the Dao in order to liberate all living beings from suffering. How much more could I do for my two parents?"[15]

The father's first question is a woman-specific one; the second is not. Lingshou answers both in ways that transcend gender. In her answer to the first question, she makes no reference to female virtues but appeals to both a set of Buddhist virtues and that of the elite. The second question is one that was frequently asked to both Buddhist nuns and monks, and Lingshou's answer is in line with standard Buddhist apologetics.[16] The father than proceeds to consult the famous magician-monk Fotucheng (d. 349). What is also striking in this record is the vision that Fotucheng produces for Lingshou's father. He sees "a monk preaching in the midst of a large assembly," and the monk's appearance "resembles his daughter." Fotucheng tells him that what he sees is the former incarnation of his daughter.[17] Therefore, in contrast to some Mahāyāna traditions, notably the Pure Land, which promise that female practitioners will become male (in this or a future life), in this account, Lingshou has gone from being a monk to a prospective nun, which was considered a proof of her innate connection with Buddhism rather than a proof of a negative rebirth. The gender component in this account is evident in the way Lingshou's father, and not Fotucheng or anyone else, treats her—as a daughter who is bound to marry to another family. Yet her ordination would turn her into something else. She no longer had to cut her family ties entirely and could perhaps still be a filial daughter in another way, but she had turned into something radically different from other women.

In another case, a woman uses the Confucian code to request a divorce. The biography of Nun Miaoxiang (4th c.) recounts that she was married to Huangfu Da, who was appointed secretary of the heir apparent at the age of fourteen. Huangfu "violated the *li* while mourning [for his parent]. Miaoxiang detested him and requested to divorce and to leave the household [i.e., to become a nun]."[18] "Violating the *li*" here most likely means that he slept with her. We do not know if Miaoxiang truly detested him or if it was more an excuse. But her appeal was that her husband had become disqualified according to the Confucian moral code, and she appealed as a qualified Confucian wife. In this narrative, she played the role of an upright wife in order to become a non-wife.

In some cases, the Vinaya helped the female renunciant when facing challenges and disadvantaged conditions—not to become a freer or more autonomous woman in the modern and secular sense, but to be able to practice renunciation with fewer distractions. The biography of Shi Huimu (5th c.) records that she left the household and received the minor ordination (*xiaojie*: commitment to the ten rules of a novice, at the age of ten). Afterward, she practiced under a nun master and lived in a monastery. As her mother became old and lost all her teeth, Huimu chewed food to feed her. Having meat and perhaps other forbidden food in her mouth, Huimu was unable to meet the full Vinaya and so had not received full ordination. But she simply "wore white, practiced arduously, and repented of her own *karma*."[19] One day she had a vision: "Seeing the ordination platform and the sky both in a golden color, she looked up and saw a person in a heavy yellow robe, who seemed now close and now far away. [The person] said to [Huimu], 'I have granted you the [full] ordination,' and soon disappeared."

Huimu had many visions like this, which she kept secret. Her brother—in the *Mingxiang ji* (ca. 490) version of the story—was a Buddhist monk curious about the content of her visions and attempted to trick her into disclosing them. He told her that since there was no proof of her progress, she might as well grow her hair back and he would find her a husband. Huimu was troubled and told her brother what she saw in her visions and subsequently received the full ordination.[20]

In this account, Huimu's care for her mother, although a manifestation of her compassion, is not extolled as a female virtue. When the figure in her vision grants her full ordination, it is recognition of her arduous practice and repentance *regardless of* her "impure mouth." But the visionary full ordination cannot prevent her from still being subject to her brother. (If her brother was indeed a Buddhist monk, Baochang was careful not to mention it.) The formal full ordination helps secure her renunciant life and practice. Baochang implies that care for family members is a condition that some female renunciants face; it is not a requirement of nor a hindrance to their renunciant practice. Huimu's care for her mother is not described as a filial duty or an expectation. She does not do it in order to match the identity of a good daughter. It is simply that she cannot leave her mother alone.[21] The identity that matters to her is that of a Buddhist nun, and that is why she insists in following the Vinaya code and postpones her full ordination. Baochang further affirms (with the details of her vision) that she should still be recognized as a full renunciant out of her arduous practice despite the contradiction between what she has to do for her mother and what the Vinaya prescribes. The Vinaya serves to facilitate the renunciants' practice and not to disqualify a pious practitioner's renunciant identity.

The practice of renunciation as seen in *Lives of the Nuns* was not about freedom or choice but piety and devotion, for the renunciant life itself was a radical reduction of a person's "choices." Neither was adoption of the renunciant life or the full ordination supposed to be solely about a person's free will. It was a person's realization of and response to the working of Dharma. The biography of Nun Kang Minggan (3rd–4th c.) describes how her

Buddhist faith and practice helped her through the hardships of ten years of abduction:

> [The bandits] made her a shepherd. Ten years went by. Her longing for her home grew more and more intense, but she saw no way to return. During all this she kept her mind fixed on the Three Treasures [the Buddha, the Dharma, and the monastic assemblies] and made the wish to become a nun. One day she encountered a Buddhist monk, and she asked him to bestow on her the five fundamental precepts [of a Buddhist householder]. He granted her request and also presented her a copy of the *Bodhisattva Guanshiyin Sūtra* [a chapter of the *Lotus Sūtra*], which she practiced chanting day and night diligently. She then made the wish to return home and build a five-story pagoda.[22]

The account continues to tell how Minggan managed to escape and was miraculously escorted by a tiger. She was abducted again in the middle of the road, and this time her husband and son learned her whereabouts and ransomed her. After she eventually returned home, her family did not let her become a nun. But she "arduously disciplined herself and practiced diligently and meticulously" for three years before she was able to leave the household. She was also described as extremely serious about the Vinaya: she repented for every minor transgression nonstop until seeing a vision.

According to this account, Minggan had been married and had children before her abduction. It was recorded that her native family had venerated Mahāyāna Buddhism for generations, but her wish to become a nun developed only during the years of abduction. The divine power helped her escape and return home, but she did not vow to become a nun simply in order to return home. Her experience and her Buddhist practice during the ten years transformed her. It turned her from one who simply wanted to return home into one who wished to leave the household, become a nun, and live the stringent life of a renunciant. Her wish to become a renunciant was not described as a *choice* to gain opportunities for better life, public career, or education, nor was it to escape an unwanted marriage or other hardships. Rather, it was a reflection of her spiritual transformation through lived experience in the secular world.

In *Lives of the Nuns*, the virtues associated with the nuns are never specifically female. Some of them take certain gendered practice or actions in order to respond to the gendered conditions in their lives and to maintain their renunciant practice rather than to create or reinforce a gendered identity. Two more examples are illustrative of Baochang's perspective on gender and his prioritization of a transgendered Buddhist renunciant identity over a gendered one.

The first is the biography of Jingxiu (418–506), and the second regards Baochang's take of the nuns' "second ordination" that took place in China around 433. Jingxiu was born to a prominent family. She was associated with numerous visions and miracles, a monastic regulation reform, as well as a restoration of the color of Buddhist monastic robes that distinguished nuns and monks from others. She received high respect and patronage from the emperors as well as imperial members of the Liu Song (420–479), the Qi (479–502), and the Liang (502–557). Her biography is the longest in the collection. Baochang very likely based his account on the "conduct description" (*xingzhuang*) that Shen Yue (441–513) wrote for Jingxiu soon after her death. Both Baochang's and Shen Yue's accounts record that about a month before Jingxiu's death, when she became ill, Monk Master Huiling of the Pengcheng Temple saw in a dream that Jingxiu was reborn in the Tushita Heaven. Huiling came to visit Jingxiu, told her what he saw, and said, "When you attain birth in that excellent place, do not forget to receive me there." Jingxiu replied, "You, Dharma master brother, are a great gentleman [*da zhangfu*], spreading the *sūtras* and propagating the teaching. You shall surely be reborn in that superlative place." In Baochang's account, the conversation ends here, and the biography concludes with Jingxiu's last words to her disciples, "I ascend to the Tushita Heaven."[23] In Shen Yue's account, however, Jingxiu further says, "I am a woman. Of what benefit can I be to you?" And Huiling responds, "This is not true. If someone, though a gentleman, is unable to practice arduously and keep the precepts, he is not comparable to you, master."[24] No matter whether this conversation ever happened, Baochang chose not to include this part of the conversation in his collection.

Jingjian (ca. 292–361), whose biography is listed first in the text, according to Baochang, received the ordination only in the presence of an assembly of monks instead of both monks and nuns. The discussion about the legitimacy of Buddhist nuns' lineage in China reached its peak in the early fifth century, when four Vinaya texts were translated into Chinese. In around 433, the "second ordination ceremony" was held in the presence of a quorum of Sinhalese nuns, and the doubt on nuns' legitimacy was resolved. The discussion about early nuns' ordination and their legitimacy continued among several Chinese Buddhist masters, especially those specialized in the Vinaya, in the succeeding centuries.

Baochang recorded Jingjian's ordination and the "second ordination" in quite some detail. In his record, we learn that the nuns were perhaps facing criticism concerning their legitimacy and observance of the Vinaya, and that the "second ordination" was carried out only at the second attempt when a sufficient number of (ten) Sinhalese nuns made their way to China and learned enough Chinese to preside over the ritual. However, as we have seen in the biography of Huimu, while recognizing the importance of observing the Vinaya, Baochang seemed to put more emphasis on the nuns' actual practice and piety than on the question of legitimacy. Jingjian's biography shows that there were already disagreements among the Buddhist monastic community when she received the full ordination. While acknowledging voices of disagreement, Baochang affirms Jingjian to be "the first *bhikṣuṇī* in the territories of the Sima Jin dynasty [265–317; 317–420]." He records that Jingjian discovered on her own the references to "*bhikṣu* [fully ordained Buddhist monk] and *bhikṣuṇī*" in the Buddhist scriptures that she borrowed from her first Dharma teacher, the monk Fashi. Jingjian then expressed to Fashi her wish to be ordained as a *bhikṣuṇī*. Her conversation with Fashi is one of the few places in *Lives of the Nuns* where gender difference is addressed:

> Fashi responded, "In the western regions [Central and South Asia] there were both male and female monastic assemblies. But the requirements for a female assembly were not yet complete in China."
>
> Jingjian asked, "Since [the scripture] says '*bhikṣu* and *bhikṣuṇī*,' why are there different rules?"
>
> Fashi said, "Foreign Buddhists say that nuns have five hundred rules to follow [as compared to fewer for monks], and that must be the difference. I shall ask the monk-master about this for you."
>
> The monk-master said, "The rules for nuns are largely the same as those for monks, with a few differences. Without acquiring the complete set of rules [for nuns], I cannot bestow on anyone the obligation to observe them [by ordaining her]. There are, however, ten precepts that a [novice] nun can receive from a monk-master, but, without a nun-master, the novice nun will have no one to rely on [for her monastic practice]."

Here Jingjian questioned, but did not challenge, the different monastic rules applied to Buddhist monks and nuns. She then received the ten precepts from the monk-master, along with twenty-four other women, and became their *de facto* nun-master. In or after 357, Jingjian and four other nuns received the full ordination from the "foreign monk Tanmojieduo." The record says that a Jin monk named Daochang objected to the ordination based on his understanding of the Vinaya texts. His objection was not acknowledged, and for this reason, he left Luoyang, the capital of the Eastern Jin, and moved south. Baochang does not make judgments regarding who is right or wrong, but he records that "on the day of the ordination ritual, everyone in presence smelled remarkable fragrance" and people respected Jingjian even more. Baochang also records that even before the ordination, Jingjian was already a qualified nun-master and an effective preacher.[25]

The "second ordination" is mentioned in the biographies of Huiguo (ca. 364–433), Sengguo (b. 408), and Baoxian (401–477). Both Huiguo and Sengguo received the "second ordination." Baoxian, however, did not. In Baoxian's biography, Baochang described the downside of the implementation of the "second ordination"—a fad of "vanity and competition" among nuns—and how Baoxian handled it. Baoxian left the household at eighteen, after three years of mourning for her mother—refraining from eating grains, wearing silks, and using a mat or an elevated bed. She was respected and patronized by three (Liu) Song emperors. Emperor Ming (r. 466–473) appointed her the abbess (*sizhu*) of the Puxian (Samantabhadra) Temple and the rector (*sengzheng*) of the (nuns') assembly in the capital.[26] Baochang describes her in this capacity as "imposing and majestic, making decisions with divine insight. She was good at discussing the principles of things and able to set errors right." Baochang continues to recount the 433 "second ordination" event presided over by Saṃghavarman and comments, "It did not mean that previous ordinations were invalid. Rather, the second ordination augmented the good value of the precepts [that had already been received]. Afterward, however, those who were fond of marking their own differences passed on [the precepts] widely, and the norms became somewhat flawed."[27]

In 474, after listening to the Vinaya master Faying's (416–482) lecture, some ten nuns wished to receive the full ordination again, supposedly in the presence of both the monks' and the legitimate nuns' assemblies. In response to this, Baoxian, as the rector, sent a messenger to the lecture hall to deliver her order that no one was allowed to receive a second ordination without permission. She issued a series of procedures for all nuns under her jurisdiction to follow if they wished to receive a second ordination. The procedures involved various examinations of the nun's condition by the assembly of nuns. After this action, Baochang records, "[the fad of] vanity and competition [among nuns] came to an end."[28]

For Baochang, the main purpose of the monastic regulations for nuns was to facilitate nuns' practice and advance in Dharma, rather than to differentiate them from monks. The piety and perseverance that the nuns cultivated in observing the precepts was crucial to their renunciant identity and was more important than determining which precepts were the most orthodox. It also seemed that Baochang cared more about the distinction between hardworking nuns and ordinary men and women than that between nuns and monks. The ultimate goal of Buddhist renunciant practice—enlightenment and liberation—transcends gender, but the process has to be gendered to various degrees particularly because the material conditions for men and for women are different. In other words, nuns' and monks' practice is gendered *precisely because* they are pursuing the same goal. In the process, however, they have already transformed into people that do not share the same gendered identity with ordinary men and women.

STUDENTS OF THE DAO

Ma Shu's *Students of the Dao* (Daoxue zhuan; late 6th c.) was the earliest collection of Daoist hagiographies that dedicated a separate chapter for female Daoists. The text exists only in fragments. Unlike *Lives of the Nuns*, it does not address why Ma Shu provided this chapter. This might be emblematic of the significant presence of priestesses and abbesses in the Supreme Purity (Shangqing) tradition.[29] Ma might have also been inspired by compilations such as *Biographies of Exemplary Women* and *Lives of the Nuns*. However, unlike the *Biographies of Exemplary Women*, the very purpose of which was to elaborate gendered virtues, the depictions of Daoist women in Ma's *Students of the Dao* resemble *Lives of the Nuns* in their emphasis on practice and qualities that apply to both male and female practitioners. In the surviving accounts of nine Daoist women, there are almost no gender-specific elements except that in two accounts the women resist marriage. The majority of the content describes practices and characteristics also seen in men's accounts. The shared descriptions include the Daoist diet (which avoids grain and ingests longevity herbs or minerals instead), seclusion in the mountains, young and robust appearance at an old age, unusual fragrance surrounding their abode or body, and ascension to heaven—many of which are characteristic of the Supreme Purity tradition of south China.[30]

One of the two women who are recorded as having resisted marriage is Song Yuxian. Ma Shu stated that because Song was "endowed with womanhood, her aspiration could not be exclusively dedicated to herself." Her "aspiration" (*zhi*) apparently refers to her devotion to the Dao. It is unclear yet what "womanhood" (*nüzhi*) means here. From the language of this sentence alone, it is also difficult to determine whether it means that Song *did not* focus on her own aspiration or that she *was unable to* do so. But it becomes clear that it was the latter as we read along the rest of the passage:

> As she approached the age of being hairpinned [fourteen], her parents arranged her marriage to a Xu family. She secretly prepared a Daoist costume and mounted the carriage. When she reached the bridegrooms's gate and it was the time for the six rituals [of marriage], she changed her clothes into a coarse yellow robe, held a magpie-tail incense burner in her hands, and did not play the bride's role in the rituals. The guests and the hosts were all stunned. Unable to bend her will by their efforts, the bridegroom's family gave up and let her return to her natal home. She therefore was able to leave the household [and become a nun].[31]

Song was so determined to become a Daoist nun that she took such a dramatic public performance to avoid marriage. More intriguing is that in this context, "womanhood," or "female quality," seems to relate specifically to Song's capacity of being a wife. By making herself unmarriageable—acting inappropriately during the marriage ritual and refusing to comply—she rid herself of her "womanhood."

RECORDS OF THE ASSEMBLED TRANSCENDENTS OF THE FORTIFIED WALLED CITY

Du Guangting's (850–933) *Records of the Assembled Transcendents of the Fortified Walled City* (Yongcheng jixian lu; compiled around 923; *Assembled Transcendents* hereafter) is entirely dedicated to records of female "transcendents" (*xian*), some of whom are from antiquity or legendary times and others closer to Du's time. Many of the legendary or real historical figures might have become "Daoist" only after their accounts were edited and incorporated into Du's work. The compilation begins with the account of the Divine Matriarch of the West (Xiwangmu), the head of all female transcendents, who resides in and governs Yongcheng, the Fortified Walled City.[32] Du distinguishes female transcendents from male ones and identifies the Divine Matriarch of the West, also named the Metal Matriarch (Jinmu), as the highest female transcendent. She is the counterpart to the Wood Patriarch (Mugong), or the Divine Patriarch of the East, the head of all male transcendents. Du explains the rationale of such a distinction by invoking the vocabulary of *yin* and *yang* and specifying a separation of ranked divine offices for male and female transcendents. There is nothing new in Du's formulaic wording for the pairings of *yin* and *yang*, Heaven and Earth, the sun and the moon, day and night; it was also common in Supreme Purity texts to list male and female transcendents separately. A clear distinction between male and female transcendents' titles, however, was rarely seen in surviving sources before Du.[33] Du seems to have tried to establish a tradition that separated the lineage of female Daoists from their male counterparts—a kind of separation similar to that between the Buddhist monks' and nuns' assemblies. Why did such distinction matter to Du?

This is not an easy question to answer—not simply because gender separation cannot be immediately equated with gender differentiation, but also because of the diversity of paths to transcendence included in Du's accounts. As Du states in his preface, "The Ways of the transcendents number in the hundreds, not limited by a single route or a single method."[34] Across the various paths to immortality, some appear to be general principles and others individual variations. While there are gendered attributes in some accounts, the general principles tend to apply to all. The varying paths presented in Du's text are certainly also a result of Du's consciously all-inclusive approach to his very heterogeneous sources. As also stated in his preface, he "collated various accounts about those [female transcendents] and gathered them within one lineage."[35] Du arguably turned many historical and legendary figures into Daoists by appropriating and editing their stories.[36] Most of the features that Du added were not specific to women but attributes frequently seen in the Supreme Purity tradition, such as extraordinary powers and signs, fasting, ingesting elixirs, various rituals, and divine descending. When describing the women's appearance, Du usually emphasized vigor and youth—characteristic signs of Daoist achievement for all practitioners.

Only two of eighteen accounts of Tang women in *Assembled Transcendents* describe the women's appearance in particularly feminine ways.[37] One is the account of Wang Fengxian (ca. 838–886), an influential sorceress and likely also a cult leader active in the late Tang whom Du depicted as a Daoist transcendent.[38] In Du's account, Wang acquired an extraordinary appearance after fasting for more than a year: "Her skin and flesh became rich and lustrous, as clean as ice or snow. With her cicada-shaped head and rounded neck, she seemed made of luminous matter with bright pupils. Her appearance was like that of a heavenly person. She was brilliant and perceptive in knowledge and argument."[39] On the one hand, some imagery in this passage was usually used to describe beautiful women (or men as beautiful as women). On the other hand, Wang's beauty was the miraculous effect of her fasting practice instead of a congenital feature, and her unusual looks were mentioned together with her outstanding intellectual capacity. In fact, judging from the abundance of details in Du's account compared to other historical records, Du very likely drew from existing folklore of Wang's cult rather than simply drafting the whole story on his own. It is hard to tell if Du added such feminine features or simply preserved them.

Du's other account that praises feminine beauty is the story of Supreme Transcendent Dong (Dong Shangxian). Like Wang, Dong was also worshiped in a local cult. When she was sixteen, people in her hometown began to call her "High Immortal" because of her extraordinary appearance (*rong*) and virtue (*de*). In describing her appearance, the text uses *yanye* (gorgeous), a term usually used for women. With regard to virtue, the text uses nongendered Daoist terminology, including her low intake of food and her inclination toward "tranquility" (*jing*) and "harmony" (*he*), two terms often used in Daoist contexts referring to the state of one's body and mind during practice. Dong was once summoned to the court during the Kaiyuan reign (713–741) of the Tang but did not stay long and soon returned home. Dong ascended to heaven three times. Each time her parents, unable to comprehend her divine achievement, cried. The first two times she came back—the text implies that she did so in consideration of her parents' feelings. The last time she did not. She left behind only the most exterior layer of her skin and her still intact clothes as a cicada sheds its shell. Her "skin" and clothes were preserved in lacquer, and the court commissioned the construction of two Daoist temples in her hometown.[40] Dong did not seem to be as active a leader as Wang Fengxian, but clearly her cult was popular and famous enough to have attracted the imperial court's attention. Du's account very likely drew from folklore about her cult or even inscriptions in her temples. It is clear that Du turned the deity of a local cult into a legitimate Daoist transcendent. But it is unclear whether Du deliberately depicted Dong in feminine ways.

In Du's accounts, we see not only alluring goddesses who came down from heaven to marry mundane men and otherworldly beautiful transcendents worshiped in local cults, but also those who have the looks of elderly women but have lived for hundreds of years. For instance, the Tea Granny of Guangling (Guangling Chalao) is said to have had the appearance of a seventy-year-old for more than a hundred years; meanwhile, her movements were quick and vigorous, her hearing and visual capacity excellent, and her hair still black.[41] When Li Quan (fl. mid-8th c.; a Tang official and Daoist) encountered another Daoist woman, the Granny of Mount Li (Lishan Lao), and received a Daoist scripture from her, she appeared to be "a granny with a hair bun on the top of her head, and the rest of her hair hanging loose." She wore "shabby clothes and walked with a stick," yet her "numinous appearance was quite extraordinary."[42] Overall, Du stresses the women's vigor and younger-than-their-age looks much more consistently than their alluring feminine beauty.[43] Sometimes Du depicts Daoist women in a particularly unfeminine fashion, such as the account of Li Zhenduo, who was said to have lived for more than eight hundred years. Du notes that Li's "numinous *qi* [manifested in her] solemnity [*shenqi zhuangsu*]; her spirit and physique were outstanding and magnificent [*fenggu yingwei*]." Terms such as *yingwei*, especially *wei*, were normally used to describe magnificent men, and only rarely used for women. Du explicitly states that Li's appearance was "different from that of a fragile woman." Instead of attracting people's eyes, Li inspired awe: "Those who saw her did not dare to look straight at her."[44]

Another motif in Du's accounts that deserves attention is that of women's divine power that protected them from assaults—especially during solitary practice in the wild mountains. Huang Lingwei, or the Flower Maiden (Huagu), who was aged eighty but looked like a child, had traveled all over the famous mountains and grottoes in the lower Yangzi area. She often spent the night in wild forests while en route, and "divinities protected her." Anyone who attempted to assault her was immediately struck down. She first established her own altar according to the divine instruction from a Daoist priest named Hu Chao. Later in 711, the Tang emperor Ruizong commissioned another Daoist priest, Ye Shanxin, to construct a temple for her, where she ordained seven priestesses. Worshippers of the temple had to remain solemn and pure; otherwise they would be admonished by anomalous signs of snakes and tigers.[45]

Transcendent Lady Xu (Xu Xiangu), skilled in magic spells (*jinzhou zhi shu*), also traveled across all the sacred mountains and frequently lodged in the wild and sometimes in Buddhist monasteries as well. Once, a gang of Buddhist monks attempted to assault her. She scolded them and simply blew out her candle and went to bed. The next morning when Xu left the mountain, all the monks were frozen still, unable to move or speak.[46] Similarly, Transcendent Lady Gou lived and practiced alone at the altar of Wei Huacun (252–334)—the matriarch of the Supreme Purity tradition—under Mount Heng for more than ten years. The altar was surrounded by tigers and wolves, and no one else could approach it. One night, ten Buddhist monks attempted to break in and to destroy the altar. In the morning, nine were found killed by tigers, while the last was spared for his reluctance to participate in the attack. Both the altar and Gou remained intact.[47] In these accounts, it is the women's divine power, rather than any conventional female virtue or institution, that prevents them from being assaulted. Moreover, the narratives do not blame their beauty or their female bodies for the assault.

This is distinct from the Tang story discussed in chapter 3 about a young widow who found no exorcist capable of stopping a male ghost from harassing her, which resulted in her having to disfigure herself.[48] Du's accounts are also in sharp contrast to the ways female bodies and feminine beauty are treated in certain Buddhist textual traditions such as the Avadāna literature. *Sūtra of Parables* (Za piyu jing; translated into Chinese by Kumārajīva in the fifth century), for example, tells a story of a *bhikṣuṇī* who was harassed by a man who loved her beautiful eyes. She gouged out one eye and handed it to the man, and his desire was quelled. She then went to the Buddha and related what happened. The Buddha restored her eye and prescribed that no *bhikṣuṇī* should live or travel alone beyond the community.[49] On the one hand, Du's accounts seem less misogynous and do not depict the female body—be it young or old, beautiful or not—in a negative light. On the other hand, one wonders whether Du's narratives would have helped or harmed female Daoist practitioners and their communities, especially if they were expected to live and practice alone and yet left to defend themselves solely by divine power.

But Du's emphasis on miracles and divine power accentuates the gap between Daoist transcendents and mundane people regardless of gender and class. Du called those who did not appreciate their daughters' or wives' practice of and achievement in the Way "ignorant" or "dumb" (*yu*), even elite men. The account of Xue Xuantong (ca. 828–882), the wife of Feng Hui, an official in present-day Shanxi, is an example. After twenty years of marriage, Xue "used illness as her pretext to stay in solitude." Du describes that Feng harbored "ignorant and jealous [or hostile] feelings" (*yu ji zhi huai*) toward Xue's practice of celibacy and solitude.[50] Du does not simply call Feng ignorant (*yu*), a term often used for illiterate or nonelite people, but also jealous (*ji*), a term usually reserved for women. Supreme Transcendent Dong's parents are also described as "always ignorant" as they cried over Dong's ascendance to heaven.[51]

Through relating stories of extraordinary female transcendents, Du aimed at constructing an ultimate truth rather than simply elevating the exceptional anomalies. By composing *Assembled Transcendents*, Du was likely more interested in propagating a specific set of Daoist doctrines and making political connections to the Wang clan in power in the Shu region than in providing practical advice for communities of Daoist practitioners. However, we have no reason to assume that the cosmological principle embodied by those female transcendents did not apply to every woman simply because transcendents were rare. While transcendents were rare and beyond the league of ordinary men and women, Du emphasized that they arose *consistently* from antiquity to the present day. They represented the ultimate reality of the universe not despite of but precisely because they were different and rare. The Way of the universe that they represented applied to every man and woman even if he or she—out of ignorance—did not respect or practice the Way. It was this embodiment of the Way that marked the difference between the divine and the mundane, a difference even more radical than that between men and women.

Such a categorical distinction between the divine and the mundane continued to matter in later Daoist records and scriptures. Treatises on Daoist female alchemy (*nüdan*) instruct women, like male Daoists, to remove the sexual attributes of their bodies and to transform into an undifferentiated, androgynous body. Once they reach that stage, their original gender identities no longer matter. Although the female body seems to require more effort than the male to reach that goal, whether or not a person devotes oneself to Daoist practice is more important than gender. As the scholar of Daoism Chang Hsun notes, "Women who do not practice the Way find no place in the Daoist texts under discussion," and "Women are divided into two kinds: ones who practice the Way and the others who do not."[52]

GENDERED NARRATIVES REVISITED

Thinking beyond a two-gender model lends new insights into gendered narratives such as those of "transforming the female body [or self]" (*zhuan nüshen*) and the "great gentleman" (*da zhangfu*) in Chinese religious traditions. We can ask two questions related to these much-studied subjects: What was the "female *shen*" and what did it entail? Was it possible to construct a (still gendered) identity distinct from the two genders?

An abundance of stories and doctrines in both Buddhist and Daoist traditions tell of women turning into men as a sign of achievement. A third-century Chinese sutra recounts that a devoted Buddhist woman, Longshi, sees a manifestation of the Buddha when getting out of a bath and vows to become a Buddha. Māra the demon, intending to frustrate her, assumes the form of her father and reminds her that no woman can become a Buddha. Longshi then vows to "practice arduously to transform this female body and to eventually receive a male one." Māra further convinces her to jump off of a wall. Longshi, considering that "father once taught me that abandoning one's own body [*qi shen*] could achieve Buddhahood," does what Māra suggests. Before reaching the ground, however, she turns into a man.[53]

The notion of male rebirth—in this or another life—echoes that of a womanless Pure Land in sutras such as the *Amitābha Sūtra*.[54] Several

Buddhist feminist scholars regard this body of sutras as evidence of the "massive institutional failure" in Buddhist history that the doctrine of equality and liberation became tainted by androcentric and patriarchal cultures.[55] Stephanie Balkwill, however, provides a new reading to the Chinese *Sūtra on Transforming the Female Form* (Fo shuo zhuan nüshen jing, T. 564). Balkwill notes that the text provides a different argument from other Mahāyāna texts as to why a woman must become a man in order to become a Buddha. That is, the Chinese author of this sutra stresses that the problem of the female body is not in its inherent impurity but rather in the social context that often subjects the female body to abuse and makes it more difficult for women to practice.[56] As Suzanne Cahill also observes, Tang Daoist women shared the same practices and goals as men but in different social contexts, specifically social practices such as marriage and motherhood.[57]

By distinguishing the social from the natural, or the intrinsic and the bodily, recent scholarship has produced more nuanced analyses of gender in Chinese religious traditions. The natural-social distinction also seems to have provided a solution to the question that has haunted scholars of gender and religion: are religious texts or traditions intrinsically misogynous? But did people in the past always distinguish the corporal from the social as modern societies do? What if the body and one's very self (*shen*) could be and should be transformed, just like one's social identity? If so, what was really the difference between the female body "itself" and the social norms attached to it? What if the "bodily" encompassed not simply the body that one was born with but also his or her embodied practice? In *Lives of the Nuns*, Baochang emphasizes the social and familial obstacles that prevent women from becoming a *bhikṣuṇī*, rather than any bodily ones. But his work shows that he considered *bhikṣuṇī* a categorically distinct identity from other women. Through renunciation, women already turned into nonwomen.

Zhuhong (1535–1615), a Buddhist monk who practiced both Pure Land and Chan Buddhism, recorded stories of rebirth in the Pure Land—including Buddhists monks, nuns, the laity, and even three cases of animals—in his *Assembled Record of Rebirth* (Wangsheng ji). Among them, a woman of the Song dynasty, Qin Jingjian, "detested the female body [*yanwu nüshen*] and lived separately from her husband." In her secluded room she arduously recited the sutras, conducted the Amitābha Repentance, and worshiped the Buddha for many years. When her time came, she sat peacefully, facing west, and passed away.[58] There is no mention in this account as to whether or not she physically turned into a man or was reborn as a man. "Living separately from her husband" was her way of ridding herself of her female body. Or to put it in another way, sex with men was closely tied to the very definition of the female body and the identity of being a woman.

One can perhaps also read this account to mean that Qin detested her female body and practiced strenuously with the hope of being reborn in the Pure Land, which she believed to have no women. However, in the end of the section for "Women's Rebirth," Zhuhong leaves an intriguing remark. He first asserts, "In the land of ultimate bliss [i.e., Pure Land], there are indeed no women. All the women who are reborn there assume the appearance of great gentlemen [*da zhangfu*]." "Great gentlemen" is a term used frequently in Chinese Buddhist literature when referring to women, especially *bhikṣuṇī*, who are advanced in their practice of Dharma; this term is adopted in Daoist literature as well. Zhuhong's assertion, according to his own writing, is his response to contemporary illustrations of the Pure Land that still depict female figures. And he immediately qualifies, "In the realm of purity, we cannot even find male appearances [*nanxiang*], not to mention female ones." He further adds that women in general have "three defects," and one of them is "aspiring to a male body/self [*nanshen*] and yet not realizing [the importance of] eradicating their female habits [*nüxi*]." As soon as a woman realizes the three problems (and supposedly eradicates them), Zhuhong asserts, she is already "notably a *bhikṣu*" [*juran biqiu*] before leaving this world.[59] Here we see again the inseparability between who one is and what one does, or that between *shen* (body, self) and *xi* (habit). Once a woman changes what she does, she changes who she is.

Focusing on the discourse of great gentlemen in seventeenth-century Chan Buddhist literature, Beata Grant observes a similar kind of continuum of what one does and who one is. That is, many Buddhist monastics assumed that for a woman, "becoming a nun meant abandoning one's female gendered identity and assuming a male one," and that transformation was as instantaneous as the sex transformations recorded in the sutras.[60] When a woman renounced her life as a woman, she transformed both her female identity (*nüshen*) and female body (also *nüshen*). But Zhuhong went even further. He asserted that in the Pure Land there were no "male appearances" but only "great gentlemen" and *bhikṣus*. According to this logic, great gentlemen and *bhikṣus* were not male (*nan*). This echoed the statement in *History of Great Jin* that Buddhist monks and nuns "renounced manhood and womanhood" (*she nan nü*). In Zhuhong's eyes, *bhikṣuṇīs* were neither women nor men but great gentlemen; *bhikṣus* were not men, either. There were four genders: *bhikṣu*, *bhikṣuṇī* (great gentleman), *nan*, and *nü*.

CHAPTER SIX

MEANINGS OF FEMALE CELIBACY

BOTH MEN AND WOMEN WERE EXPECTED TO MARRY AND TO PRO-
duce offspring—but social expectations differed for male and female sexuality. For a married man, keeping away from his wife was rarely grounds for
suspicion of illness or involvement with demonic spirits; if anything, it
could gain him a reputation for being a supreme gentleman. To be free of
desire and to reduce or even eliminate sexual activity with women was a
much-discussed ideal among elite men, regardless of their marital status.
As discussed in chapter 1, at least one bedchamber author claimed that
"supreme gentlemen" slept in separate beds from women. In general, bedchamber literature both advised men to do away with their desire for
women and warned against the danger of women without men. Men were
cautioned against losing control over their desire for women or over their
own pleasure during sex; they were also told to turn women's desire and
pleasure to their own uses.[1]

Discussion of women's desire for men, in contrast, appeared before the
twelfth century mainly in the contexts of women's jealousy and men's bodily
or affective sublimation.[2] In tales and biographies of jealous women and in
bedchamber literature's warnings about manless women's unfulfilled desire
and illnesses born thereof, an interesting pair of narratives of control
emerges: the latter reveal men's fear of losing control if women do not desire
them—as men would in these cases be unable to manipulate female bodies
as instructed in bedchamber texts—while the former caution against
women's desire to control men. Goddesses, by contrast, were often depicted
as desireless beings, free of jealousy, though they might associate intimately
with men of their choosing. Although both Buddhist and Daoist traditions
in medieval China often expected women to practice in the same ways as
men, the treatment of sexual desire was rarely part of a discussion germane

to women's own bodily or moral cultivation within those traditions. In anomaly accounts and literary tales, a recurrent concern in stories of women's enchantment disorder was the women's unmarriageability or lack of interest in their husbands, whereas stories about men who had erotic encounters with female spirits never mentioned the men losing interest in marriage or their wives. While women were frequently praised for not being jealous of their husbands' other consorts, they were rarely praised—except in hagiographies—for being indifferent to their husbands.

The different expectations for (elite) men and for women situated their practice of religious celibacy in opposite positions: celibate men conformed to the expectation that a morally cultivated man should be immune to desire, whereas celibate women defied the norm that women's sexuality should be guarded by their husbands.[3] The distinct social and cultural contexts of men's and women's celibacy not only subjected male and female practitioners to different material conditions for their practice, but also contributed to distinct narratives about them. A shared identity existed between Buddhist monks and nuns and between male and female Daoist adepts— an identity that was still gendered but was not constrained in a binary model. This chapter emphasizes the uniqueness of female celibacy and the construction of sexuality and subjectivity of celibate women.

ATTITUDES TOWARD MARRIAGE AND CELIBACY

It is common knowledge that Chinese Buddhist monks and nuns practice celibacy. In comparison, the attitudes toward marriage and celibacy appear to be more diverse in the Daoist traditions. But the Buddhist authorities never unequivocally supported all devout women to become nuns, and we see almost as many stories about women rejecting marriage in Daoist hagiographies as we see in Buddhist ones. What matters is whether or not and in what circumstances men and women were encouraged to be celibate, especially vis-à-vis lay practice, and how society responded to their renunciation. What also matters here is whether or not marriage status was a major factor in her path to renunciation.

Among the sixty-five biographies in *Lives of the Nuns*, thirteen mention the clash between the women's will to become a nun and her family's expectation for her to marry. We see a variety of confrontations in this collection. The author Baochang did not emphasize how to be a good *female* Buddhist renunciant but rather emphasized how to be a good Buddhist renunciant in the face of all kinds of obstacles, including marriage. Some parents compromised when promised greater blessings. An Lingshou's father was an example. He granted his daughter's wish when the eminent monk Fotucheng showed him a vision and promised that having a daughter who became a Buddhist nun would bring blessings to the family.[4]

Some women threatened their families with suicide. Sengji protested against the marriage that her mother arranged for her with a hunger strike. Her fiancé, "a man of devout faith," seeing that she was dying, voluntarily relinquished the marriage arrangement.[5] Tanhui swore not to marry at the age of eleven and was prepared to burn herself to death if her family forced her to marry. A monk and a nun helped her hide in a temple. A sympathetic regional inspector heard about this and persuaded the mother of her fiancé to let her go.[6] Sengduan ran away from home before her wedding and hid in a Buddhist temple, where she recited the *Guanyin Sūtra* in tears day and night. After three days, she saw a vision where the Buddha informed her that her bridegroom would soon die. The next day, the bridegroom was gored to death by an ox. She was therefore free to leave home and become a nun.[7] Jingxiu changed her parents' minds partly by adopting unwomanly behavior—not wearing beautiful clothes and makeup.[8] Miaoxiang accused her husband of violating sexual restrictions during a mourning period and divorced him to become a nun.[9] In these narratives, the conflict between celibacy and marriage serves to emphasize the power of Dharma and the resolution of the women—two major themes in *Lives of the Nuns*. Baochang did not suggest a solution to the conflict other than miracles and piety; nor did he defend celibacy for Buddhist nuns in non-Buddhist terms.

In contrast to Baochang's narrative, some women during the same time period in north China and during the Tang assumed renunciant identity for obvious political reasons. Some temporarily joined a nunnery in order to gain political power and prestige.[10] Others used renunciation as a means to avoid political persecution.[11] Most of those women were widows, for whom marriage and celibacy were not in conflict. Nevertheless, epigraphic writings from the Northern Dynasties (386–581) and the Sui (581–618) did not emphasize the link between widow chastity and Buddhist celibacy; in other words, epitaph writers did not feel the need to justify Buddhist women's practice of celibacy by associating it with familial virtues such as widow chastity. Rather, some epitaphs addressed these widowed women's lifestyle and virtues in ways beyond a traditional state-familial framework and similar to Baochang's narrative—perseverance and arduousness in their Buddhist practice, resolution toward liberation from samsara, bringing blessings for all sentient beings, and so on. The link between widow chastity and religious celibacy in epigraphic writings only became more pronounced after the sixth and seventh centuries.[12] In the meantime, Tang sources indicate that Buddhist mothers influenced and actively supported their daughters and sons in their practice of Buddhism and even in their efforts to become nuns and monks. While the mothers themselves were only able to fully devote themselves to Buddhist practice in their old age, they made it possible for their children—both sons and daughters—to become renunciants before marriage.[13]

The number of Buddhist monks and nuns increased during the Song along with a boom in the population and economy. In 1021, according to Song imperial documentation, the number of officially registered monks was 397,615 and the number of registered nuns was 61,239.[14] Rising dowry expenses might have prompted some parents to send their daughters to a nunnery.[15] Still, some elite men and women during the Song supported their unmarried female family members to pursue renunciant lives out of their respect for Buddhism.[16] Meanwhile, elite women seem to have been more regularly encouraged to practice Buddhism at home than to become a nun. Many elite men of the Song held a positive attitude toward elite women's domestic Buddhist practice.[17] Huang Tingjian (1045–1105), a prominent Northern Song scholar-official and also a devout Buddhist, recorded the story of a contemporary Buddhist nun of his time, Fawu (Dharma Enlightenment), an elite woman who had married her maternal cousin. Her family was supportive of her Buddhist practice at home, and her aunt/mother-in-law was "particularly fond of her." But when she expressed the wish to become a nun, her family panicked. Huang's account records,

On the first day of the second month in the third year of Yuanyou [1088], Fawu suddenly cut her hair with a pair of scissors in the Buddha hall of her natal home. Having seen this, her mother held the cut hair and cried. In a moment, all her siblings and sisters-in-law gathered and tried every means to dissuade her. Appearing peaceful and content, Fawu simply smiled and said, "I, Fawu, have come to a realization. I have taken the great vow. If encountering another sensible and wise soul, I may dare to say a few words." No one in the family knew what to do. Another day, the family summoned a senior monk Jianlong, who preached to Fawu the *prajñā* doctrine of the immense sin of not paying a child's [filial] debt. Before Jianlong finished, Fawu came forward, burned incense and bowed. She said,

"On the first day of the first month this year, in the late afternoon, I was sitting [meditating] in the Buddha hall, and everything suddenly went dark. I saw a light of fire from afar and walked toward it. In a few miles, I entered a gate with a panel inscribed 'Gate of Retribution.' A judge in a green robe held in his hand a book of documents and said to me, 'It is not your turn. What brought you here? But there will be retribution awaiting you. Are you aware?' I was startled and asked, 'I have done no evil since the day I was born. What wrongdoings could there be?' The judge said, 'Your current husband was your wife in your previous life. In your previous life, she hurt your left ear out of jealousy and caused your death. Now she/he became your husband in this life, and that is her/his destiny [to receive retribution].' I said, 'Even though he owes me the retribution, I do not wish to take revenge.' The judge said, 'She/he is to be punished. It is not up to you.' I said, 'If I take revenge, the vengeance would lead to another retribution, and there would never be an end.' The judge said, 'That is not true. Just like all the murder cases in the world, the feuds would not be resolved without the culprits atoning for their crimes.' I said, 'I simply do not hold any hatred. The feud would itself dissolve. . . .' Seeing all the worldly feuds still documented in the judge's book, I wanted to fetch a torch to burn the scroll to liberate all the hatred and feuds. The judge raised his eyebrows furiously and scolded, 'Who are you to meddle with our law!' . . . I found myself outside the city gate. I cried, 'What vicious karma it is to make people kill in retribution! Bodhisattva Guanyin come rescue me!' Suddenly an old monk appeared and said to me, 'Come over, child. You should take a vow.' I responded, 'I vow to never serve men [as a wife] or else my body will be shattered as the sand in the river and I will never be reborn as a human for aeons.'" . . . Having heard this, Jianlong no longer opposed Fawu and simply said, "Marvelous!" . . . This happened in the residential area inside the northern gate of Yangzhou.[18]

This story presents quite a different narrative from hagiographies written by Buddhist monks or epitaphs by elite men that scholars have studied so far. In An Lingshou's account in *Lives of the Nuns*, the monk Fotucheng persuaded Lingshou's father to let her be ordained as a Buddhist nun by showing him a miraculous vision; Tanhui and Sengduan hid in Buddhist temples with the help of monks and nuns when running away from marriage. The situation was reversed in Fawu's case: her family summoned an eminent monk in order to dissuade their daughter and daughter-in-law from becoming a nun. But it was Fawu herself rather than any prominent Buddhist figure who had visions. Furthermore, in contrast to most epigraphical writings about Buddhist women, this story places emphasis on Fawu's visionary dream and her comprehension of the Dharma rather than her contribution to the family, if any. According to Huang's record, Fawu was his contemporary, and her hometown, Yangzhou, was a place where Huang and many of his friends had lived. It is likely that Fawu was a renowned Buddhist nun in this elite circle. This story could potentially be read by nonbelievers as sarcastic or cynical, especially considering how Fawu's vision could be seen as threatening her family with karmic retribution targeted toward her husband. But that would not have been Huang's intention to relate the story as a devout Buddhist, if Huang was indeed the original author of the story. Regardless of the authorship, the depiction of the monk Jianlong's cooperation with the family should reflect the attitude of at least some members of Song Buddhist clergy, especially those who maintained good relationships with the elite. They would not have proactively encouraged married women whose husbands, parents, and parents-in-law were alive to become a nun, even though they might still be open to exceptional cases like Fawu.

Compared to the positions taken by Chinese Buddhists, attitudes toward marriage and sex have been diverse and even controversial in the Daoist traditions. It is the consensus among scholars that the early Celestial Master community in the late second and the third centuries practiced a sexual ritual of some sort as a part of its initiation rites, and that from the very beginning the Celestial Masters clearly distinguished their ritual from the sexual techniques taught in the bedchamber literature.

Xiang'er Commentary to Laozi (Laozi Xiang'er zhu; early 3rd c.), the earliest extant Celestial Master text, criticized those who taught the techniques of "not releasing [the semen] during intercourse with women" and "returning its essence to fortify the brain" as "false practitioners." The true practitioners "do not borrow from others."[19] *Xiang'er Commentary*, however, shares with the bedchamber tradition the notion that "essence" (*jing*) is the precious source of life and that men tend to lose it during (ordinary) sexual intercourse. It thus advises practitioners to exercise caution and to only have sexual intercourse for reproductive purposes. Ideally, one should refrain from sexual intercourse altogether. As the text states, "heaven and earth lack ancestral thrones, dragons lack offspring, Transcendents lack wives, and Jade Maidens lack husbands."[20] In other words, even though the early Celestial Master clergy or congregation did not take a vow of celibacy, sexual intercourse was not encouraged—even between married couples. Meanwhile, other sources suggest the possibility that certain sexual techniques were used in early Daoist communities also as a means to secure pregnancy and birth.[21]

The sexual rite practiced within the Celestial Master community is called *heqi*, or "merging the pneumas," in reformist and polemical sources written a century or two after the time when the early community was active. Due to the esoteric nature of the rite and the scarcity of available sources, we do not know exactly how it was conducted or whether or not it involved physical intercourse. What we do know is that it was a part of the early Celestial Master's initiation ritual that transformed individuals into "Seed People," who would survive a near apocalypse, and that the rite should have generated the same effect for both male and female members.[22] While it is unclear whether or not the rite involved physical intercourse between male and female members in the early church, leaders of the early community juxtaposed it with the sexual cultivation techniques in the bedchamber tradition. In other words, from the Celestial Masters' own perspective, what this rite involved was of the same category as, or at least of similar appearance to, the bedchamber arts, although its method, purpose, and supposed effect were different. We also know that the bedchamber cultivation tradition predated the early Celestial Master community and that the latter consciously adopted (and adapted) the former's techniques.[23] However, considering how soon and how thoroughly *heqi* was internalized and no longer involved physical intercourse, we may entertain the conceptual distance between this "sexual" rite and our modern notion of "sexuality." Meanwhile, just like the modern invention of sexuality is inseparable from power and affect dynamics, the practice of *heqi* was also subject to power abuse and affective tensions such as jealousy in practitioners' eyes.[24]

In Celestial Master texts from the fourth century that record reformulated versions of the rite, the practice is already internalized. Much emphasis is placed on meditation and visualization rather than physical intercourse. Also in the fourth century, leaders of the newly emerged Supreme Purity Daoism claimed that they received a higher revelation from the gods. While sharing the goal of merging the pneumas in order to create a new and transcendent life, Supreme Purity leaders discouraged all sexual activities and viewed celibacy as a precondition to perfection. They condemned the Celestial Master's sexual rite, which was now called by its critics as the method of "the yellow and the red," and they provided alternative and sublimated methods that involved visualizing and connecting the spirits within one's own body and with those of the gods, rather than intercourse or interaction between two adepts.[25] The Buddhists and the Lingbao Daoist scriptures in the fourth and the fifth centuries also vehemently criticized the Celestial Masters' sexual rites.[26]

Although the principles of self-cultivation and celibacy apply to both men and women, the wording is often androcentric, such as in these two passages found in *Declarations of the Perfected* (Zhen gao; comp. Tao Hongjing, late 5th c., including mid-4th c. teachings transmitted by Yang Xi and Xu Mi):

> The calamity caused by one's attachment to his wife and wealth is greater than imprisonment. Imprisonment may be pardoned. Yet the sin cannot be redeemed for those who relentlessly indulge themselves in affection and desire toward their wives despite [knowing it to result in] calamity equivalent to being thrown in front of a tiger.[27]
>
> Those who pursue immortality should not be with women. On the ninth day of the third month, the second day of the sixth month, the sixth day of the ninth month, and the third day of the twelfth month, one should enter a chamber and must not see women. . . . On these days, the three male *shi* [corpse; death-bringer] and three female *shi* come out from the pupils of one's eyes. The female *shi* attract men, and the male *shi* attract women. Their interaction causes calamities, extinguishes one's *shen*-spirit, and damages the upright.[28]

Both passages clearly speak to a male audience and warn male practitioners of the dangers inherent in desire for women—even their wives. Both are instructions given by female deities. The first passage is the admonishment of Madam Dark Purity, and the second is a part of the mnemonic instructions of Madam Fan; both were said to have reached transcendence during the Eastern Han.[29] The first passage in fact situates sexual desire within a variety of emotions and obsessions that are considered obstacles to Daoist practice, but the desire and affection toward one's wife is condemned as the most dangerous and distracting. The second passage specifies the dates when people are the most susceptible to attraction to the other sex. Taken together, heterosexual attractions and sexual relationship between husband and wife were considered common, ordinary, and also destructive for Daoist practice.

The biography of Wei Huacun (252–334), or Madam Wei, first composed in the late fourth or early fifth century, represents both the Supreme Purity's ideal of celibacy and female practitioners' negotiation and compromise. Wei was a major deity featuring in the initial Supreme Purity revelation.

Record has it that Madam Wei was dedicated to the Way of transcendence since childhood. She read Daoist scriptures and other classics, adopted a Daoist regimen to regulate her *qi*, and refrained from seeing even her relatives. She wished to live in seclusion and not to marry, but her parents did not allow it. She was married to an official and, after fulfilling her familial duties—giving birth to and raising two sons—she began to live in a separate room. Three months after that, an assembly of deities suddenly descended to her chamber and transmitted to her several sacred scriptures.[30]

During the Tang, Daoist monasticism was fully developed under strong imperial patronage and out of the Daoists' conscious effort of integrating various traditions. Cases of royal women and palace ladies ordained as Daoist priestesses were particularly well documented. A few princesses did not marry and remained renunciant throughout their lives, while more did so only temporarily. The official record indicates that during the Kaiyuan reign (713–741), about one-third of Daoist abbeys were convents. The Tang Code addressed Daoist priests, priestesses, Buddhist monks, and nuns as a distinct legal category. Monasteries were granted financial privileges and enjoyed certain degrees of economic independence, provided that they observed monastic precepts including celibacy. The procedures of ordination for Daoist priests and priestesses were the same, and priestesses could reach the highest ranks in ritual status.[31] A group of female Daoist adepts were active and associated closely with men and women in the Tang imperial palace. These adepts distinguished themselves from both ordinary women and Buddhist nuns by a set of practices and performances such as making parts of their bodies more visible to men.[32] The biography of Xie Ziran (d. 794), a particularly well-known adept among the crowd, records that Xie not only practiced celibacy but also instructed her followers to distance themselves from family members and relatives.[33]

According to the Song imperial census, in 1021 there were 731 registered Daoist nuns, only about 3.7 percent of the number of registered Daoist monks (19,606) and 1.2 percent of the number of Buddhist nuns (61,239). Up to the year 1077, the numbers of Daoist nuns and monks remained stable, while those of Buddhist nuns and monks dropped by half.[34] No official record of the total number of Daoist nuns survives from the Southern Song. In the north, records are scarce before the formal establishment of Complete Perfection (Quanzhen) monastery by Qiu Chuji (1148–1227).

Sources about the famous female Daoist, Sun Bu'er (1119–1183), provide a glimpse of the attitude toward celibacy and women's participation in the early Complete Perfection community in north China during the Jin dynasty (1115–1234). Sun was one of the "Seven Perfected"—first-generation disciples of Wang Zhe (Chongyang; 1113–1170), the founder of Quanzhen Daoism. Sun was born into an elite family and was well educated; she married Ma Yu (1123–1184; who left the family first and also became a disciple of Wang Zhe) and gave birth to three children before divorcing Ma and starting a renunciant life.[35] Wang Zhe's poems regarding Sun's renunciation emphasize the superiority of a renunciant life; Sun's own poem also asserts her resolution to "transform ignorance and delusion" and to "separate from husband and children in the Burning House [i.e., *saṃsāra*]."[36] Under Qiu Chuji, Complete Perfection became a highly organized community with a clear self-identity; it also earned the imperial endorsement and patronage of the Yuan dynasty (1271–1368). Information gathered from stone inscriptions suggests that four thousand Quanzhen monasteries and twenty thousand clerics, about one-third of whom were nuns, existed during the Yuan.[37]

Compared to doctrinal scriptures and records produced within organized Daoist communities, some hagiographical collections preserve more diverse practices and forms of transcendence, especially those collections that aim at being inclusive. An early example is *Arrayed Records of Transcendents* (Liexian zhaun; 1st c. BCE), which records several male adepts who either never married or who abandoned their wives; one account specifically states that the adept "did not take a wife and [hence] did not age."[38] The same collection's depictions of female transcendents, however, are different. It includes the tales of two goddesses who had an erotic encounter with a man, women who became transcendents after following and/or mating with male transcendents, and a woman who received longevity sexual techniques from a transcendent and practiced with several young men.[39] Ge Hong's *Traditions of Divine Transcendents* (early 4th c.) portrays both male and female adepts' defiance of social norms including marriage and familial duties.[40] Ma Shu's *Students of the Dao* (late 6th c.) records two women who resolutely resisted marriage and succeeded. One of them was Song Yuxian, who wore a Daoist renunciant's robe at her wedding in order to express her will.[41] The other was Qian Miaozhen, who "shed tears and firmly declined" when her family tried to force her to marry.[42] Among the nine accounts of female transcendents included in Ma Shu's reconstituted work, six explicitly indicate that the women did not marry. In the other three accounts, there is no mention of a husband.

In *Assembled Transcendents*, Du Guangting claims that marriage is "the Way of one *yin* and one *yang*" in the preface, while recording in the main text many female transcendents who rejected marriage. The latter conforms to the emphasis on celibacy in early Supreme Purity teachings. The incongruity between the preface and the main text might have been a result of

Du's dual purpose, that is, to propagate the Supreme Purity tradition and at the same time to cater to the ruling Wang clan of the Former Shu (907–925). The account of Xue Xuantong, as already discussed in the previous chapter, is an example of Du's depiction of a female transcendent's practice of celibacy. Xue "stayed alone with the excuse of sickness" after being married to her "jealous and ignorant" husband, Feng Hui for twenty years.[43] Another example is Xiaoyao, a girl who supposedly lived in the eighth century. Xiaoyao differed from most other cases in that she was said to be a village girl and did not share the same experience with other elite women who practiced the Dao. Her initiation was prompted by her encounter with the manifestation of Madam Fan. Xiaoyao immediately began to follow Madam Fan upon the encounter. Her parents "chased after her, beat her with sticks, scolded and forced her home." She protested by attempting to hang herself until her parents conceded.[44] The accounts of female transcendents to whom marriage was not a hindrance in Du's collection are all adopted from previous hagiographies, such as those from *Arrayed Records of Transcendents*.

Shen Fen's *Continued Traditions of Transcendents* (10th c.) also contains mixed attitudes toward marriage and celibacy and, compared to *Assembled Transcendents*, adopts a more eclectic approach. Some accounts resonate with Supreme Purity's tradition of celibacy and similarly depict divinities descending in the adepts' secluded rooms. The account of Jin Keji, a Daoist practitioner from Silla (Korea) who visited the Tang during Emperor Xuanzong's reign (712–756), tells that Jin was uninterested in the court ladies that the emperor bestowed on him. He "stayed alone in a quiet chamber" and did not allow court ladies or eunuchs to approach. Every night, court ladies and eunuchs heard sounds of people chatting and laughing from his room, and some even saw male and female divine figures in the room.[45] Two women, Qi Xiaoyao and Pei Xuanjing (to be discussed later), were also determined to practice celibacy and yet encountered many more obstacles from their families than men such as Jin Keji.

Another account in *Continued Traditions* praises a married couple for practicing with each other. Old Wang of Yijun and his wife "shared the aspiration [to practice the Dao] diligently." One day an old Daoist master visited them and stayed for several months. After drinking a miraculous wine made by the master, Old Wang, his wife, and the whole family including their livestock, together ascended to heaven.[46] The text does not mention whether or not the Wang couple practiced sexual abstinence.

Still other accounts record the practice of sexual cultivation in a positive light, but the practitioners were all men. For example, Song Xuanbai, "wherever taking lodgings, always purchased at a high price a couple of beautiful concubines; he left them behind when he departed." People were convinced that he had acquired the art of "fortifying the brain and returning to the primordial" (*bu nao huan yuan*), a term that combines the goal of ancient bedchamber arts ("[retaining *jing* and] fortifying the brain") and that of Daoist inner alchemy ("returning to the primordial").[47] Another man, Qian Lang, followed a Daoist master at Mount Tai during Emperor Tang Wenzong's reign (827–841) and also "acquired the art of fortifying the brain and returning to the primordial, and that of ingesting and producing alchemical elixirs for longevity." Both Song and Qian were said to have become transcendents—Song ascended to heaven, whereas Qian was "liberated from the corpse" (*shijie*).[48]

In sum, within Buddhist and Daoist communities, there were always members and leaders who advocated the superiority of celibacy for both men and women and supported women's pursuit of renunciation regardless of their marital status. However, it seemed more common, especially when the monasteries became more developed in later imperial times, for religious leaders to cooperate with the family system and not encourage women who were not orphaned or widowed to become renunciants.[49] Epigraphical sources recorded many renunciant women who remained connected to their families, and members of the elite often praised women's religious piety by making references to their contribution to the family and the community. Meanwhile, significant elements in female renunciants' epitaphs were different from conventional women's biographies, such as a new vocabulary of religious virtues that were not particularly gendered and the emphases on temple building, ritual expertise, institutional leadership, and so on.[50]

CELIBACY, ISOLATION, AND POSSESSION

Female celibacy provoked both reverence and opposition; it also generated suspicion and confusion. Let us read again the statement in "Tree Lodgers" in *Record of the Listener* that associates enchanted women with *wu* (spirit-mediums; sorcerers) and *xian* (transcendents; gods or goddesses; semi-divinities; adepts of esoteric arts): "Women afflicted by [Wutong] are all in unbearable pain, emaciated and pale, losing all their energy. Some become *wu*. People regard them as *xian* and call their condition 'transcendent illness' [*xianbing*]."[51] It is fairly clear that the narrator of this passage believed that some of these women indeed became *wu*. This might have been the narrator's observation of a social phenomenon in which some women who were believed to have a certain connection with spirits—and were therefore considered unfit for conventional marriage—might turn to being a *wu* by trade. It is also clear that the narrator did not believe such women to be transcendents, even if others regarded them as so. Less clear is what the narrator himself thought of female transcendents per se: it could be that the narrator believed in transcendents, who were not to be confused with those enchanted women or *wu*, or it could also be that the narrator simply did not believe in the lore of transcendents and thought that the so-called *xian* were simply women afflicted by demonic spirits like Wutong. In either case, there was a perceived confusion about the identity of such women. This confusion was specifically related to women's unfitness for marriage, untamable sexuality, and loss of subjectivity.

Who or what is a transcendent, or *xian*? As scholars of Chinese religions have noted, in early Chinese texts, *xian*, though often translated as "immortal," refers not to those who have entered a static state of immortality and escaped time and change, but rather to those who "have ascended to links in the chain higher than those occupied by even the best human beings."[52] Robert Campany illustrates in his study of Ge Hong's *Traditions of Divine Transcendents* how *xian* as a cultural and historical category was necessarily shaped in an "interpersonal and interactive process," despite *xian* often being presented—by themselves and by others—as recluses who maintained their distance from society. As Campany puts it, "to become a *xian* was to be recognized as one by some community of other persons."[53] A "cultural repertoire" was used—by *xian* seekers and others—to distinguish *xian* from ordinary human beings. The distinctive dietary practice of "avoiding grains" (*bigu*), for instance, could be seen as the rejection of conventional values in an agricultural society.[54] Such countercultural practices and behaviors did not come without risks. The repertoire of transcendents not only distinguishes transcendents from ordinary human beings but often also overlaps with the repertoires of demons and ghosts.[55] Sometimes such figures were viewed as an "extraordinary person" (*yiren*); other times they were deemed "demonic and heretical" (*yaowang*).[56] Xie Ziran, a female Daoist adept who lived in the late eighth century and was said to have ascended to heaven in 794, was also "suspected of being demonic and heretic" by her father and the local official because of her fasting. According to her hagiography, the suspicion only lifted after the two men separately locked Xie in an isolated chamber only to see her emerge more than a month later, radiating vitality and strength.[57]

Some elements in the transcendents' repertoire are more gendered than others. For women, celibacy and isolation, or particularly claiming an undisturbed space, seem to have aroused more suspicion than for men. While both men and women were subject to their parents (and perhaps the ancestors that their present families represented), women were also subject to their husbands. Although it was also countercultural for men to refrain from contributing to the succession of their patrilines, men were rarely suspected of being demonic or possessed by spirits on account of indifference to their wives. Social isolation was a constant motif in both male and female transcendents' stories. A major function of transcendents' isolation, or restricting access to themselves, was to protect their "secrets." Secrecy was valuable cultural capital for the *xian*-seekers, who carefully manipulated the concealment and the display of their arts.[58] Isolation and restriction of access easily aroused curiosity.

Several hagiographies and anecdotes about female transcendents, however, show that women's isolation triggered not only curiosity but also fear, and was associated with demonic possession. The association of women's isolation with spirit possession brings us back to the confusion of identities between enchanted women, female transcendents, and female *wu* in "Tree Lodgers." In early hagiographies, a transcendent's "mastery of non-human others" can also be viewed as "on a par with or superior to shamans or spirit-mediums [*wu*]."[59] The *wu*–transcendent–enchantment conflation in women, however, was due not to their mastery of spirits, but simply their connection to them; that connection was often perceived as indicating some sort of possession and lost or tainted subjectivity on the part of the women. As discussed in chapter 4, not all female *wu* were thought to be possessed by spirits and not all spiritual possessions were sexual, but the cases in which spiritual and sexual possession intersected were almost exclusively women. Narratives and folklore related to such intersections shaped and were shaped by a construction of female sexuality. While this female sexuality constituted the core of women's identity and subjectivity, it was recognizable only in relation to its accessibility to men. When a woman was not sexually available to men or was available to the wrong "men," she was no longer herself.

Narratives of Suspicion

Chapters 3 and 4 have examined the recurrent motifs in narratives about "enchanted women," including seclusion, indifference to one's husband, speaking and laughing to oneself, and superfluous self-adornment. We may view these motifs as constituting another repertoire—one that allowed people to recognize enchanted women. The repertoire of enchanted women overlapped with that of female transcendents in aspects concerning a woman's manlessness and isolation. The emphasis on divine revelation and the practice of seclusion in the Supreme Purity tradition might have contributed to a growing number of narratives that contained this overlap.

From the tenth century onward, similar motifs of women in seclusion and related suspicion of demonic possession were also present in both Daoist hagiographies and in tales and anecdotes. For those who believed in transcendents, these were simply superficial resemblance; the true meanings of these anecdotes, as determined by the true identity of the woman involved, were categorically different. For skeptics or critics of transcendent practice and cults, such as the narrator of "Tree Lodgers," there were not necessarily different meanings behind a woman's manlessness and isolation. But even for believers, it was difficult to tell what a woman's behavior actually meant. The overlap of repertoires generated confusion, uncertainty, and suspicion. This suspicion, in turn, became a useful element in both hagiographical and anecdotal narratives, serving to depict the contrast between the ignorant and the divine.

The biography of Xie Ziran is an example; Xie's father's and the local official's suspicion of her fasting underscores both the ignorance of the two socially superior men and Xie's true superiority. In other words, for people in a community—especially the community leaders—the confusion of repertoires was troublesome, if not threatening. For hagiography narrators, however, confusion, uncertainty, and suspicion could be turned into useful narrative devices. For a manless woman, this brought both risks and possibilities. Celibate and secluded women could be deemed sick, possessed, and demonic; women thought to be sick, possessed, and demonic could also claim divinity or divine affinity. Several pre-Song hagiographical narratives placed an emphasis on female transcendents' celibacy and isolation and depicted people's suspicion of their involvement with spirits.

In Du Guangting's account, Wang Fengxian started to receive visitations from goddesses when she was twelve or thirteen years old—at first in the field where she worked during the day and later in her home at night. Hearing voices chatting and laughing in her room and yet not seeing anything, her parents "suspected that she was enchanted by demonic spirits" (*yi yao-mei suo huo*). Whenever they questioned her, Wang always responded with excuses. After Wang was confronted with questions, the goddesses no longer came during the night but instead did so during the daytime when her parents were out working and could not spy on her. The goddesses took Wang to journeys far away from home—soaring in the sky—and always returned at dusk. One day near dusk, Wang's mother, witnessing that Wang had just landed from the sky, persistently questioned her. Under pressure, Wang divulged her experience with the goddesses, and yet her parents "eventually failed to understand what happened."[60]

Xue Xuantong, after being married for twenty years, began to stay in a separate room from her husband. In her solitude, she burned incense and chanted *Scripture of the Yellow Courtyard* (Huangting jing; a Supreme Purity canon of bodily cultivation). After thirteen years, the Primal Lord of the Purple Void (Zixu Yuanjun; the divine title of Wei Huacun after her ascension) and attending transcendents descended to her room. The Primal Lord taught her the essence of Huangting meditation, left her an elixir, and promised to send escorts to guide her ascension in eight years. In the meantime, Xue began to fast. According to the account, "Although perfected transcendents descended in her presence, although radiant phosphors lit up the space while numinous winds carried unusual fragrances and the harmonious music of cloud harps was performed in her room, [her husband] Feng Hui was not aware of any of this." Simply because Xue made herself inaccessible, she was "often suspected [by her husband in the same way as was] the Holy Mother of Dongling [Dongling Shengmu]."[61] A tenth-century edition of the Holy Mother of Dongling's biography tells that her husband "did not believe in the Dao" and filed an official complaint that she was "rebellious and heretic, not attending to her domestic duties."[62]

Suspicion and failure in understanding are crucial to the narratives in that they create a contrast between the transcendent and the ignorant. Suspicion comes from lack of knowledge and control. The lack of knowledge is presented in two ways: in Xue's husband's case, even when something is happening, he is not aware. In Wang's parents' case, even if they hear something, they cannot see it; even if something is disclosed to them in words, they still cannot understand. Wang's parents are only suspicious of her after perceiving something unusual—hearing voices without seeing anyone and witnessing Wang descending from the sky. Xue's husband, however, is suspicious simply because she is "distant and cannot be [intimately] approached" (*miao buke qin*), emblematic of the husband's lack of control. The suspicion of spirit possession or enchantment in Wang's story, furthermore, is specifically related to Wang's divine visitation.

Two accounts in the tenth-century *Continued Tradition of Transcendents* contain similar and yet more elaborate narratives of suspicion. One is the biography of Qi Xiaoyao:

> Miss Qi, Daoist name Xiaoyao, was a native of Nangong, Jizhou [in present-day Hebei]. Her father earned his living as an

instructor. When Xiaoyao was in her teens, she was quite self-contained in temperament; she did not play children's games and had her mind directed toward the Dao. Her parents were aware of all this. Xiaoyao frequently conducted hidden merits on people. When her father taught her to read *Admonishment for Women* [Nü jie; composed by an elite woman, Ban Zhao, in the first century], she looked at it and said, "this simply concerns ordinary people's affairs." She turned instead to chant diligently *Laozi's Canon of Transcendents*.[63] When she reached the age at which one wears a hairpin [fourteen], a matchmaker visited, and she sensed the ominous. When she was nineteen, her parents married her to Ji Xun, the son of a peasant family in the same village. Her parents-in-law were severe and reprimanded her for neglecting agricultural work. However, day and night Xiaoyao was preoccupied with purification practice, paying no attention to their livelihood. Ji Xun also frequently reproached her. Xiaoyao then asked her parents-in-law to send her back to her natal home. As she returned, her parents also rejected her. She then excused herself for being unable to manage mundane affairs and expressed her wish to live alone in a quiet chamber [*jingshi*] to practice the Dao in order to bring blessings to her parents-in-law. Ji Xun and her parents were all suspicious of her behavior [*ju you ta yi*] and hence abandoned her in a chamber. Xiaoyao, in the meantime, simply stored fragrant water and practiced fasting and meditation. . . . The Ji family and neighbors all deemed her to be demonic and manic [*yaokuang*]. One night, people heard sounds of various people talking in her room; at dawn people saw her sitting alone and not frightened. Three days later, in the morning, the whole family heard the house breaking apart as loudly as the thunder, and all they saw in Xiaoyao's room was her clothes and shoes. They looked up into the sky and saw splendid and magnificent clouds and smokes, divine birds and cranes flying and singing, transcendent music and fragrant sedans, and an array of heavenly attendants in colorful garments. Xiaoyao was in the clouds and accompanied by a group of transcendents. People could hear clearly her words of farewell. Ji Xun rushed to inform her parents, who could still see her in the clouds when they arrived. The whole village ran over to see her and were marveled.[64]

The ignorant people in this story include both Xiaoyao's peasant husband and parents-in-law and her own literate but nonbelieving father. This story not only accentuates the incompatibility between the expected labor of a peasant woman and Daoist practice, but also explicitly states the irrelevance of elite womanly virtues (as represented by *Admonishment for Women*) to the Daoist ideal of transcendence. The family's suspicion of Xiaoyao begins as she requests a separate, secluded room for herself. The suspicion escalates and becomes more specific when the family and neighbors start to hear voices from her room. It is only lifted when the most astonishing scene happens in front of the entire village. The narrative also creates a contrast between the ways Xiaoyao is perceived and treated by her families before and after marriage. She, while not changing her lifestyle and practice, goes from a bright and composed daughter of understanding parents to a demonic, crazy wife and daughter-in-law who is abandoned by everyone. At the core of this dramatic shift is Xiaoyao's unchanging attitude. This kind of contrast rarely appears in male transcendents' accounts, which do not relate a radical change after marriage.

The other account, the biography of Pei Xuanjing in the same collection, provides a case for comparison. Unlike Xiaoyao, Pei is surrounded by an understanding husband and parents. And yet the motif of suspicion is still present:

> Pei Xuanjing was the daughter of Pei Sheng, the magistrate of Goushi, and the wife of Li Yan, the district defender of Hu. From childhood she was smart and quick in memorizing *The Book of Odes* and *The Book of Documents*, which her mother taught her. Upon reaching the age at which one wears a hairpin, she loved the Dao and adorned herself with garments she made by herself. She asked her parents to let her stay in a quiet chamber and wear these clothes. Her parents also loved the Dao and granted her requests. Every day she offered incense and paid homage to Daoist images. When maids served her, she never allowed them to enter the room. While she lived alone, at times there were sounds of women chatting and laughing in her room. But when her parents peeped inside, they saw no one. When they asked her about it, she said nothing. Her thoughts were clear, and her desires few. She used proper etiquette and was never impolite, even to her close family. At the age of twenty, her parents wanted to marry her to Li Yan. Upon hearing of it, she strongly objected and expressed the desire to devote herself to the Dao and

cultivate perfection in order to save people in this world. Her parents tried to dissuade her and said, "Women belong to [the families they marry into], and that is what rituals [*li*] are for. The timing for a woman [to marry] cannot be missed, and the rituals should not be incomplete. If you devote yourself to the Dao and yet your practice does not bear fruit, there will be no place where you belong. Madam Wei of Nanyue [Wei Huacun] also married and had children before ascending to the highest rank of transcendents." Xuanjing then married Li Yan, and all the marriage rituals were properly conducted. Not a month after the wedding, however, she told Li, "Since I have been practicing the Dao, the gods do not allow me to be your wife. Please stop [treating me as your wife]." Li also admired the Dao and hence consented to her request. She then lived alone in a quiet chamber, burned incense, and practiced [the Dao]. At night, Li heard sounds of chatting and laughing and was somewhat curious [*yi*]. Afraid of disturbing his wife, he peeked through a chink in the wall. He saw that the whole room was bright and had an unusual fragrance. There were two elegant and beautiful ladies, around seventeen or eighteen years old, wearing phoenix haircoils and colorful dresses, and a few maids, wearing cloud haircoils and silk robes, gracefully attending at the ladies' side. Xuanjing was talking with the two ladies. Li Yan was amazed and left. The next morning, he asked Xuanjing about what he saw. She answered, "Yes, it happened. What you saw were my transcendent companions visiting me from Kunlun [where the highest female transcendent, Divine Matriarch of the West, resides]. The supreme transcendents already knew that you peeked and blocked you with magic without your awareness. In the future, you shall be cautious and not peek again lest the divine officials chastise you. Even so, we are not destined to be husband and wife for long, and this is not the way for me to stay long in this world. I am concerned that you have no progeny yet. When the supreme transcendents come again, I will ask them for help." Later, one night, a celestial lady descended to Li's room. After a year, she came again, gave Li a baby, and said: "This is your son. Xuanjing will leave soon." Three days later, five-colored clouds hovered in the sky, celestial ladies played music, and a white phoenix carried Xuanjing to the sky and flew toward the northwest. It was in the eighth year of Dazhong [854], on the eighteenth day of the eighth month, at Li's villa in Gongdao village, Wen district.[65]

As mentioned earlier, in hagiographical accounts Wei Huacun was said to have married against her will and waited until after her sons grew up to resume full practice. In this story, Xuanjing's parents use Wei as a role model in the opposite way: to persuade Xuanjing to do both in the socially pre-scribed sequence—to first marry and bear sons in order to secure a place in the patrilineal family, and then to devote oneself fully to Daoist practice. If this attitude represents a (mis)use of Wei Huacun's example, the second half of the story subtly criticizes such opportunist half-heartedness. After mar-riage, rather than following her parents' suggestion to raise children before resuming her practice, Xuanjing almost immediately adopts celibacy and seclusion by claiming divine authority. The husband in this case respects Daoist practice and is not as ignorant as Xiaoyao's husband and in-laws—perhaps that is why he can see part of the divine congregation. But he is still blocked from sacred knowledge and not allowed to participate or to see any further. In the end, Xuanjing uses her divine connection to grant Li Yan a son as a favor (rather than a duty) and perhaps also as a reward for his rev-erence for the gods and her practice. As readers, supposedly as respectful as Li Yan, we also do not know anything beyond what Li Yan knows and sees. Li's curiosity, or suspicion, becomes crucial for the narrative to disclose to its readers what we need to know.

Both accounts mention a "quiet chamber" (*jingshi*), an oratory where the women practice the Dao in seclusion.[66] For early Celestial Master Daoists of the late second and early third centuries, "quiet chambers" were a kind of ritual space for members of the community to retreat and repent in.[67] The rites of the quiet chamber were crucial for the Supreme Purity tradition, founded in the 360s. Wei Huacun was said to have revealed the revised rite for "entering the oratory" to the founders of the tradition. In the oratory, practitioners visualized Daoist divinities, who in turn descended to and inhabited the sacred space.[68] A fifth-century source still attested to the importance of such a sacred space and its solemn qualities.[69] In later sources the term was generally used in referring to a solemn and secluded space for various religious practices. Historian Man Xu notes that many lay Buddhist women in Song Fujian made themselves such a "separate, undisturbed room" at home for religious practice, and that women's activities in such a space "transcended the mundane boundary between inner and outer, and trans-formed these private rooms into sacred facilities for communication with the supernatural world."[70] As is also demonstrated by the accounts of Qi

Xiaoyao and Pei Xuanjing cited earlier, a woman's secluded room at home complicated the domestic space and, if the woman's husband was still alive, could even undermine her role as a wife.

DIFFERENT SUBJECTIVITIES

Women's seclusion and celibacy continued to be associated with both divine and demonic connections in Song anecdotes. Celibate women were more often suspected than their male counterparts of losing their subjectivity, or the consciousness of their own state and actions. There were multiple constructs of manless women's subjectivity. Two Northern Song accounts (mid-11th c.; late 11th–early 12th c.) about a female deity, Yanhua, offer an interesting basis for comparison. Both accounts describe the incompatibility of wifehood and divine connections, but each depicts a different subjectivity of the woman in question.

The first account relates that at the age of seventeen, the daughter of an official named Wang Lun (*jinshi* degree sometime between 1008 and 1017) one day suddenly began referring to herself as Lady Yanhua and her father as Student Qingfei after waking up from a nightmare. Though originally illiterate, the daughter was now suddenly versed in the "thirty-six celestial seal scripts," which men of this world could not read, and she started to exchange poems with her father. The account includes several of her poems, which were later transcribed by another scholar-official, Jiang Zhiqi (1031–1104), and inscribed on steles. Twenty-four scrolls of her calligraphy in "celestial seal script" were presented to Emperor Renzong in 1040 or 1041. After being married into the Lü family in Guangling, she no longer remembered any of these events, nor was she capable of composing poetry.[71] It is clear from the narrative that, until her marriage, the daughter had been possessed by the deity, Lady Yanhua, who composed all the poems and interacted with the father. The style of the narrative is a combination of literary tale and remarks on poetry (*shihua*); Lady Yanhua's poems comprise the majority of the account. In this account, the anonymous author shows no interest in the relationship between the deity and the daughter, or the exact identity of the deity. The other account, however, differs greatly in both style and content.

The author of the later account was Huang Shang (1044–1130). It begins with the remark that "Transcendent Yanhua [Yanhua Xianren] is a woman who has attained the Dao." The narrative describes in great detail a daughter's dream, in which she encountered the transcendent/deity on a sacred mountain. One day, the deity "descended through writing [*bijiang*] to Wang Lun's official compound. Wang had already purified the room in expectation of her arrival. The deity chatted cheerfully with the maiden daughter [*chuzi*] and stayed with her, as if they were companions of this world. And yet only the daughter was able to see her and hear her voice. Everyone else, including Wang Lun, could not."

Wang's communication with the deity was mediated entirely through the writing of his daughter, who was able to communicate with the deity directly. Wang asked the deity if the daughter could marry. The deity "responded to his questions but never gave him a decisive answer." When the daughter's marriage was arranged, the deity left, and the daughter no longer remembered anything that was transmitted to her.[72] In clearly identifying the deity at the beginning as a Daoist transcendent, this account resembles a hagiography. As in the earlier account, the daughter plays the role of a spirit-medium. But in the first account she is passively possessed, while in the second she is an active participant in the revelation and communication. The incompatibility between wifehood and the daughter's connection to the deity in both accounts is intriguing because the deity is female and the relationship is not depicted as sexual. In other words, the possession or connection does not have to be (hetero-)sexual in order to be considered incompatible with wifehood. This is a sharp contrast to "Tree Lodgers," which assumes that women became *wu* because they are sexually and spiritually possessed by spirits.

Three anecdotes from *Record of the Listener*—relating, respectively, certain divine experiences of a maiden, a wife, and a concubine that came along with fasting and celibacy—suggest yet a different kind of subjectivity: that of a divine female body. The first story tells that a maiden daughter of a gentry family, after eating a peach-like fruit that mysteriously appeared beside her pillow, suddenly found all food and drink repulsive. Her parents summoned both medicinal and ritual healers, but they were powerless to help. The girl's condition continued for more than ten years, yet her body did not waste away. Everything else about her remained as before, but the girl's parents "did not dare to arrange marriage" for her. One day she suddenly asked for a cup of wine; after drinking it, she became hungry and started eating again. Her parents then married her into another gentry family from the same county.[73] It seems that the girl has either temporarily become a *xian* or gained certain divine qualities through the power of the mysterious peach, a fruit often associated with transcendent qualities and Daoist paradise— but neither the girl's parents nor the narrator know for sure what has happened. The only "symptom" that the girl has is refraining from food, which is already sufficient for her parents to seek help through exorcism. Only after her appetite returns is the girl considered suitable for marriage. As in Xie Ziran's biography, fasting can be seen as either divine or demonic. Here, the potential divine or demonic connection in this story is more likely perceived as one of spirit possession, since exorcism is deemed necessary despite being ineffective. The fact that the girl's body does not waste away seems to suggest a divine connection. But whether divine or demonic, the girl is deemed unfit for marriage until she resumes an ordinary diet, even in the absence of other unusual behavior.

The second account tells the story of Lu, the wife of an official named Zhang; both were natives of modern-day Zhejiang. A few years after giving birth to a boy, Lu suddenly began to refrain from eating anything except for a small amount of wine and fruit. She continued to attend to housework as usual but no longer shared a bed with her husband. Her mother-in-law suspected that she was affected by ghosts or other spirits. Upon being questioned, Lu apologized but offered no explanation. The maidservants told the mother-in-law that Lu claimed to have eaten peaches in the rear yard that only she could see. Lu stopped consuming even wine and fruits fifteen years later and subsisted on only cold water for another seven years, after which she consumed nothing at all. The account does not associate her with any specific religious tradition or lineage but records that in 1194, decades after Lu began to fast and practice celibacy, she cured her brother-in-law of a chronic illness that "multiple physicians had failed to treat." She did so simply by massaging the area that hurt. After that, people were convinced that she must have encountered the divine. The account ends with the remark that Zhang Lüxin (fl. 1174–1190), a former colleague of Lu's husband Zhang and the source of this story, once invited Zhang and other colleagues, including their wives, to a banquet at his home; Lu alone declined. By the time the story was recorded, Lu was seventy years old.[74]

The concubine story contains descriptions that resemble narratives of ghost fetuses, spirit possession, Daoist transcendents, and a mixture of Buddhist and Daoist elements. It relates that the commander-general Pan Zhang once bought a concubine in the Southern Song capital of Lin'an and brought her to Hanzhong (northern Sichuan), where Pan and his family resided. The entire family liked her. Two years later, however, she "caught an illness that resembled pregnancy" and refrained from eating. Less than four months later, she gave birth to a son; three months after that she had a second son; and then a third after another four months. From then on, she ate rarely and irregularly "as if being possessed." She asked for, and was given, a "purity chamber" for herself to "practice the Dao." Day and night she locked herself inside the chamber. Anyone who peeked into her room only saw her sitting with her legs crossed, reciting scriptures. No suspicious voices could be heard in her room, but when Pan Zhang forced his way in, he found the room filled with Buddhist scriptures, some of which were printed copies from South Asia and other foreign lands. When asked about these, she simply said, "the celestial ladies gave them to me." Over the following years, she performed several miracles and magic tricks for the family, and her soul traveled with Pan when he moved postings. A visiting cousin of Pan's once said to Pan, "I heard that you, my brother, bought a concubine who turned out to be a *xian*!" Whenever the concubine went out, she was always accompanied by a little tiger. Eventually, when Pan returned to the capital, she disappeared.[75]

In these stories, although *xian* qualities are still incompatible with wifehood (or concubinage), the women's marital status does not seem to affect their chances of encountering the divine (or the demonic). Fasting, here, was a prelude to celibacy, whether imposed or voluntary, temporary or long-term. Indeed, in these three cases, fasting seems to have aroused more suspicion and concern among the women's families than solitude or celibacy. The three stories were not hagiographies, they were records of the narrators' (mostly elite men in these cases) accounts of the extraordinary women within their own circles. The narratives consist of some familiar elements in the transcendents' repertoire, and yet suspicion does not function here as it does in the hagiographical narratives. In these three stories, suspicion serves not to distinguish the transcendent from the ignorant, but to distinguish the marvelous and unknowable (whatever it is that has happened to the women) from the curious (the narrators themselves, acquaintances and relatives of these women). Hagiographies and the three anecdotes, though, share the similar construct of a divine female body, of which manless sexuality is an aspect but not the entirety. It is a closed system with a celibate and fasting body in a purity chamber of her own. This differs from what we have seen in the narratives that conflate female *wu* and *xian* with enchanted women, in which female sexuality (as constructed in relation to men) occupies the center of female subjectivity, and in which manless sexuality thus indicates the loss of subjectivity.

CONCLUSION

ON AUGUST 25, 2006, A TAIPEI COUNCILWOMAN, A CATHOLIC PRIEST, and a number of Christian pastors held a press conference to criticize the Taipei municipal government's official sponsorship of the LGBT movement. The government had sponsored the city's seventh LGBT festival, Tongwan Jie, which was to take place the following month. Panelists at the press conference claimed that "tolerance of homosexuality would accelerate the spread of AIDS and cause severe social problems," that "homosexuality was deviant behavior and could be rectified," and that same-sex marriage would lead to "the demise of the nation and the extinction of mankind." Activists for LGBT and women's rights, gender equality in education, and advocates for patients with HIV responded with another press conference the following day, asserting that "medical research proved long ago that homosexuality cannot be changed." Their rebuttal cited the Department of Health's HIV statistics for the year and the comments of Dr. Chang of the Infectious Disease Division at NTU Hospital, and added, "Only diversity can accelerate Taipei's development; only openness can broaden Taiwan's horizons to see the world."[1] Despite the extreme disparity in the two sides' use of facts, both groups appealed to the authority of medical knowledge and to the desire to see the nation progress. This is emblematic of a present-day public debate.

Medicine and "knowledge" worked very differently in the premodern world in at least three ways: the unique discursive power of medical knowledge, multiple and competing sources of authority, and a different constitution of norms and normalcy. The Southern Song physician Chen Ziming cited the Confucian classics to buttress his medical theory; the elite and the ruling class, however, rarely needed medical theory to justify their claims about sex, marriage, and gender roles. Chen, moreover, was an anomaly

163

among medical writers up to his day in two respects: his assertion of a sex–desire–procreation link and his normalization of that link through the creation of the medical category of *guafu*, which encompassed all women without sexual contact with men. His *guafu* theory contradicted the (Neo-)Confucian ethics that he attempted to incorporate, as it implied that it was unhealthy and unnatural (or against "the principle of Heaven and Earth") for young widows to remain chaste. This theory was rebuked a century later by a more dedicated Confucian-physician, Zhu Zhenheng, who asserted that desire could and should be controlled and that sex with men was not a necessary condition for women's health. Zhu was more successful than Chen—more thorough and more coherent—in his medicalization of Confucian ethics and his moralization of medicine, but the family and the marriage system at large never needed Zhu's or any other physicians' opinion to maintain its legitimacy.

Medical writers often disagreed with one another. In the Song dynasty and throughout most of imperial Chinese history, medicine was not a standardized profession; medical specialists did not enjoy special institutional or social status.[2] Although elite physicians shared a similar reading list of medical texts by this time, thanks to the development of printing and the Song state's sponsorship of medical compilations and publications, physicians did not always share a common ground when constructing their own theories and engaging in debates with one another. Moreover, medicine was not the most authoritative source regarding matters of the body, sex, and sexuality; it was itself a composite tradition and was only one among many sources from which people drew to navigate discomfort and uncertainties. While Song anecdotes about spirit possession and ghost enchantment made reference to medicine, physicians played a minor role in dealing with such problems. The diverse narratives about enchanted women in Song folklore not only contradicted the concurrent medical explanations of women's "intercourse with ghosts" but also went beyond the relatively coherent gendered patterns seen in pre-Song literary tales. Song physicians were not known for their exorcism skills; people often distrusted the professional ritualists that they brought in as well. Narratives of absolute failure emerged during the Song, where no method of treatment was effective and no one had the privilege of knowing the truth.

Chen Ziming and Zhu Zhenheng did have one thing in common, though. Their assessment of health was based not on the descriptive (the average condition of most women) but on the prescriptive (what *all* women should strive for). For both Chen and Zhu, the norm of women's health bore more similarities to the original meaning of the Latin word *norma*, meaning "a square used by carpenters, builders, and surveyors to obtain a right angle," than to the modern notion of norm and normalcy, which conflates "statistical regularity derived from quantitative analysis" and "evaluative judgment attached to a model or type."[3] Throughout the sources cited in this book are norms about health, illness, the body, and sexuality established on the basis of what was considered right or superior, not on what was perceived as common or average. Daoist self-cultivation and exorcism texts treat ghost intercourse and other illnesses not as deviations, but as ordinary bodily expressions of ordinary people. Buddhist and Daoist writers who promised sexual transformation for pious women seemed to have found no need to reconcile between the doctrine that "all women who [follow a certain program of practice] will turn into men" and the empirical fact that such things rarely happened. Gender and sexual norms were not more flexible in premodern China. But the complexity and constitution of norms in a world where there was no single most powerful common ground of public debate is worth our attention and future research.

Women's manless condition was understood very differently in different sources. For several physicians, and for varying reasons, it was a cause of illness; for a few bedchamber texts, it was the major cause of women's intercourse with ghosts; in literary tales and popular anecdotes, it was a symptom or an outcome of women being enchanted by spirits; in hagiographies, it was a part of the woman's religious practice and/or a prerequisite for her transcendence. If there was one thing that almost all the sources shared when it came to the subject of manless women, it was the need for explanation.

Heterosexuality as an institution, according to Adrienne Rich, is a "cluster of forces within which women have been convinced that marriage and sexual orientation toward men are inevitable."[4] This notion of "compulsory heterosexuality," as literary scholar Tze-lan Sang argues, is not applicable to premodern China, where there was little interest in women's sexual desire (whether heterosexual or same-sex); there was simply a "marriage imperative" for women. Depictions of female same-sex desire in Ming-Qing literature served either to perpetuate the "utopian polygamy" or to trivialize eroticism between women.[5] Indeed, the marriage system in premodern China rarely needed a discourse on women's sexual desire to sustain itself, at least until female sexuality became inconvenient and women appeared uninterested. Bedchamber texts' discussion of women's ghost intercourse and narratives about women's enchantment disorder in literary tales and popular anecdotes complicate this picture. In these, we see not only the gaze at young and desirable female bodies, but also fears that women might not desire men. Rich's analysis of men's fear that "women could be indifferent to them altogether" is relevant here.[6] However, while ghost enchantment made women unmarriageable and in some cases marriage was the indication of successful treatment, none of the sources assumed that marriage solved the problem; marriage itself was never a cure.

When people began to make sense of women's bodies and lives apart from wifehood and motherhood, new questions about normalcy, desire, sexuality, and gendered identities emerged. The most contentious, puzzling, and unstable discourses on and expressions of female sexuality in sources discussed in this book lay in women's manlessness, rather than in their desire for other men or women.

CHINESE CHARACTER GLOSSARY

An Lingshou 安令首

Ban Zhao 班昭
Baochang 寶唱
Baoxian 寶賢
Beishi tongzhi hunli, yiyuan pi
    fangzong 北市同志婚禮，
    議員批放縱
Bencaojing jizhu 本草經集注
bieli san 別離散
bigu 辟穀
biji 筆記
bijiang 箄降
Bintui lu 賓退錄
biqiuni 比丘尼
biyao 必要
bu ke yan 不可言
bu nao huan yuan 補腦還元
bu yu jian ren 不欲見人
buji luan 不及亂

Cai Jing 蔡京
caiqi 採氣
Cao Pi 曹丕
chali 差戾
Chao Buzhi 晁補之
Chao Yuanfang 巢元方
chaochang 超常
Chen Shao 陳邵/劭
Chen Yanzhi 陳延之

Chen Zhi 陳埴
Chen Ziming 陳自明
Chenggong Zhiqiong 成公智瓊
chimei 魑 / 螭魅
chonghun 重婚
chongmai 衝脈
chongqie 寵妾
Chu Cheng 褚澄
Chu Yong 儲泳
chuangi 傳奇
chuanshi 傳屍
Chunyu Yi 淳于意
chuzi 處子
Cuishi zuanyao fang 崔氏纂要方

da qi xinghuai 達其性懷
da zhangfu 大丈夫
Dai Fu 戴孚
Dai Liang 戴良
dan 丹
Daoliu 道流
Daonü 道女
Daoren 道人
Daoshi 道士
Daotang 道堂
Daoxin 道心
Daoxue 道學
Daqing jing 大清經
de 德
de yinshi zhi zheng zhe 得飲食之正者

167

Deng Zhi (style name: Duanruo)
鄧植 (端若)
dihuang 地黃
Ding Jie 丁介
Dong Feng 董奉
Dong Jingchen 董經臣
Dong Shangxian 董上仙
Dongling Shengmu 東陵聖母
Dou Weiwu (or Weixian)
竇維鋈 (維鋈)
du 獨
Du Guangting 杜光庭
Duan Chengshi 段成式

enyi shuge 恩義殊隔
ewei 阿魏

fa 法
fanchang 反常
fangnei 房內
fangshi 方士
fangzhong 房中
Fangzhong buyi 房中補益
faren 法人
fashi 法師
Fawu 法悟
Faying 法穎
feichang 非常
fenbie ren gui 分別人鬼
Feng Hui 馮徽
fenggu yingwei 風骨英偉
fengxie 風邪
Fo shuo zhuan nüshen jing
佛說轉女身經
Fotucheng 佛圖澄
fu 腑 viscera
fu 婦 married woman; wife
fu 符 talisman
Fu Shan 傅山
Fu Wenxiu 傅文秀
Fu zi yu qi qin 父子欲其親
fuke 婦科
funü 婦女

furen 婦人
Fushi lun 服石論

Gan Bao 干寶
gan mai dazao tang 甘麥大棗湯
ganjie 感接
gantong 感通
ganying 感應
ganyun 感孕
gong tong qing 共通情
gou 媾
gu 孤 young and without a father
gu 蠱 a kind of poison
gua 寡
gua er wu yu 寡而無欲
guafu 寡婦
guai 怪
guan 鰥
Guangling Chalao 廣陵茶姥
Guangyi ji 廣異記
gui 鬼
guijiao 鬼交
guimei 鬼魅
guiqi lin shen 鬼炁臨身
guitai 鬼胎
guzheng 骨蒸

Han Qi 韓琦
he 合 conjoin
he 和 harmony
heqi 合氣
Hong Hao 洪皓
Hua Shou 滑壽
Huagu 花姑
Huang Lingwei 黃靈微
Huang Shang 黃裳
Huang Tingjian 黃庭堅
Huangting jing 黃庭經
huanjing bunao 還精補腦
huanmei fakuang 患魅發狂
Huichang jieyi lu 會昌解頤錄
Huiguo 慧果
Huiji Fa 穢跡法

hun 魂
hunkuang 昏狂

ji 笄 hairpin
ji 疾 illness
jia 瘕
jian 姦
Jiang Guan 江瓘
Jiang Zhiqi 蔣之奇
jianguishi 見鬼師
jiangyao 將要
Jiankang 建康
jiao 蛟 aquatic dragons
jiao 交 intercourse
jiao 醮 Daoist rite
jiaogan 交感
jiaogou 交媾
jiaohe 交合
jiaojie 交接
jiaoqi 腳氣
jiaotong 交通
Jiaozheng Yishu Ju 校正醫書局
jieshen 潔身
Jin Keji 金可記
jing 精 essence
jing 靜 tranquility
Jing Huan 景煥
jing wei tong 精未通
Jing xie 精血
Jingjian 淨撿
jingmei 精魅
jingqin jiexing 精懃戒行
jingshen huanghu 精神恍惚
jingshi 靜室; 淨室; 靖室
Jingxiu 淨秀
Jinmu 金母
jinyi huashen dan 金液華神丹
jinzhen 禁針
jinzhou zhi shu 禁呪之術
Jiyi ji 集異記
ju you ta yi 俱有他疑
jue qi 厥氣
juran biqiu 居然比丘

Kang Minggan 康明感
Kou Zongshi 寇宗奭
kuang 曠
kujie 苦節

lai 癩
lao 勞
Lao er wu fu yue gua 老而無夫曰寡
laozhai 癆瘵
Laozi Xiang'er zhu 老子想爾注
li 禮
Li Quan 李筌
Li Zhenduo 李真多
liangxing guanxi 兩性關係
liaoxie 療邪
Liaozhai 聊齋
Libin Fushi 禮賓副使
Lienü zhuan 列女傳
Lieyi zhuan 列異傳
lijing kuxing 勵精苦行
Lingbao 靈寶
Lingbao lingjiao jidu jinshu
　　靈寶領教濟度金書
Lishan Lao 驪山姥
Liu Jingshu 劉敬叔
Liu Jixian 劉繼先
Liu Yiqing 劉義慶
Longshi 龍施
Lü Fu 呂復
Lu xiansheng daomen kelüe
　　陸先生道門科略
Lu Yanghao 盧養浩
luan 亂
lun 論
Luo Jin 羅禁

Ma Shu 馬樞
Ma Yu 馬鈺
mei 魅
meiji 魅疾
miao buke qin 邈不可親
Miaoxiang 妙相
Mingdao 明道

Mingseng zhuan 名僧傳
Mugong 木公
Muke 木客

nan 男
nan nü you bie 男女有別
nanshen 男身
nanxiang 男相
neijiao 內交
Ning Quanzhen 寧全真
nizheng 尼正
nü 女
nü Daoshi 女道士
Nü jie 女誡
nüdan 女丹
nüe 瘧
nüshen 女身
nüxi 女習
nüxing 女性
nüzhi 女質

Pei Xuanjing 裴玄靜
ping 憑
po 魄
Pu Songling 蒲松齡
Puji benshi fang 普濟本事方

qi 氣
qi shen 棄身
Qi Xiaoyao 戚逍遙
Qian Lang 錢朗
Qian Miaozhen 錢妙真
Qianjin yifang 千金翼方
Qin Jingjian 秦淨堅
qinxi 寢息
Qiu Chuji 丘處機
qu 渠
Quanzhen 全真
qubie 區別
Quyi shuo 祛疑說

re ru xieshi 熱入血室
Ren shi zhuan 任氏傳

renxin 人心
renyu 人欲
rong 容
ru jian gui zhuang 如見鬼狀
ruyi 儒醫

sanshi jiuchong 三尸九蟲
Santan Fa 三壇法
seng 僧
Seng Shen fang 僧深方
Sengduan 僧端
Sengguo 僧果
Sengji 僧基
sengzheng 僧正
shamen 沙門
shan zhigui zhe 善制鬼者
Shanghan jiushi lun 傷寒九十論
Shanghan lun 傷寒論
Shangqing tianpeng fumo dafa
　　　　　上清天蓬伏魔大法
shangxue zhi shi 上學之士
shanling 山靈
shanxiao 山魈
shaqi 煞炁
she ling 設令
she nan nü, wei seng ni 捨男女, 為僧尼
shen 神 spirit; deity
shen 身 body; self
shen da qi xing 深達其性
shen wei qi xing 深違其性
shen wu xin 深無忻
shen ya xie 身厭邪
Shen Yue 沈約
shengsheng 生生
Shennong bencao jing 神農本草經
shenqi zhuangsu 神氣莊肅
Shenxiao 神霄
shi 士 gentleman; scholar-official
shi 尸 corpse; deathbringer
Shi Huimu 釋慧木
Shi Xuanzao 釋玄藻
shihua 詩話
Shihua zonggui 詩話總歸

shijie 尸解
shipo 師婆
shixing 濕形
shuo jin 說今
shushi 術士
si 思
si nanzi he 思男子合
Sima Qian 司馬遷
sizhu 寺主
Song Xuanbai 宋玄白
Song Yuxian 宋玉賢
sudie 訴牒
sui 祟
sui pingfu 祟憑附
suiyun 祟孕
Sun Bu'er 孫不二

Taiping huimin hejiju fang
　　太平惠民和劑局方
taishang wugu wan 太上五蠱丸
taixia 胎下
Taiyi Yinhun Fan 太一引魂旛
tan 壇
Tang Gongfang 唐公房
Tang Song yishi 唐宋遺史
Tanhui 曇暉
tanyu 貪欲
Tao Hongjing 陶弘景
Tiandi 天帝
tiangui 天癸
Tianli 天理
Tianpeng 天蓬
Tianshi 天師
tianyi 天醫
tong 通
tongqi wan 通氣丸
tongqin 同寢
tongta 同榻
Tongwan Jie 同玩節
Tongyou ji 通幽記

wai xie 外邪
waishu 外屬

wana qi 膃肭臍
Wang Fengxian 王奉仙
Wang Xichao 王希巢
Wang Zhe (style name: Chongyang)
　　王嚞 (重陽)
Wei Huacun 魏華存
wei jingguai suo huo 為精怪所惑
wei mei suo bing 為魅所病
wei mei suo huo 為魅所惑
wei wu suo huo 為物所惑
wei yaowu suo mei 為妖物所魅
weichang 違常
weichang de xing 違常的性
Wen zi 問子
wenjing tang 溫經湯
wu 巫
wu fu zhi fu 無夫之婦
wu nanzi he 無男子合
wu'ao 巫媼
Wulang 五郎
Wumu 五木
Wutong 五通/統

xiali 下利
xian 仙
Xian Chao 弦超
Xian jing 仙經
xianbing 仙病
xiang ru shenling suozuo 象如神靈所作
xiang wenxun 相問訊
xiangyao 想要
xiangzhe 相者
xiani 狎昵
Xiao Guang 蕭廣
Xiao Yuan 蕭淵
xiaojie 小戒
Xiaopin fang 小品方
Xiaoyao 逍遙
Xici 繫辭
xie ni jie 血逆竭
xie sheng 血盛
Xie Ziran 謝自然
xiemei 邪魅

xieqi 邪氣
xindong 心動
xing 性
xingzhuang 行狀
xinnian buzheng 心念不正
xinshen xufan 心神虛煩
Xiwangmu 西王母
xu 虛
Xu Chunfu 徐春甫
Xu Mi 許謐
Xu Shuwei 許叔微
Xu Xiangu 徐仙姑
Xue Xuantong 薛玄同
Xue Yongruo 薛用弱
Xulao 虛勞
xulao ximeng 虛勞喜夢
xuyao 需要

yang jing 陽精
Yang Xi 楊羲
yangsheng 養生
Yanhua 燕華
Yanhua Xianren 燕華仙人
yanwu nüshen 厭惡女身
yanye 豔冶
yao 要 want; need
yao 藥 medicine; medicinal
yao 妖 demon; anomalous beauty
yaokuang 妖狂
yaoni 妖尼
yaowang 妖妄
yaoyu 要譽
yasheng 厭勝
Yeren xianhua 野人閑話
yi 醫 medicine; physician
yi 疑 suspicion; doubt; curiosity
yi shi ru ren 意事如人
yi wu buneng zhi 醫巫不能治
yi yaomei suo huo 疑祅魅所惑
yichang 異常
Yijing 易經
Yikan 義堪
yin 淫 with a "water" radical

yin 姪 with a "female" radical
yin shui 陰水
yin xie 淫邪
yin yi wei 陰已痿
yinhuo mengxiang 淫惑夢想
yinyu 姪欲
yiren 異人
Yiwen zonglu 異聞總錄
yiwu 醫巫
yiyu 醫諭
yizhe 醫者
Yongcheng jixian lu 墉城集仙錄
yongju 癰疽
Yongle dadian 永樂大典
youshen 有娠
yu 欲 need; desire
yu 愚 ignorant
yu ji zhi huai 愚嫉之懷
yu ni bu de 欲溺不得
yu si 欲死
Yu Tuan 虞搏
Yu Yunwen 虞允文
yu zhi jie hao 與之結好
yuan 怨
yuanjun 元君
Yufang mijue 玉房秘訣
Yufang zhiyao 玉房指要
yunü 御女
Yunü sunyi 御女損益
yuxin 慾心
yuyan 寓言

zaiyi 災異
zang 臟
zangzao 藏躁
Zhan Daozi (given name: Kangzong) 詹道子 (亢宗)
Zhan Jie 詹玠
Zhang Ji 張機
Zhang Shunlie 章舜烈
Zhang Xujing 張虛靖
Zhang Yuchu 張宇初
Zhang Zhuo 張鷟

Zhao Yushi 趙與時

Zhen gao 真誥

Zhen Quan 甄權

zheng 正 orthodox

zheng 癥 conglomerate

zhengchang 正常

Zhengyi 正一

zhenjiu 針灸

zhenjun 真君

zhiguai 志怪

Zhu Conglong 朱從龍

Zhu Duanzhang 朱端章

Zhu Xi 朱熹

Zhu Zhenheng 朱震亨

zhuan nü shen 轉女身

Zhuihun Fa 追魂法

Zichen xuanshu 紫宸玄書

Zifu Zhai 資福齋

zihui ruci 自會如此

zineng gaiyi xinzhi 自能改易心志

ziqing 恣情

Zixu Yuanjun 紫虛元君

Ziying Lingshu Shezhao Fa
　　紫英靈書攝召法

zong qing jian yu 縱情兼慾

Zunsheng (mi)jing 尊生(秘)經

NOTES

INTRODUCTION

1 *Zhubing yuanhou lun* 40.1149–50.
2 *Xu xian zhuan* 1.20a–21b.
3 *Qingsuo gaoyi* bieji.1.1169.
4 Important monographs on gender in the Song period include Bernhardt, *Women and Property in China*; Birge, *Women, Property, and Confucian Reaction*; Bray, *Technology and Gender*; Blanchard, *Song Dynasty Figures of Longing and* Desire; Bossler, *Powerful Relations*; Bossler, *Courtesans, Concubines, and the Cult of Female Fidelity*; Ebrey, *The Inner Quarters*; Ebrey, *Women and the Family in Chinese History*; Furth, *A Flourishing Yin*; Xu, *Crossing the Gate*; Yü, *Kuan-yin*.
5 Epitaphs of female renunciants, for instance, are mostly those of widows or women who were orphaned at young age.
6 For example, Campany, *Making Transcendents*; Bokenkamp, "Sisters of the Blood."
7 For example, Ebrey's *The Inner Quarters* collects substantial information about Song women's lives from *Yijian zhi* stories. *Yijian zhi* is also one of the major source materials in Valerie Hansen's *Changing Gods in Medieval China*, Edward Davis's *Society and the Supernatural*, and Richard von Glahn's *The Sinister Way* in their investigation of various aspects of Song popular religion. Ronald Egan shows how *Yijian zhi* contains records of what "would rarely if ever be deemed fit for inclusion in orthodox historiography," including "violence against women, corruption among the official class, scams targeting young men with a weakness for sexual fantasy, cases of haunting and madness, and infidelity in and outside of marriage" ("Crime, Violence, and Ghosts," 149–50).
8 Hansen, *Changing Gods in Medieval China*, 17–23; Liu Ching Cheng, *Bujuzi*, 2–6, 655–56; Davis, *Society and the Supernatural*, 17–20; Inglis, *Hong Mai's*

Record of the Listener, 2. See chap. 4 for more discussions on using *Yijian zhi* as a historical source.

9   For instance, Song civil examination takers frequently sought help from spirits and visited popular temples for divination (Chaffee, *The Thorny Gates*, 177–81; Shih-shan Huang, "Tianzhu Lingqian," 284–88). *Yijian zhi* shows that Hong Mai's belief in the ubiquity of spirits was a widespread way of thinking of his day (Egan, "Crime, Violence, and Ghosts," 175–78). For a study on the shared ground between elite and commoners' religious practice and beliefs during the Song, see Liao, "Popular Religion and the Religious Beliefs."

10 For instance, Du Zhengzhen uses the inscriptions in Yuhuang Temple in Jincheng, Shanxi, to uncover the changing organization and leadership of local communities during the Song-Jin-Yuan period ("Beike zhong de difang jiceng zuzhi"); Anne Gerritsen's study of temple inscriptions from Song-Yuan Jizhou shows that, even though the link between temple cults and local community during the Song-Yuan period was not yet as close as that in Ming-Qing times, literati authors used temple inscriptions to depict the image of their ideal community and local identity ("Visions of Local Culture").

11 Hansen, *Changing Gods in Medieval China*, 15–17, 84–95; Pi, *Songdai minzhong cishen*, 279.

12 Both cases are mentioned in Xu, *Crossing the Gate*, 115–18, 122.

13 *Yijian zhi* bu.1690–92. This story is also discussed in chap. 4.

14 *Yijian zhi* jia.19.173–74.

15 It is likely that the character *Dao* here refers to some form of Daoism and that the *Daotang* was a kind of Daoist nunnery. But the context is not entirely clear.

16 *Yijian zhi* yi.16.317.

17 *Yijian zhi* jia.20.161.

18 On economic change during the Song, see McDermott and Yoshinobu, "Economic Change in China."

19 There were a few texts on female bodily cultivation written by women during the Tang-Song period, mostly in verse. I will discuss them in chaps. 5 and 6.

20 Dorothy Ko in her study of the history of footbinding challenges the existence of an "authentic" female voice by pointing out that oftentimes the language itself does not serve to convey one's actual feelings; that is why, from Ko's point of view, modern researchers and ethnographers who interviewed women with bound feet still failed to listen to the "murmurs from within their bodies." What Ko proposes to pay attention to, instead, is the hybrid nature of footbinding's history: "there is not one footbinding but many" (*Cinderella's Sisters*, 2, 12–13).

21 Marcus, "The State's Oversight," quotations on 509 and 517.

22 Sommer, *Sex, Law, and Society*, 9 and 15.

23 Rocha, "Xing."

24 For an overview, see Weeks, *Sexuality*.

25 The six categories are "normal" (*zhengchang*), "transgression" (*weichang*), "perversion" (*fanchang*), "unusual" (*feichang*), "abnormal" (*yichang*), and "extraordinary" (*chaochang*); see Liu Yuan-ju, *Shenti, xingbie, jieji*, 61–63. All of these terms exist as lexemes in modern Chinese, and some can be found in classical Chinese. However, their usages differ from Liu's definitions, which (like her classifications) are entirely her own. Since these categories are not present in historical or contemporary Chinese, the English translations here are tentative and provided purely for the sake of convenience.

26 Liu Yuan-ju, *Shenti, xingbie, jieji*, 67. The English translation is mine.

27 In the family system at that time, it was not procreation as a natural phenomenon that mattered, but giving birth to sons. Giving birth to sons could improve that status of a woman in the family, especially that of a woman other than the legitimate wife. But failure to give birth to sons alone was rarely a threat to a wife's legitimacy. See Huang and Goldin, "Polygyny and Its Discontents," 25; Cheng Ya-ru, *Qinggan yu zhidu*, chaps. 1 and 4.

28 *Soushen ji* 7.125–27. Daniel Hsieh regards this story as one of the "beginnings of [the] literati love story," a genre which always involves a man and a woman who is not his wife. Wives belong to a different domain from women such as courtesans. Hsieh calls it "the division or splitting of women" that inhibited the development of "love" (*Love and Women*, 19).

29 This is the case in many Tang tales as well. In the stories about "mating with spirits" in the *Guangyi ji* (mid-late eighth century) studied by Glen Dudbridge, for instance, a man's welfare depends upon the identity of the spirit that he encounters. A high-ranking goddess brings happiness, fortune, good health, and sometimes even sons—unless the man rejects and offends her, while a demon or minor spirit often causes harm or death. As for encounters with the ghosts of deceased women, it "depends on the need and the plight of the women" (*Religious Experience and Lay Society*, 154–73).

30 Mei Chia-ling, "Liuchao zhiguai," the quote is on 108–9.

31 *Soushen houji* 7.545.

32 *Soushen ji* 4.75–77.

33 Furth, *A Flourishing Yin*, 91; Hsiu-fen Chen, "Between Passion and Repression," 51–53.

34 Sang, *The Emerging Lesbian*.

35 Sommer, *Sex, Law, and Society*.

36 For example, Jinhua Chen, "Family Ties and Buddhist Nuns"; Cahill, "Discipline and Transformation"; Chao, "Good Career Moves"; Yao, "Good Karmic Connections" and "Tang Women in the Transformation of Buddhist Filiality"; Pang, "Eminent Nuns And/Or/As Virtuous Women"; Balkwill, "The Sutra on Transforming the Female Form" and "When Renunciation Is Good Politics."

37 Ding-hwa Hsieh, "Buddhist Nuns in Sung China," 65.

38　Bumbacher, *The Fragments of the* Daoxue zhuan, 504, 507, 523.

39　Chao, "Good Career Moves," 135; Cahill, *Divine Traces of Daoist Sisterhood*, 1–2; Tsai, *Lives of the Nuns*, 7.

40　Tsai, *Lives of the Nuns*, 7; Chao, "Good Career Moves," 135; Cahill, *Divine Traces of the Daoist Sisterhood*, 2; Wang Rutong, *Biqiuni zhuan jiaozhu*, 8. Along with the separation of social from religious factors, there is often a conflation of motives and conditions in scholarly analysis. For instance, widowhood could create a more positive condition for women to become renunciants, but it was not necessarily the motive for women to do so.

41　Cahill, "Discipline and Transformation," 253.

1. "HUSBANDLESS WOMEN" IN MEDICINE

1　For the naturalization of sex and gender in early twentieth-century China, see Dikötter, *Sex, Culture, and Modernity in China*; Rocha, "Xing."

2　Wu, "Ghost Fetuses"; Hsiu-fen Chen, "Zai mengmei zhi jian" and "Between Passion and Repression."

3　Furth, *A Flourishing Yin*, 91.

4　On the compilation and inclusiveness of Song medical books, see Leung, "Medical Learning from the Song to the Ming."

5　For the organization of Chen's book and its textual history and significance, see Ng, "Male Brushstrokes and Female Touch," especially chap. 3.

6　*Furen daquan liangfang* 6.4a–b (emphasis added). For other translations of parts of this passage, see Furth, *A Flourishing Yin*, 89, and Hsiu-fen Chen, "Between Passion and Repression," 53–54. What Hsiu-fen Chen quotes and translates is Xue Ji's (1487–1558) summary and paraphrase of the original passage. My translation is based on the original text of Chen Ziming.

7　For studies on Chunyu Yi and his case histories, see Sivin, "Text and Experience"; Loewe, "The Physician Chunyu Yi"; Hsu, *Pulse Diagnosis in Early Chinese Medicine.*

8　This statement occurs in the context of Tao noting that physicians, when using drugs, should take into consideration patients' various individual conditions, such as their locales and whether they are the depleted or replete type, men or women, old or young, or in joy or in agony (*Zhenglei bencao* 1.21a). Chu's original text is no longer extant, and we do not know the original context of the sentence that Tao quotes. The extant version of *Chu's Posthumous Work* makes no mention at all of nuns and widows or separate treatment for manless women; but there is one place that mentions the right age for men and women to start having sexual contact with the other sex. See the discussion below.

9　*Mengzi zhushu* 2.35b.

10　In addition to widows, nuns, and maidens, other medical writings around or after Chen's time also include palace ladies (*Nüke baiwen* 1.60b–61a), betrothed maidens (*Danxi yiji*, 331), and women whose husbands were away from home for a long time (*Jiaozhu furen liangfang* 6.10). Courtesans and prostitutes were never included in this category.

11 *Shiji* 105.2808–9 (emphasis added). For another translation of part of the passage, see Hsiu-fen Chen, "Between Passion and Repression," 51.

12 *Shiji* 105.2804.

13 *Xu Shuwei yixue quanshu*, 83; *Yijian zhi* jia.5.38; Chang Bide, *Songren zhuanji ziliao*, 2177; Okanishi, *Song yiqian yiji kao*, 442–43.

14 *Xu Shuwei yixue quanshu*, 76.

15 Xu used the word *guafu* for widows. When Chen adopted Xu's sentence, he replaced the term with "*wu fu zhi fu*" (women without husbands), reserving *guafu* for a larger category.

16 On the rise of scholar-physicians in the Song, see Chen Yuanpeng, *Liang Song de shangyi shiren*; Chu, "Song Ming zhiji de yishi."

17 Hymes, "Not Quite Gentlemen."

18 On the plurality of Chinese medicine, see Scheid, *Chinese Medicine in Contemporary China*, chap. 2; Wu, *Reproducing Women*, 9–11.

19 See Yi-Li Wu's critique in *Reproducing Women*, 11.

20 *Zhuzi yulei* 78.2011.

21 *Zhuzi yulei* 78.2012.

22 *Zhuzi yulei* 6.112–13.

23 *Wenzhou fuzhi* 20.7a–b.

24 *Maijing jiaozhu* 9.359–60. *Zheng* and *jia* often refer to tumor-like conglomerates inside the body that are caused by stagnation of *qi* or blood. *On the Origins* defines *zheng* as static and *jia* mobile (*Zhubing yuanhou lun*, 589).

25 Physicians in pre-twentieth-century China, like those elsewhere in the world, were never able to be completely certain about whether or not a woman was pregnant until she gave birth. For a thorough discussion of the issue of medical uncertainty and the diagnoses of true and false pregnancy in traditional Chinese gynecology, see Wu, "Ghost Fetuses."

26 The text was said to be inscribed on a sarcophagus when first discovered. When Yikan "discovered" it again in 1126, it came with an additional stone slab inscribed with Xiao Yuan's preface dated to 935. Chu Yong (ca. 1101–1169) in his *Quyi shuo* refers to the text as *Zunsheng (mi)jing*. It was given the title *Chushi yishu* when printed by Liu Jixian in 1201 and postscripted by Ding Jie. No one during the Song seems to have doubted its authenticity. Xu Chunfu (1520–1596) was the first to raise doubts over what he deemed an "absurd" distinction between male and female pulses. The *Siku quanshu* editors in the late eighteenth century and Tanba no Mototane (1789–1827) of Edo Japan also found its discovery story dubious. See Tanba, *Zhongguo yiji kao*, 651–54.

27 *Chushi yishu*, 33, emphasis added to indicate the sentence quoted by Chen Ziming.

28 *Chushi yishu*, 57. The context is that the king asks Chu Cheng why he cannot have sons even though he has drafted "women below the age of *ji*" into his court.

29 Most bedchamber texts were lost during the Song, though their techniques might still have been practiced among esoteric groups. See Li Jianmin, *Fangshu, yixue, lishi*, 66–79; Furth, "Rethinking Van Gulik."

30 Furth, "Rethinking Van Gulik"; Pfister, "Gendering Sexual Pleasures." See also Lee, "Han Tang zhijian qiuzi yifang"; Lin Fu-shih, "Lüelun zaoqi Daojiao"; Goldin, "The Culture and Religious Background of Sexual Vampirism." Several early medieval Daoist lineages claimed that their sexual practices "allow[ed] men and women to gather living pneuma and nourish their essence and blood together" and also criticized the "exoteric method which focuses on 'plucking yin to augment yang'" (Raz, *The Emergence of Daoism*, 185).

31 The text has traditionally been attributed to Tao Hongjing and Sun Simiao. Michael Stanley-Baker dates it between 650 and 763, compiled by an unknown author ("Cultivating Body, Cultivating Self," 6–21). Zheng Canshan argues that Sun Simiao is its author (*Liuchao Sui Tang daojiao wenxian lunkao*, 163–83).

32 *Ishinpō* is the earliest extant medical book in Japan, compiled by the imperial doctor Tanba no Yasuyori of the Heian (794–1183) court. It was finished in 982 and included materials from more than two hundred Chinese texts circulating in Japan at the time (Lee, "*Yixinfang* lun 'furen'"). For the organization of *Ishinpō*, see Pfister, "Gendering Sexual Pleasures."

33 Many Song medical books, including Chen Ziming's *Good Formulas for Women*, quote and cite Sun's *Invaluable Formulas* extensively. *Invaluable Formulas* was also included in the curriculum of the medical school that Emperor Huizong established (Goldschmidt, *The Evolution of Chinese Medicine*, 53).

34 *Beiji qianjin yaofang* 27.489b. On the theory and practice of *huanjing bunao* (retrograding the essence and fortifying the brain), see Li Jianmin, "Dumai yu Zhongguo zaoqi yangsheng shijian"; Goldin, "The Culture and Religious Background of Sexual Vampirism."

35 *Beiji qianjin yaofang* 27.489b; *Yangxing yanming lu* 6.254.

36 *Yangxing yanming lu* 6.242.

37 For the conditions of successful conception mentioned in pre-Song bedchamber texts, including reference to bedchamber methods in general medical texts, see Lee, "Han Tang zhijian qiuzi yifang." In addition to the timing of ejaculation, conditions also included taboos of location and certain physical and social conditions for both parties. A few texts include descriptions of women's responses during intercourse. One recipe prescribes specific actions for the woman to take during intercourse to treat her infertility.

38 *Beiji qianjin yaofang* 27.489a–b.

39 *Yangxing yanming lu* 6.250.

40 *Beiji qianjin yaofang* 27.490a–b.

41 Chen Yanzhi's *Xiaopin fang* (ca. late 5th c.) has a similar opinion. *Ishinpō* 21.842.

42 *Ishinpō* 28.1131. The title of *Yufang mijue* is included in the bibliography of *Sui History* (Ma, "Yixin fang," 354).

43 *Ishinpō* 28.1132. A similar passage is seen in *Beiji qianjin yaofang* 27.489a. The date of *Yufang zhiyao* is unclear. The title is not included in any contemporary bibliography. Its content (as seen in *Ishinpō*) is very similar to the *Yufang mijue* and Sun Simiao's "Bedchamber" section; there are overlapping passages in the three texts. For this reason I date it to around the seventh century.

44 For example, *Sunü jing*, included in *Ishinpō* 28.1132.

45 *Beiji qianjin yaofang* 27.490a, emphasis added. An identical passage with minor verbal variations is seen in *Yangxing yanming lu* 6.248.

46 *Yangxing yanming lu* 6.245.

47 Furth, "Rethinking Van Gulik," 136. See also Pfister, "Gendering Sexual Pleasures."

48 Only one short passage, quoted from a "Xian jing" (Classic of Immortality), refers to "the Way for both men and women to reach immortality." See *Beiji qianjin yaofang* 27.489b; *Yangxing yanming lu* 6.269.

49 Those passages are reorganized into *Ishinpō*'s own chapters, including the chapter "Inside the Bedchamber" (*fangnei*) and two sections in the chapter for women's various illnesses—"Recipes for Women Wanting Men" and "Recipes for Women Having Intercourse with Ghosts."

50 For a discussion of sexual vampirism in ancient Chinese texts, see Goldin, "The Culture and Religious Background of Sexual Vampirism."

51 *Ishinpō* 21.862, 28.1156–57.

52 "Let the woman have intercourse with men [single or plural uncertain] without the men ejaculating. Continue to do it day and night and do not rest. She would surely recover in less than seven days. If the man is fatigued and cannot conduct it on his own, it would be fine simply inserting deeply without moving," *Ishinpō* 21.862.

53 The smoking treatment produces the effect that "the ghosts leave in tears" (*Ishinpō* 21.862).

54 *Ishinpō* 28.1157. The passage further explains that the phenomenon is due to "the *qi* of *yuan* [women without men] and *kuang* [men without women] being governed by the malign."

55 Date unknown. The text does not appear elsewhere in extant texts (Ma, "Yixin fang," 59). Judging from what is preserved in *Ishinpō*, it is a *yangsheng* (bodily cultivation) text about longevity diet, mineral and plant ingestion, bedchamber techniques, and so on.

56   *Ishinpō* 21.862. My translation is adapted from Yates, "Medicine for Women in Early China," 128.

57   *Beiji qianjin yaofang* 3.53b.

58   Preserved in Wang Tao's (670–755) *Waitai miyao* (Arcane essentials from the imperial library), 34.970.

59   Ibid.

60   *Zhouhou fang* 31.144, 18.83–84; *Zhubing yuanhou lun* 4.129–30, 40.1149–50; *Beiji qianjin yaofang* 3.51b, 4.64b, 12.227b, 18.327a, 24.437b, 26.469b. None of these texts treat suppressed or excessive desire or sexual inactivity as the cause of such a disorder. For more discussion see chap. 2.

61   *Nüke baiwen* 1.60b–61a, emphasis added.

62   *Maijing* 9.359–60.

63   Another minor but intriguing textual variation is in the first two characters of both sentences: *she ling* (if) in the original and *shuo jin* (says nowadays). The resemblance of both sets of characters makes one wonder if there was a mistranscription. It is unlikely to be the problem of the transmitted text of the *Pulse Classic* because both *she* and *she ling* are frequently used in the text, and multiple editions all have the same characters. Could Qi or one of the later copiers of his book have mistranscribed? But "says nowadays" fits surprisingly better the new context. Could this have been a Freudian mistake of Qi? We may never know the answer, but the question itself is interesting.

64   This is not to say that the Song medical interest in female sexuality came solely from the bedchamber tradition, merely that there was a noticeable continuity.

65   See the following section for more Song medical discussions of female sexual desire.

66   A late imperial manuscript copy of the text (photocopied and reproduced by Xinwenfeng in 1980) mistranscribed the last sentence, "*shen da qi xing*," as "*shen wei qi xing*" and therefore inadvertently changed the meaning of the entire sentence into "widows, nuns, and monks . . . suffer from distressed thoughts because [celibacy] is deeply against their innate tendency" (*Taiping shenghui fang* 61.3). This could perhaps be seen as the reflection of a late imperial perspective of female sexuality.

67   *Taiping shenghui fang* 69.41.

68   *Bencao yanyi* 1.5b–6a.

69   Kou can be seen as a part of an old tradition that places more emphasis on exhaustion, or depletion (*xu*), and associates emotions and mental activities with physical exhaustion. Chen, in contrast, associates women's sexual desire with "ample" blood, the same source of women's reproductive capacity.

70   *Jiaozhu furen liangfang* 6.9–10.

71   *Xueshi yi'an* 3.26b.

72   *Danxi yiji*, 331. Nathan Sivin has translated and analyzed this and other cases of what he terms "emotional counter-therapy" included in Wu Kun's *Yifang*

kao (1584; Sivin, *Medicine, Philosophy and Religion*, 4). See also discussions in Hsiu-fen Chen, "Zai mengmei zhi jian" and "Between Passion and Repression."

73 *Danxi yiji*, 332. Both cases are recorded in Zhu's biography written by Dai Liang (1317–1383).

74 I disagree, however, with Hsiu-fen Chen's reading of Zhu Zhenheng and Xue Ji that "sex [was] seen as an essential need for both sexes" and that "the necessity of marriage as a social system in which sex is sanctioned, was also assured" ("Between Passion and Repression," 57). As discussed earlier, Zhu never claimed sex or desire to be essential. Marriage in traditional China was never about fulfilling women's (or men's) sexual desire. I also doubt that the necessity of marriage in traditional China ever needed physicians' opinions to be assured.

75 See, for instance, Goldman, "The Nun Who Wouldn't Be."

76 Kuriyama, "Angry Women," 182, 186.

2. GHOST INTERCOURSE IN MEDICAL AND DAOIST CONTEXTS

1 *Huangdi neijing lingshu yijie* 43.330–31. For an English translation, see Unschuld, *Huang Di Nei Jing Ling Shu*, 421–24.

2 *Zhouhou fang* 18.83–84. According to the *Zhenglei bencao* (an eleventh-century compilation of materia medica that includes a wide range of such texts up to its time), realgar "kills goblins, demonic ghosts, malign *qi*, and the poison of all worms" and also breaks *qi*-conglomerates; deer antler "treats malign sores and tumors, expels malign *qi*, and [clears] stagnant blood in the *yin* [reproductive organs]" (*Zhenglei bencao* 4.6a, 17.8b). There was no significant distinction between intercourse with ghosts and dreams of intercourse with ghosts (or other entities) because dreams were considered movements of the *shen*-spirits, which were also a part of the body.

3 *Zhouhou fang* 31.144. The major effect of both leek seed and dragon bone was to cure *jing* leaking (*Zhenglei bencao* 28.10b, 16.3b).

4 For instance, *Waitai miyao* 13.367a–69b, 16.455a–56b; *Taiping shenghui fang* 30.2621–25, 70.6940–43.

5 *Ishinpō* 21.862 quotes from Chen Yanzhi's (ca. 5th c.) *Xiaopin fang*; *Waitai miyao* 15.404b–5a quotes from *Cuishi zuanyao fang* (ca. late 7th–mid-8th c.).

6 *Shennong Bencao jing*, preserved in *Zhenglei bencao* 1.16a.

7 *Ishinpō* 11.556–58.

8 *Beiji qianjin yaofang* 12.227b–28a.

9 *Seng Shen fang*, cited in *Beiji qianjin yaofang* 18.326b–27a and *Waitai miyao* 10.297b.

10 *Beiji qianjin yaofang* 24.436b–37a.

11 *Zhenglei bencao* 2.46b–47a.

12 *Zhubing yuanhou lun* 4.129–30.

13 *Zhubing yuanhou lun* 40.1149–50.

14 In anecdotal sources and medical case histories from Song and pre-Song, however, there was no reference of any physician diagnosing ghost intercourse by taking the patient's pulses. Physicians rarely played a role in pre-Song stories about ghost or demonic possession and exorcism. In Song anecdotes we begin to see more cases where medicine (*yi*) or medicinals (*yao*) were used for spirit possession or "enchantment" (*mei*), but medicine rarely worked. Among the few cases where physicians or medicinal recipes were effective, the effect was usually to abort a monstrous fetus or to nourish the body after the exorcism was done. See chap. 4.

15 *Waitai miyao* 13.369a.

16 *Zhenglei bencao* 17.52b, 18.15b.

17 *Zhenglei bencao* 18.27a.

18 *Zhenglei bencao* 9.34b.

19 *Ishinpō* 19.796–97.

20 *Ishinpō* 19.775, 793–94, 802–4.

21 *Rumen shiqin* 6.48a–b. Zhang made the woman vomit three times, defecate three times, and sweat three times. In ten days she had no more dreams. In a month she became pregnant.

22 *Danxi yiji*, 673.

23 *Zhubing yuanhou lun* 4.129–30, 40.1149.

24 Both men and women had *jing*, and women could lose *jing* as well. *Formulas at Hand*, for example, specifically stated "men and women dreaming of intercourse with someone and hence leaking *jing*." But descriptions of women leaking *jing* were less frequently seen in the medical texts of later times. Meanwhile, leaking *jing* was often juxtaposed with men's illnesses such as leaking urine.

25 *Taiping shenghui fang* 30.2621–25.

26 *Taiping shenghui fang* 70.6940–42.

27 *Taiping shenghui fang* 70.6873 explains, "bone fever is caused by hot and poisonous *qi* attached to the bones . . . also called corpse transmission [*chuanshi*]."

28 *Taiping shenghui fang* 70.6873–74.

29 *Jinkui yaolüe* 3.6a. The "blood chamber" can refer to the penetrating vessel (*chongmai*), the liver, or the womb. In this context, it can mean either the penetrating vessel, which governs menstrual circulation in a more general sense, or the womb specifically.

30 The bureau was established in response to a large number of epidemics in the mid-eleventh century. For studies on the bureau, see Goldschmidt, *The Evolution of Chinese Medicine*; Fan, *Bei Song Jiaozheng yishu ju*.

31 *Xu Shuwei yixue quanshu*, 61.

32 *Xu Shuwei yixue quanshu*, 162.

33 *Furen daquan liangfang* 15.440.

34 *Ishinpō* 21.862, 28.1156.

35 Wu, "Ghost Fetuses," 173.

36 *Zhubing yuanhou lun* 42.1183.

37 *Taiping shenghui fang* 77.7620–23.

38 Such as moutan, pangolin scales, realgar, croton fruit, otter's liver, centipede, mylabris, and genkwa.

39 *Weisheng jiabao chanke beiyao*, 101. The recipe uses Shu pepper, green onions, and peach twigs: boil in water and let the patient squat on top of the steam.

40 *Furen daquan liangfang* 14.398–99.

41 This was in sharp contrast to the late imperial medical debates over whether or not there was in fact a ghost or demonic spirit at work in the formation of a "ghost fetus." See Wu, "Ghost Fetuses"; Hsiu-fen Chen, "Zai mengmei zhi jian" and "Between Passion and Repression."

42 *Weisheng jiabao chanke beiyao*, 101.

43 There were many records of anomalous births and "affected pregnancies" in pre-Song sources. The former usually appeared in records about political portents; anomalies in the natural and human worlds were considered signs of anomalous *qi* in the realm, which was caused by significant political success or failure. The latter were frequently seen in myths about ancient sage kings.

44 *Soushen houji* 6.531; *Taiping guangji* 450.3683; 470.3872–73. See chaps. 3 and 4 for discussions of women's "enchantment disorders" in tales and anecdotes.

45 See chap. 4 for more discussion.

46 *Yijian zhi* zhigui.3.1238–39. Another account in the same collection also records that Wutong caused some women to have "spirit-inflicted pregnancy" (*suiyun*), which basically meant the same as *guitai* (*Yijian zhi* ding.19.695–97). On the cult of Wutong, see von Glahn, *The Sinister Way*. More discussions follow in chap. 4.

47 *Yijian zhi* zhigui.8.1280–81. Hong Mai notes that this account was told by Zhou Shaolu. Zhou offered seven other accounts in *Yijian zhi*. But his life and deeds were otherwise unknown.

48 For a history of abortion in the Song, see Liu Ching Cheng, *Bujuzi*.

49 *Yijian zhi* jia.8.69. These cases are incorporated into Jiang Guan's (1503–65) anthology of medical case histories, *Ming yi lei an* 11.326. See also Wu, "Ghost Fetuses," 200–201.

50 *Zhubing yuanhou lun* 42.1185; *Weisheng jiabao chanke beiyao* 1.11. See also Wu, "Ghost Fetuses,"195.

51 For instance, *Yixue zhengchuan* 1.25b–26a; *Jingyue quanshu* 38.55a. See also Wu, "Ghost Fetuses"; Hsiu-fen Chen, "Zai mengmei zhi jian" and "Between Passion and Repression."

52 *Yixue zhengchuan* 1.25b–26a.

53 *Ming yi lei an* 11.311.

54 *Fu Qingzhu nüke* shang.23a.

55 For instance, *Wushang jiuxiao yuqing dafan ziwei xuandu leiting yujing* 15a–b; *Taishang tiantan yuge*, in *Daofa huiyuan* 250.1a.

56 Some traditions placed more emphasis on self-cultivation; others were known for their specialty in exorcism. But the two kinds of practice were not mutually exclusive.

57 For a study of Daoist rituals included in Song medical texts, see Cho, "Ritual and the Occult" and "Healing and Ritual Imagination."

58 The character *yin* with a water radical is usually translated as "excessive" or "illicit." Its variant, *yin* with a female radical, normally indicates men's sex with women. The term *yinyu* here uses the latter character and is better translated as "sexual desire" and not "excessive/illicit desire" or "excessive/illicit sexual desire" because in this context, any form of sex leaks the vital substance of the body, not just the illicit or excessive ones; or put in another way, any sexual desire is excessive (*Dongxuan lingbao ziran jiutian shengshen yuzhang jingjie* 1.25b).

59 The text explains that the human body contains three *hun*-spirits and seven *po*-spirits (*Yuanshi wuliang duren shangpin miaojing tongyi* 1.30b).

60 *Yuanshi wuliang duren shangpin miaojing tongyi* 1.31a–b. In the Stems and Branches calendar system, a person has six birthdays in a year.

61 *Shi* was male by definition and usually translated as "gentleman." It could refer to men of letters in general or those who held official posts specifically. The readers of this text were most likely men, but the term did not exclude women. A Daoist priestess could be called *nü Daoshi* (literally, "female official of the Dao").

62 Davis, *Society and the Supernatural*, 21.

63 Davis, *Society and the Supernatural*, 39–43. Illness was still a kind of divine punishment—for the lay wrongdoers and the priests who violated the precepts. But it was also a result of capricious spirits and ghosts, the main target of exorcist rituals. Nevertheless, as Chuang Hung-I points out, the ritual masters' rigorous self-cultivation and strict adherence to the Daoist precepts were often the prerequisite for their efficacy (Chuang, "Songdai Daojiao yiliao," 130–32). Philip S. Cho also notes that the Daoist therapeutic rituals included in the *Shengji zonglu* (a medical book compiled from 1111 to 1117 under Emperor Huizong's command) emphasize the ritualists' moral conduct and mindset as crucial for carrying out efficacious rites (Cho, "Healing and Ritual Imagination," 80–81).

64 *Lingbao lingjiao jidu jinshu* 273.39b–42b, 286.23a–26b.

65 *Lingbao lingjiao jidu jinshu* 273.13a–39b, 286.1a–23a.

66 For exorcist rituals recorded in Song anecdotes, Daoist and Buddhist scriptures, see Davis, *Society and the Supernatural*. For Song anecdotal accounts about "enchantment disorders," see chap. 4 of this book.

67 *Lingbao lingjiao jidu jinshu* 260.25a–26a. *Shengji zonglu* has a pair of similar diagrams and the ritual process as described is also similar. But the section designations are different (195.18b). See discussions in Cho, "Healing and Ritual Imagination," 80–84.

68 *Taiqing jinque yuhua xianshu baji shenzhang sanhuang neimiwen* 1.12a–b. For a study of Wutong, see von Glahn, *The Sinister Way.*

69 *Shangqing lingbao dafa* 20.10b–12b, 22.26b.

70 *Fahai yizhu* 18.9a, 13a–b.

71 *Daofa huiyuan* 162.39a–b.

72 *Fahai yizhu* 45.25a–b.

73 The meaning of *wu* varies according to the context. See chaps. 4 and 6 for more discussion.

74 *Fahai yizhu* 45.1a–7b.

75 *Fahai yizhu* 45.3b–4a.

3. ENCHANTMENT DISORDER AND PRE-SONG TALES

1 On the genre and cultural significance of *zhiguai* literature, see Campany, *Strange Writing.*

2 The translation of *wu* is a much debated issue. I translate it as "exorcist" here because in this specific context, exorcism is the only thing the *wu* does. Chap. 4 will discuss the term in more detail.

3 There is at least one other story from around the same time period about an alligator (or "Chinese alligator," *tuo*) demon that enchanted women. See *Yiyuan* 8.668.

4 This account appears in both Liu Jingshu's *Yiyuan* 8.668 and Liu Yiqing's *Youming lu* 737. The translation here synthesizes the two accounts, which differ only in a few minor points.

5 Medical texts include medicinals and recipes that expel ghosts and demonic entities. Some ritualists used medicinals as well. But texts and practitioners in the medical (*yi*) tradition usually focused on the patients, whereas tales often pitted ritualists against demons.

6 Lin Fu-shih examines textual references to *mei* from the pre-Qin to the Six Dynasties and derives three categories: the wild *mei* (*chimei*), the ghostly *mei* (*guimei*), and the transformative *mei* (*jingmei*). The English translations for the three terms are mine, based on Lin's description of them ("Shi mei," 109–34). They differ in locale and appearance, while sharing the commonalities of being nonhuman, enchanting, and harmful. I concur with Lin's observations and would add that at least in the tales I examine here, *mei* is not necessarily an identity but a kind of interaction in which nonhuman beings engage with humans. Although interactions of this kind were considered to be harmful to humans and to constitute wrongdoing on the part of the nonhumans, the creatures involved were not intrinsically evil.

7   Richard von Glahn's *The Sinister Way* makes an insightful point about the inseparability of good and evil, divine and demonic, and sacred and mundane in his study of the concept of the sinister in Chinese religious traditions.

8   Dudbridge, *Religious Experience and Lay Society*, 154–73.

9   Mei, "Liuchao zhiguai."

10   There are only two exceptions: one man loses his hair and semen, suffers from abdomen pain, and eventually dies; the other gradually turns into a fox and no longer responds to other humans. Lin, "Renjian zhi mei," 111–12.

11   Lin, "Renjian zhi mei."

12   *Taiping guangji* 456.3726. All the English translations of the titles of anomaly account collections from the second to the fifth centuries follow Campany, *Strange Writing*.

13   *Taiping yulan* 934.4283b.

14   *Yiyuan* 8.669.

15   Manling Luo, "Tangdai xiaoshuo." In at least one story that Luo examines, the enchanted woman, a court lady of Emperor Wen of the Sui, is not entirely passive—she runs the demon through with a sword (*Taiping guangji* 46.3868). In another account, to be discussed later, the woman (a young widow) becomes a moral agent and successfully expels the ghost with her unflinching resolution (*Chaoye qianzai* 3.2b–3a).

16   Zeitlin further shows how, through a process of feminizing ghosts, female ghosts became the corporealization of emotions and desire. The frightening and malignant female ghosts of earlier times were further transformed in seventeenth-century elites' production of ghost fiction into "timid, vulnerable, fragile creatures in need of male sympathy, protection, and life-giving power." This power is gained mainly through sexual contact (*The Phantom Heroine*, 14–15, 24).

17   Huntington, "Foxes and Sex," 109–13. Huntington also notes that although vixens were imagined in these stories as the embodiment of lust, their sexual desire is instead veiled by the focus on men's desire and the link between vixens' sexual behavior and other parasitic aims, such as absorbing men's *jing* in order to attain immortality (86–91).

18   Lin, "Renjian zhi mei."

19   *Shenxian zhuan* 10.335.

20   *Soushen ji* 19.321.

21   *Youming lu*, 745.

22   *Soushen houji* 6.539. I follow Robert Campany, who dates *Soushen houji* to the late (Liu) Song or early Qi (late 5th c.) by an unknown author, "most likely an official with some connection to the court archives" (*Strange Writing*, 70).

23   *Soushen houji* 6.531.

24   *Yiyuan* 6.653.

25   *Youming lu*, 703.

26 Sometimes even an elder woman is not quite a qualified guardian. In one story in *Guangyi ji*, after a man leaves for military service, a fox spirit disguised as a bodhisattva comes to live with his mother and sister and impregnates his unmarried sister. Upon the man's return, the "bodhisattva" tells the mother that it "does not want to see a man." In the end the man's brother hires a Daoist to exorcize the fox (*Taiping guangji* 450.3683). For an English translation of this story, see de Groot, *The Religious System of China*, 5:592–3.

27 Many authors of spirit-affliction stories from the pre-Tang were themselves religious or ritual specialists. Lin Fu-shih believes that this explains why those stories are often told from an exorcist's perspective (Lin, "Renjian zhi mei," 145). Sarah Allen also notes that, compared to earlier times, there were more collections of eclectic stories from the mid-eighth century on, although "doctrinally inspired collections" never disappeared (*Shifting Stories*, 12).

28 Daniel Hsieh, *Love and Women in Early Chinese Fiction*, 25–26.

29 Allen, *Shifting Stories*, 23. This characteristic of Tang tales makes them quite different in method and in style from Hong Mai's *Yijian zhi*, which will be discussed in chap. 4.

30 *Taiping guangji* 449.3674–75.

31 *Taiping guangji* 470.3872–73.

32 *Taiping guangji* 456.3733.

33 *Taiping guangji* 450.3679.

34 *Taiping guangji* 454.3709–10.

35 *Youyang zazu*, 211–12.

36 *Taiping guangji* 79.504.

37 *Zhubing yuanhou lun* 40.1149–50.

38 *Beiji qianjin yaofang* 12.227b. More discussion of women's enchantment disorder in medicine in the following section.

39 Medical writers through later imperial times generally took a similar position. Some physicians in the Ming and the Qing began to repudiate the existence of ghosts or demons in this kind of case and focused their treatment on the women's mental state; see Hsiu-fen Chen, "Dang bingren jiandao gui."

40 To the best of my knowledge, there are only two extant pre-Song accounts in which the exorcist treats the woman directly rather than engaging in battle with the demon. Neither uses anything that corresponds to the treatments described in surviving medical texts. One tells that the exorcist Wang Zuan used a needle on the woman and the demon left (*Yiyuan* 8.669). The other says that a Buddhist monk, Fazhou, used two pills of some mysterious elixir (*dan*) to cure a girl enchanted by a fox (*Huichang jieyi lu*, included in *Taiping guangji* 454.3709–10). *Youyang zazu* records another Buddhist monk, Zhan, who after a series of battles with two demons used an "interdict needle"

(*jinzhen*) to cure a sore on the arm of the possessed woman, an after-effect of the disorder (*Youyang zazu*, 211–12).

41 Medicine and exorcism were, of course, not mutually exclusive categories. Medical texts often include exorcist recipes—recipes that "expel ghostly/demonic/malign *qi*." The exorcists (be it a shaman, a Daoist master, or a Buddhist monk) were considered healers too, and many ritual healers also used medicine. The distinction was not between medicine and exorcism but among different specialist skills.

42 *Ishinpō* 21.862, 28.1156–57.

43 *Youming lu*, 737.

44 *Taiping guangji* 450.3679. A similar Tang tale is discussed later in the chapter.

45 More discussions in chap. 6.

46 *Chaoye qianzai* 3.2b–3a. *Chaoye qianzai* is one of the many "historical miscellanies" that flourished from the Tang onward. It contains anecdotes about figures and events from the early Tang, mostly from the mid-seventh to mid-eighth centuries. It was compiled before the An Lushan Rebellion (755–63) and differs in style from postrebellion compilations, which, according to Manling Luo, contain "a much wider spectrum in terms of the storyteller's personal predilections in choice and arrangement of entries, revealing their diverse, even contending, views of literati sociality" (*Literati Storytelling*, 61).

47 The name Dou Weiwu is not seen in other extant sources. Li Jianguo proposes that he is either the same person as or the brother of Dou Weixian, who has a short biography in the *Jiu Tangshu* 183.4726 (Li, *Tang Wudai zhiguai*, 221).

48 *Taiping guangji* 469.3868.

49 *Taiping guangji* 454.3709–10.

50 *Taiping guangji* 460.3766.

51 *Taiping guangji* 450.3679.

4. ENCHANTED WOMEN IN SONG ANECDOTES

1 I translate *wu* as "exorcist" here because exorcism is the only thing that we know this *wu* did from the context. It is unclear whether the *wu* performed shamanism or anything considered to be illicit witchcraft.

2 *Qingsuo gaoyi* bieji.1.1169.

3 According to Li Jianguo's study, *Qingsuo gaoyi* (including three installments—*qianji, houji,* and *bieji*) contains tales of multiple origins and various styles. Some are edited or simply adopted from Tang works; others are authored by Song literati, including Liu himself. The authors of fourteen accounts are noted. At least eight other longer ones are likely Liu's own work. There are also a few shorter accounts that seem to be Liu's record of contemporary anecdotes (Li, *Songdai zhiguai*, 15, 179–89).

4   *Qingsuo gaoyi* bieji.1.1162–69.

5   Allen, *Shifting Stories*, 13.

6   Allen, *Shifting Stories*, 24.

7   Davis, *Society and the Supernatural*, 18.

8   All we know about Liu's life is in the preface and his self-reference in *Qingsuo gaoyi*. See Li Jianguo, *Songdai zhiguai*, 179.

9   For a table of the completion dates of the installments, see Inglis, *Hong Mai's Record of the Listener*, 21–22. For a detailed textual history of *Yijian zhi*, see Inglis, "A Textual History."

10 For a list of scholars and their reconstitutions of *Yijian zhi*, see Inglis, "A Textual History," 289–90. Synopses of the prefaces to the lost installments are preserved in Zhao Yushi's *Bintui lu* (*Yijian zhi*, 1817–21). For English translations and discussions of all the prefaces, see Inglis, *Hong Mai's Record of the Listener*, 24–55.

11 I do not call them supernatural because for most Song people, spirits were a part of the natural world.

12 *Yijian zhi, yi*, preface, 185.

13 For a comprehensive list and biographical references of Hong's informants, see Inglis, "Hong Mai's Informants." As Inglis points out, there are significant inconsistencies in Hong's citation of his sources, especially in the later installments, and the textual integrity of the first four installments is superior to the rest (85).

14 *Yijian zhi, bing*, preface, 363. Translation adapted from Inglis, *Hong Mai's Record of the Listener*, 28.

15 Inglis, *Hong Mai's Record of the Listener*, 29.

16 *Yijian zhi, ding*, preface, 537. Translation adapted from Inglis, *Hong Mai's Record of the Listener*, 32.

17 *Yijian zhi, ding*, preface, 537.

18 For instance, in the preface to the fifth installment, Hong points out the absurdity of the story that a giant fish ate everyone on a ship. If no one survived, who is there to tell such a story? *Yijian zhi*, 1818.

19 *Yijian zhi, zhiding*, preface, 967. My translation.

20 *Yijian zhi, zhigeng*, preface, 1135. Translation adapted from Inglis, *Hong Mai's Record of the Listener*, 43.

21 There are many occurrences of vernacular language in *Yijian zhi*. For instance, using the word *qu* as a third-person pronoun. Robert Hymes observes that in some *Yijian zhi* accounts the use of literary or vernacular language is not random but reflects the social status of the speaker and the context of the conversation ("Getting the Words Right," 47–52).

22 Some of Hong's notes might have been lost or misplaced during the textual transmission (Inglis, "Hong Mai's Informants," 85), but Hong certainly did not name all his sources.

23 Davis, *Society and the Supernatural*, 18.

24 Egan, "Crime, Violence, and Ghosts," 150.

25 Hymes, "Truth, Falsity, and Pretense."

26 For example, "Guanyin ji," *Yijian zhi* jia.1.4–5; "Duan Zai qie," *Yijian zhi* jia.3.22; "Jiang jiaoshou," *Yijian zhi* yi.2.195–97.

27 Inglis, "Narratological Ambiguity," 39. "Meta-anomaly" is Robert Campany's term; in his own words: "the expected sequence of events established early in the tale is itself a sequence involving a type of anomaly; the latter portion of the tale then frustrates the reader's expectations of one sort of anomaly and replaces them with another sort of anomaly" (*Strange Writing*, 234).

28 Inglis, "Narratological Ambiguity."

29 Inglis has also made the point about the similarity between *Yijian zhi* and oral history, as both contain imperfect memories, inconsistent details, and incremental exaggeration (*Hong Mai's* Record of the Listener, 2).

30 Dates according to Li Jianguo, *Songdai zhiguai*, 194.

31 *Kuoyi zhi* 9.103. Zhang noted that the source of the story was Dong Jingchen (11th c.). It is not clear in the account whether it was the exorcist Luo or the ghost who gave the woman the abortive medicine. My translation assumes that the subject follows the previous sentences and does not change.

32 The Orthodox Unity lineage of the Celestial Masters migrated to Mount Longhu in Jiangxi. Many ritual masters of the Song claimed affiliation with the Orthodox Unity. See Davis, *Society and the Supernatural*, 79.

33 *Yijian zhi* bing.10.446–47. Hong notes that the story was told by Zhan Daozi (named Kangzong, b. 1117, *jinshi* 1148).

34 Richard von Glahn points out the "interpenetration of the divine and the demonic in Chinese religious culture" (*The Sinister Way*, 16) and the ways in which socioeconomic changes impacted perceptions of the divine power. Von Glahn notes that, during the Song, "Wutong became closely associated with the acquisition and loss of wealth. . . . Wutong's emergence as a god of wealth betokened a burgeoning phenomenon in Song society: success or failure in a competitive money economy brought about abrupt changes in personal fortunes" (*The Sinister Way*, 186).

35 *Yijian zhi* zhijia.1.717–18. Translations adapted from von Glahn, *The Sinister Way*, 1–2. Hong Mai noted that this account was told by Zhu Conglong, an otherwise unknown figure but the source of a number of accounts in *Yijian zhi*.

36 For examples in Tang tales, see Dudbridge, *Religious Experience and Lay Society*, 154–60. Two Song examples are *Yijian zhi* bing.11.459; ding.19.692.

37 One story tells of an official's son who saw a beautiful woman smiling at him in their compound. He was attracted to her but thought that it was impossible for an ordinary woman to enter a well-guarded office compound. For this reason he did not approach her; instead, he tricked the woman into revealing her true identity—an aged piece of wood—and burned it (*Yijian zhi*

zhigui.6.1264). Two other examples are *Yijian zhi* bing.2.373–7; ding.4.566–67.

38   *Yijian zhi* zhijia.7.762–63. The comment could also be that of Deng Zhiqing, who was the source of this account and three *juan* of the eleventh installment of *Yijian zhi*.

39   *Soushen houji* 3.504–5.

40   *Yijian zhi* zhiyi.1.796; zhiyi.1.797; sanyi.7.1356–57; sanyi.9.1375–76; bu.1690–92; sanbu.1804.

41   Wutong folklore was not homogeneous. In another story, a female medium was possessed (*ping*) by a ghost who also called himself Wulang. Through this possession the medium gained a reputation of efficacy. But there is no indication in the account that their relationship was sexual. Besides, this Wulang was much less powerful—once, the medium was summoned to a high official's mansion but failed to invoke the spirit because he was blocked outside by the guardian deities at the gate (*Yijian zhi* jia.11.97).

42   *Yijian zhi* bu.1690–92.

43   Edward Davis notes that in *Yijian zhi* and other Song anecdotes, an exorcist is often called a *fashi* (ritual master) regardless of his (or in a few cases, her) denomination. The afflicted is usually depicted as a patient-customer rather than a religious follower. A Daoist ritual master competes with other healers (Daoist or not) for the recognition of their power and efficacy (*Society and the Supernatural*, 41–42).

44   For instance, "Raoshi fu," *Yijian zhi* bing.12.468; "Shi wong nü," ding.18.686; "Hongye ru huai," ding.20.703; "Jiankang san yun," zhiji.6.836.

45   *Chaoye qianzai* 3.2b–3a.

46   *Taiping guangji* 454.3709–10.

47   This account is in the nineteenth *juan* of the fourth installment. In the end of the twentieth *juan* Hong notes that all the accounts included in *juan* eighteen to twenty, except for one, are all from Deng Zhi, a scholar-official from Jianchang, styled Duanruo (*Yijian zhi*, 709). Deng served as notary of the administrative assistant in Jiangyin garrison (in present-day south Jiangsu) (Li Guoling, *Songren zhuanji ziliao suoyin bubian*, 1752.) If this account is not misplaced from other *juan*, the opinion expressed in it perhaps belongs to Deng Zhi instead of Hong Mai.

48   In other *Yijian zhi* accounts, as well as in Tang-Song tales, this is often a sign of ghostly possession or harassment, but is not necessarily sexual.

49   *Yijian zhi* ding.19.695–97.

50   For studies on fox spirits in Chinese literature, religion, and folklore, see Huntington, "Foxes and Sex" and *Alien Kind*; Kang, *The Cult of the Fox*.

51   According to Lin Fu-shih, the office of *wu* was a part of the governmental institution in the Zhou system. As communicators in between the divine and the mundane, they were in charge of rain conjuration, burial rituals, plague expelling, and sacrifice. They were also specialists of medicine and

divination. Private and commercial *wu* appeared as late as in the Spring and Autumn period (770–476 BCE), which marked a radical change of the old sociopolitical order. It was also during this time that doubts and criticisms against *wu* and their "magic" emerged. By Han times (202 BCE–220), *wu* had become a commoners' profession, and the chances for a *wu* to become an official were extremely low. See Lin, "Zhongguo gudai wuxi."

52 Nakamura, *Chūgoku shamanizumu*, 59.

53 Davis, *Society and the Supernatural*, 2–3.

54 Cho, "Healing and Ritual Imagination," 79n17.

55 Sivin, *Health Care in Eleventh-Century China*, 16.

56 *Yijian zhi* ding.12.639.

57 *Yijian zhi* zhijing.5.919.

58 *Yijian zhi* ding.20.708.

59 More discussions in chap. 6. There were stories before the Song about women's erotic relationship with deities and spirits and the cults surrounding them. The account about Wu Wangzi cited earlier is an example. It tells that Wu Wangzi had a romantic relationship with the deity and shared his power (*Soushen houji* 3.504–5). But the text does not call her a *wu*, or a *shipo* (elder woman master) or *jianguishi* (ghost-seeing master), two alternative terms for *wu*. Nor does the text describe her as being possessed by the deity. When Wu was not interested in an exclusive relationship with the deity anymore, he simply left her.

60 Nakamura, *Chūgoku shamanizumu*, 133–35.

61 *Taiping guangji* 67.416–18.

62 For the gendered patterns in Ming-Qing ghost and fox stories, see Huntington "Foxes and Sex" and *Alien Kind*; Zeitlin, *The Phantom Heroine*.

63 *Yijian zhi* ding.19.692.

64 Examples of men who took replenishing medicines include "Tu'ou tai," *Yijian zhi* jia.17.146; "Xihu nüzi," *Yijian zhi* zhijia.6.754–44. Cases of women who were treated with purgatory therapies include "Fu Wenxiu," *Kuoyi zhi* 9.103; "Er gou guai," *Yijian zhi* ding.20.703; "Cheng shanren nü," *Yijian zhi* sanxin.5.1425.

65 The healers might also be known as a *yi* elsewhere (such as Dong Feng), but they are not called so in the enchantment accounts, nor do they use medicinal treatment in those records. Lin Fu-shih calls one of the healer-exorcist (Wang Zuan) a "physician" (*yizhe*) ("Renjian zhi mei," 142). But the text simply calls him "someone named Wang Zuan from Hailing, who could cure demonic [disorders]." Wang's treatment is most likely not "acupuncture and moxibustion" (*zhenjiu*) as Lin puts it but a kind of exorcist interdict needle (*jinzhen*) instead (*Yiyuan* 8.669).

66 *Yijian zhi* ding.20.703.

67 *Kuoyi zhi* 9.103.

68 *Yijian zhi* jia.17.146.

69 *Yijian zhi* zhijia.6.754–55.

70 *Yiwu* could refer to *wu* who specialized in healing rituals or to *yi* (physicians, medicine) and *wu* in general. The meaning is dependent on the context and not always clear. *Daoren* could refer to a Buddhist monk, a Daoist practitioner, or someone who appeared to be affiliated with either.

71 *Yijian zhi* zhigeng.3.1158–59; zhiding.8.1033–34; ding.9.611.

72 For the roles that spirit-mediums and ritual masters played in Song exorcist culture and the developments of Daoist and Buddhist exorcist rituals, see Davis, *Society and the Supernatural*. As Davis points out, sometimes the exorcist rituals also functioned as reconciliations among family members or between the living and the dead.

73 *Yijian zhi* sanxin.9.1458. Hong Mai noted that the source of this story was Xiong himself.

74 *Yijian zhi* zhigeng.6.1182.

75 One could still learn multiple skills and switch jobs. A story tells that two physicians, Liu and Shu, worked in a prefectural court. Once Liu made a diagnosis that was later proven to be a fatal mistake. Shu disagreed but was unable to win the argument. The patient pledged revenge in his dying bed. Liu died soon afterward. Frightened, Shu resigned from the medical post and learned the Rites of the Three Altars (Santan Fa). Since then he "treat[ed] spirit afflictions with talisman water and still earn[ed] enough to support himself" (*Yijian zhi* zhigeng.10.1219). For a detailed study on the Rites of the Three Altars, see Davis, *Society and the Supernatural*, 115–23.

76 *Yijian zhi* jia.5.41; zhigeng.7.1189–90. Some spirits were bound to a certain location, and the haunted could simply (or only) be rid of them by leaving the place. Another example is in *Yijian zhi* bing.2.373. For a discussion of the connection between spirits and their locations, see Li Jianmin, "Suibing yu changsuo."

77 *Yijian zhi* bing.10.446–47.

78 *Yijian zhi* zhiding.2.982.

79 *Yijian zhi* zhiwu.9.1120–21. Hong Mai commented that this anomaly was a portent of misfortune for all the evils Cai had done to the country.

80 *Yijian zhi* ding.5.574–75.

81 *Yijian zhi* ding.18.684–885.

82 *Yijian zhi* sanxin.2.1396–97.

83 *Yijian zhi* bu.15.1690–92.

84 *Yijian zhi* bu.22.1750–51. Such kind of efficacious narrative is also seen in pre-Song accounts and other Song anecdote collections, for example, *Shenxian zhuan* 10.335; *Kuoyi zhi* 9.88–89.

85 *Yiyuan* 8.668; *Soushen hou ji* 6.531. The Tang story is in *Chaoye qianzai* 3.2b–3a.

86 *Yijian zhi* bing.7.421. Hong Mai noted that he received all the stories in the same *juan* from Wang Riyan, who in turn received most of the accounts from his brother Wang Pan.

87   *Yijian zhi* ding.19.699–700. Hong Mai received this account along with the others in *juan* 18–20 from Deng Zhi, chap. 4, n47.

88   Zhu Conglong was the source of at least six *juan* in *Yijian zhi*. He is not seen in other extant Song biographical accounts. But just based on the information in *Yijian zhi*, as Barend ter Haar notes, we know that Zhu "once held an official post and his father had been friends with two *xiucai*" (ter Haar, "Newly Recovered Anecdotes," 20–21).

89   *Yijian zhi* zhiyi.1.801.

90   Davis, *Society and the Supernatural*, 25–26.

91   *Yijian zhi* zhiyi.1.796–97.

92   *Yijian zhi* zhiyi.1.797; zhiyi.1.798–800.

93   *Yijian zhi* bing.12.468. Hong Mai received this story from a literatus of Linchuan (a county of Fuzhou), who was also the source of four other stories that took place in Fuzhou.

94   For the emergence of the Wutong cult and its connection to the economic development in Song society, see von Glahn, *The Sinister Way*, especially chap. 6.

95   *Yijian zhi* ding.20.730. Hong Mai received this story from Deng Zhi, who attributed the source of this story to a man named Zhu Cheng.

96   *Yijian zhi* zhijing.2.893. The source of this story is a literatus named Yu Zhongyong. This account does not give specific information regarding the class or social status of Yu Liuqilang and his wife Cheng. But Yu's name, Liuqilang, or "the sixth-seventh man," indicates that he was likely from a family that kept a genealogy for multiple generations. "Six(th)" might indicate his generation, and "seven(th)" his seniority in that generation.

97   *Yijian zhi* zhijing.8.940. The source of this account is a man named Wang Shunbo.

98   *Soushen houji* 7.545. See also Schafer, *The Divine Woman*, chap. 1.

99   *Yijian zhi* bu.1690–92.

5. GENDERED PRACTICE AND RENUNCIANT IDENTITY

1   See, for example, Mohanty et al., *Third World Women*.

2   Chern, "Jiedu biqiuni," 322.

3   Salgado, *Buddhist Nuns and Gendered Practice*, 6–7.

4   Salgado, *Buddhist Nuns and Gendered Practice*, 7–8.

5   For a discussion of the changing meanings of *funü* and the nomenclature of *nüxing* in the twentieth century, see Barlow, *The Question of Women*, 37–63. We may not go so far as to say that there was never such a category in traditional China, but it was extremely rare that a discussion of women took place without reference to women's familial roles. Even when *nü* was used loosely in referring to all women, it did not emphasize a universal womanhood rooted in biology as the term *nüxing* does.

6   Heirman, "Chinese Nuns and Their Ordination."

7   *Song huiyao* 2.1a–b. See also Ding-hwa Hsieh, "Buddhist Nuns in Sung China," 78–81.

8   *Da Jin guozhi jiaozheng* 36.517.

9   The three collections have often been studied, especially with regard to the sociopolitical and monastic contexts of religious women's lives of those times. On the *Biqiuni zhaun*, see Tsai, *Lives of the Nuns*; Wang Rutong, *Biqiuni zhuan jiaozhu*; Heirman, "Chinese Nuns and Their Ordination." On *Daoxue zhuan*, see Bumbacher, *The Fragments of the* Daoxue zhuan. On *Yongcheng jixian lu*, see Cahill, "Practice Makes Perfect"; Cahill, "Discipline and Transformation"; Cahill, *Divine Traces of the Daoist Sisterhood*; Luo Zhengming, *Du Guangting Daojiao xiaoshuo*; Jia, *Gender, Power, and Talent*.

10 *Mingseng zhuan* is now lost, with fragments preserved in *Mingseng zhuan chao*. For a brief comparison between *Biqiuni zhuan* and *Mingseng zhuan*, see Wang Rutong, *Biqiuni zhuan jiaozhu*, 9–12. The majority of nuns recorded in *Biqiuni zhuan* came from the upper class, whereas the monks in *Gaoseng zhuan* (6th c.) were often of obscure origin (Tsai, *Lives of the Nuns*, 8). In the "edifying miracle tales" about Buddhist nuns from the Six Dynasties and the Tang, however, many women do not have high level of literacy (Georgieva, "Representation of Buddhist Nuns").

11 On the adoption of Vinaya for nuns in early medieval China, see Georgieva, "Representation of Buddhist Nuns"; Heirman, "Chinese Nuns and Their Ordination."

12 *Biqiuni zhuan* 1.934b.

13 "Arduous practice" (*kujie*) includes seven subcategories: erudition, divine senses (*gantong*), bodily immolation, asceticism and vegetarianism, pilgrimage (to Central or South Asia), icon production, and stupa and temple construction.

14 The only deed that is not seen in the nuns' biographies is a pilgrimage to Central or South Asia.

15 *Biqiuni zhuan* 1.935a. Translations adapted from Wright, "Biography of the Nun An-ling-shou," 195; Tsai, *Lives of the Nuns*, 20.

16 Tsai, *Lives of the Nuns*, 119.

17 The original text says that the father sees the image of a *shamen*. *Shamen* is the Chinese transliteration of *śramana*, or renunciant. In the Chinese context, it often refers to a Buddhist monk. On the life of Fotucheng, see Wright, "Fo-t'u-teng."

18 *Biqiuni zhuan* 1.935b.

19 White clothes distinguished her from a fully ordained nun, who would have worn black, crimson, or a dark color (Wang Rutong, *Biqiuni zhuan jiaozhu*, 27–28).

20 *Biqiuni zhuan* 2.938c. For translations of the *Mingxiang ji* version, see Tsai, *Lives of the Nuns*, 46–48; Campany, *Signs from the Unseen Realm*, 212–13.

21 Baochang values one's care for family members just as for nonfamily members. The biography of Fasheng (5th c.) records that she treated a

Madame Shan, whose parents and husband had all died, "as her own parent." Fasheng's devotion and meticulous care for Madame Shan won her high respect among the contemporaries (*Biqiuni zhuan* 2.939a).

22   *Biqiuni zhuan* 1.935c. Translations adapted from Tsai, *Lives of the Nuns*, 24.

23   *Biqiuni zhuan* 4.945c. Translations adapted from Tsai, *Lives of the Nuns*, 90–91.

24   *Guang hongming ji*, 271c.

25   *Biqiuni zhuan* 1.934c. Translations adapted from Tsai, *Lives of the Nuns*, 18–19.

26   Puxian Temple was commissioned by Empress Zhoulu (412–466), who raised Emperor Ming. The office of *"sengzheng"* was initiated during the Yao Qin dynasty (384–417), in charge of governing the Buddhist monastic assemblies. Zanning's *Da Song sengshi lüe* records that in the Southern Dynasties (including the Liu Song under discussion here), there were both *sengzheng* and *nizheng*, in charge of the monks' and the nuns' assemblies respectively. Zanning lists Baoxian as the first *nizheng*. Baochang, however, simply uses *sengzheng* to refer to Baoxian's position (*Da Song sengshi lüe*, 242c–243a; Tsai, *Lives of the Nuns*, 136n122).

27   This could be either Baochang's own words or his record of what Saṃghavarman said. Translations adapted from Tsai, *Lives of the Nuns*, 63.

28   *Biqiuni zhuan* 2.941a.

29   Bumbacher, *The Fragments of the* Daoxue zhuan, 522.

30   For a detailed study and English translations of the fragments of *Daoxue zhuan*, see Bumbacher, *The Fragments of the* Daoxue zhuan.

31   Part of my translation follows Bumbacher, *The Fragments of the* Daoxue zhuan, 296.

32   For detailed studies of this text, see Luo Zhengming, *Du Guangting Daojiao xiaoshuo*; Cahill, *Divine Traces of the Daoist Sisterhood*; Jia, *Gender, Power, and Talent*. I follow Jinhua Jia to date the text to around 923 (*Gender, Power, and Talent*, 198).

33   According to an obscure "supreme canon," Du states, "the highest position for a man who obtains the Dao is perfected lord [*zhenjun*]; the ultimate position for a woman who obtains the Dao is primal lord [*yuanjun*]" (*Du Guangting jizhuan shizhong*, 567).

34   *Du Guangting jizhuan shizhong*, 566. The translation follows Cahill with minor revisions; *Divine Traces of the Daoist Sisterhood*, 36.

35   *Du Guangting jizhuan shizhong*, 567. My translation.

36   For a comparison between Du's account and other historical records of Tang women, see Jia, *Gender, Power, and Talent*, 195–208.

37   Eighteen according to Jinhua Jia's reconstitution, including two additional accounts that Jia collects from *Xianzhuan shiyi* (*Gender, Power, and Talent*, 199–201).

38 The dates follow Cahill, *Divine Traces of the Daoist Sisterhood*, 176. *Xin Tangshu* calls Wang a "female *wu*"; *Zizhi tongjian* refers to her as a "sinister Buddhist nun" (*yaoni*). For a comparison between Du's account and other historical records of Wang Fengxian, see Jia, *Gender, Power, and Talent*, 199, 202–3.

39 The translation follows Cahill, *Divine Traces of the Daoist Sisterhood*, 181.

40 *Taiping guangji* 64.398.

41 *Du Guangting jizhuan shizhong*, 684.

42 *Du Guangting jizhuan shizhong*, 721.

43 Examples of the former also include the accounts of Huang Lingwei, Transcendent Lady Xu, and Transcendent Lady Gou (*Du Guangting jizhuan shizhong*, 679–83).

44 *Du Guangting jizhuan shizhong*, 719.

45 *Du Guangting jizhuan shizhong*, 679–80.

46 *Du Guangting jizhuan shizhong*, 681.

47 *Du Guangting jizhuan shizhong*, 682–83.

48 *Chaoye qianzai* 3.2b–3a.

49 *Za piyu jing*, 529b. Li Yu-chen notes that in Avadāna literature, both men and women are taught to visualize the impurity of the female body in order to do away with their sexual desire (Li, "Fojiao piyu," 54–55).

50 *Du Guangting jizhuan shizhong*, 697–98.

51 *Taiping guangji* 64.398.

52 Chang Hsun, "Jizhong Daojing," 262; my translation. On female alchemy, see also Valussi, "Female Alchemy and Paratext," "Men and Women in He Longxiang's *Nüdan hebian*," and "Blood, Tigers, Dragons."

53 *Foshuo Longshi nü jing*, 909c–910a. This story was adapted into the Daoist tradition and appeared in early Lingbao scriptures (Bokenkamp, "Sources of the Ling-Pao Scriptures," 474–75).

54 For reviews of scholarship on this subject, see Balkwill, "Why Does a Woman Need to Become a Man"; Hsiao-wen Cheng, "Before Sexual and Normal," 18–22.

55 Owen, "Toward a Buddhist Feminism"; Paul, *Women in Buddhism*, 230–31; Gross, *Buddhism after Patriarchy*, 55–77.

56 Balkwill, "The Sutra on Transforming the Female Form," 140–43.

57 Cahill, "Discipline and Transformation," 269–70.

58 *Wangsheng ji*, 145b.

59 *Wangsheng ji*, 146b.

60 Grant, "Da Zhangfu," 203.

6. MEANINGS OF FEMALE CELIBACY

1 This ideal of self-control and abstinence was not in contradiction with elite men's construction of identities and social bonds by speaking among

themselves about their desire for and relationships with women. For the culture of elite men's intimate relationships with women in the Tang-Song period, see Daniel Hsieh, *Love and Women*; Manling Luo, *Literati Storytelling*; Bossler, *Courtesans, Concubines, and the Cult of Female Fidelity*.

2   As argued in chap. 1, the bedchamber depictions of female sexual desire have to be considered in the context of elite men's bodily sublimation. Examples of elite men's affective sublimation are most salient in literary tales and narratives of romance; see Daniel Hsieh, *Love and Women*; Allen, *Shifting Stories*; Manling Luo, *Literati Storytelling*.

3   Widowhood is one condition under which women's religious celibacy seems to have converged with general expectations regarding female sexuality, though this does not mean that the goals of religious celibacy and widow chastity were the same. Many widows who wished to join a religious order still had to justify their decision and emphasize that they had fulfilled all their familial duties. There has been much scholarship on elite men's depictions of religious women, many of them widows, in epitaphs and inscriptions; see Chao, "Good Career Moves"; Yao, "Good Karmic Connections" and "Tang Women in the Transformation of Buddhist Filiality"; Pang, "Eminent Nuns And/Or/As Virtuous Women"; Jinping Wang, *In the Wake of the Mongols*, esp. chap. 2; Cheng Ya-ru, "Lixiang rensheng." This chapter focuses on female celibacy that was not shielded by widow chastity.

4   *Biqiuni zhuan* 1.935a.

5   *Biqiuni zhuan* 1.936a.

6   *Biqiuni zhuan* 4.945c–946a.

7   *Biqiuni zhuan* 2.939a. *Guanyin Sūtra* refers to chap. 25 of Kumārajīva's translation of the *Miaofa lianhua jing* (T. 262); see Tsai, *Lives of the Nuns*, 122n53.

8   *Biqiuni zhuan* 4.945a.

9   *Biqiuni zhuan* 1.935b.

10 Balkwill, "When Renunciation Is Good Politics."

11 Jinhua Chen, "Family Ties and Buddhist Nuns."

12 Cheng Ya-ru, "Lixiang rensheng," 70–72. Cheng's sources are epitaphs of lay Buddhist women during the Northern Dynasties and the Sui. Epitaphs of Buddhist nuns from this time period were much fewer than those of lay women and were predominantly of elite women who adopted renunciation after their husbands died.

13 Yao, "Good Karmic Connections." Yao notices that such influence is only found among Buddhist mothers and not Buddhist fathers.

14 These were the highest numbers during the Northern Song. *Song huiyao* daoshi.1.13a–14a. Ding-hwa Hsieh, "Buddhist Nuns in Sung China," 81. The surviving parts of the *Song huiyao* do not contain numbers after 1077. On Buddhist nuns in the Song, see also Huang Minzhi, "Songdai funü de lingyi

cemian"; Levering, "Miao-tao and Her Teacher Ta-hui" and "Women Ch'an Masters."

15   Ding-hwa Hsieh, "Buddhist Nuns in Sung China," 75–76.

16   Such as Chao Buzhi (1053–1110) and his wife. See Ding-hwa Hsieh, "Buddhist Nuns in Sung China," 66–67; *Jile ji* 70.5b–5a.

17   Halperin, "Domesticity and the Dharma."

18   Huang's original account no longer exists. Wang Mingqing (b. 1127) claimed that he had seen Huang's original handwriting and preserved its entirety in Wang's *Touxia lu* (Records from my guests), 3863; see also Li Jianguo, *Songdai zhiguai*, 175–76.

19   Rao, *Laozi Xiang'er zhu jiaojian*, 12, 38. Bokenkamp, *Early Daoist Scriptures*, 87, 125. Bokenkamp dates the text to 215 CE at the latest (31).

20   Rao, *Laozi Xiang'er zhu jiaojian*, 10. Bokenkamp, *Early Daoist Scriptures*, 44–45, 84. The translation follows Bokenkamp.

21   Lin Fu-shih, "Lüelun zaoqi Daojiao," 267–70; Raz, *The Emergence of Daoism*, 188, 193.

22   Kleeman, "The Performance and Significance of the Merging the Pneumas," 110. Both Stephen Bokenkamp (*Early Daoist Scriptures*, 46) and Stephen Eskildsen (*Daoism, Meditation, and the Wonders of Serenity*, 71) note possible references to the genitals in the text. Gil Raz believes that the rite was still practiced throughout the Six Dynasties and continued into the Tang despite heavy criticism even from within the Daoist communities (*The Emergence of Daoism*, 208).

23   Raz, *The Emergence of Daoism*, chap. 4.

24   Raz, *The Emergence of Daoism*, 202–3; Kleeman, "The Performance and Significance of the Merging the Pneumas," passim.

25   Bokenkamp, "Declarations of the Perfected"; Bokenkamp, "Tianshi dao hunyin yishi"; Raz, *The Emergence of Daoism*. Raz suggests that Supreme Purity's complete rejection of sexual cultivation was related to its core doctrine that viewed the ideal body as "a closed system, self-sufficient unto itself for attaining transcendence" (*The Emergence of Daoism*, 209).

26   Lin Fu-shih, "Lüelun zaoqi Daojiao"; Bokenkamp, "Tianshi dao hunyin yishi"; Raz, *The Emergence of Daoism*, chap. 4; Kleeman, "The Performance and Significance of the Merging the Pneumas."

27   *Zhen gao* 6.53a.

28   *Zhen gao* 10.97a; see also Lin Fu-shih, "Lüelun zaoqi Daojiao."

29   *Shenxian zhuan* 6.224–25.

30   *Taiping guang ji* 58.356–57. Wei's biography has many editions, and all are based on a now lost "Inner Biography of Madam Nanyue" from the Eastern Jin (317–420). The two most complete versions are seen in *Taiping guan ji* and *Taiping yulan*. On Wei's biography, its transmission and textual history, and the doctrines and worship associated with Wei, see Chang Chaojan, *Xipu, jiaofa, ji qi zhenghe*, 173–224; Cheng Su-Chun, "Tang Song shiqi Wei Huacun."

31 Jia, *Gender, Power, and Talent*, chap. 1.

32 Bokenkamp, "Sisters of the Blood."

33 *Taiping guangji* 66.412. The biography was likely written by Xie's contemporary Li Jian. See Bokenkamp, "Sisters of the Blood."

34 *Song huiyao*, daoshi 1.13–14.

35 The earliest biography of Sun is dated to 1241. For a detailed study of Sun Bu'er's biographies and works and her roles in early Quanzhen Daoism, see Komjathy, "Sun Buer." See also Despeux and Kohn, *Women in Daoism*, 140–49.

36 The translation follows Komjathy, "Sun Buer," 178–79, 221. Catherine Despeux and Livia Kohn argue that one of Wang Zhe's poems suggests that "by becoming a renunciant herself . . . the woman frees her husband to realize his immortal potential. Leaving the family is thus the ultimate in the fulfillment of wifely duty" (*Women in Daoism*, 145).

37 Goossaert, "The Invention of an Order," 117–18. On the history of early Quanzhen Daoism, see also Eskildsen, *The Teachings and Practices of the Early Quanzhen*; Komjathy, *Cultivating Perfection*; Chao, "Good Career Moves"; Jinping Wang, *In the Wake of the Mongols*.

38 *Liexian zhuan* 2.265b, 2.266a.

39 *Liexian zhuan* 1.256b–257a, 1.251b, 1.254a–b, 1.259b, 2.262a–b, 268a.

40 On the significance of *xian* adepts' social defiance, see Campany, *To Live as Long as Heaven and Earth* and *Making Transcendents*.

41 Bumbacher, *The Fragments of the* Daoxue zhuan, 295–96. See also discussions in chap. 5.

42 Bumbacher, *The Fragments of the* Daoxue zhuan, 305. The translation is my own.

43 *Du Guangting jizhuan shizhong*, 697–98.

44 *Taiping guangji* 60.373.

45 *Xu xian zhuan* 1.11b–12b.

46 *Xu xian zhuan* 1.3b–4b. The motif of "one person practicing the Dao and the entire household ascending to heaven" existed in immortality cults as early as the second century, as seen in the inscription of Tang Gongfang; see Raz, *The Emergence of Daoism*, 69.

47 *Xu xian zhaun* 1.12b–14a. Some Daoist authors and traditions were more open to sexual cultivation than others. No Daoist scripture though, to my knowledge, claims that adepts can achieve the ultimate goal of "returning to the primordial" through sexual cultivation alone.

48 *Xu xian zhuan* 1.12b–14a, 2.20a–b. "*Shijie*" (liberation from the corpse) is a form of postmortem immortality performed by less advanced adepts who "seemingly die like any other mortal, but in reality achieve purification of their body in a smelting process in the Extreme Yin palace" (Seidel, "Post-Mortem Immortality," 230–31).

49   The trend was even more salient in late imperial sources. Despeux and Kohn
     state that in Quanzhen Daoism, "women were not allowed to become nuns
     while still of childbearing age" and that "they had to pass through a period of
     family service before dedicating themselves to the Dao" (*Women in Daoism*,
     159). The sources for this statement, though, are prescriptive texts from late
     imperial times. A religious teacher Tanyangzi's (1557–1580) letters to her
     followers were another example; see Waltner, "Life and Letters."

50   Cheng Ya-ru, "Lixiang rensheng," 27, 70; Chao, "Good Career Moves," 150.

51   *Yijian zhi* ding.19.695–97. In Song sources, including the other *Yijian zhi*
     accounts from the same source-informant Deng Zhi, "*xian*" refers to a god or
     goddess that one serendipitously encounters, a deity in a local cult, a Daoist
     deity, or an adept of transcendent arts. I use Robert Campany's translation,
     "transcendent," for two reasons: First, most of the descriptions of *xian* in
     Song sources still resonate with the "transcendents' cultural repertoire" that
     Campany observes in Ge Hong's *Shenxian zhuan*. Second, most *xian* in Song
     sources do not exceed Campany's definition of transcendents, who "have
     ascended to links in the chain higher than those occupied by even the best
     human beings" (*To Live as Long as Heaven and Earth*, 5).

52   Campany, *To Live as Long as Heaven and Earth*, 5. Campany elaborates what
     is first proposed in Bokenkamp, *Early Daoist Scriptures*, 22–23.

53   Campany, *Making Transcendents*, 25.

54   Campany, *Making Transcendents*, chap. 3.

55   Campany, *Making Transcendents*, 48–51.

56   Chen Anshi and Li A were both examples of the former (*Shenxian zhuan*
     3.76–77, 87; Campany, *To Live as Long as Heaven and Earth*, 137–38, 212–13);
     Mao Ying (Lord Mao) and Liu Gen were examples of the latter (*Shenxian
     zhuan* 5.182, 8.298; Campany, *To Live as Long as Heaven and Earth*, 241, 327).

57   *Taiping guangji* 66.408; *Du Guangting jizhuan shizhong*, 726.

58   Campany, *Making Transcendents*, chap. 4.

59   Campany, *Making Transcendents*, 54–55.

60   *Yunji qiqian* 116.2566.

61   *Yunji qiqian* 116.2569–70. Translation adapted from Cahill, *Divine Traces of
     the Daoist Sisterhood*, 190.

62   *Taiping guangji* 60.374.

63   The title *Laozi xianjing* is not seen elsewhere or in the Daoist Canon. It could
     refer to the *Dao de jing*, a text of another title, or simply a lost text.

64   *Xu xian zhuan* 1.21b–22b.

65   *Xu xian zhuan* 1.20a–21b.

66   In Daoist sources, the term *jingshi* is written in various characters with the
     same or similar pronunciations meaning purity chamber or pacified
     chamber.

67   Robinet, *Taoism*, 58–59; Bokenkamp, *Early Daoist Scriptures*, 35.

68 Kleeman, *Celestial Masters*, 250–51.

69 Kleeman, *Celestial Masters*, 225. The source is *Lu xiansheng daomen kelüe*.

70 Xu, *Crossing the Gate*, 179–80.

71 *Songdai chuanqi ji*, 147–48. This story first appeared anonymously in Zhan Jie's *Tang Song yishi* (1067), which only survives in fragments. The text discussed here is Li Jianguo's reconstitution from *Shihua zonggui* (1167); see Li, *Songdai zhiguai*, 93–96.

72 *Songdai chuanqi ji*, 371–72.

73 *Yijian zhi* zhiyi.8.854–55. The account also notes that the two younger brothers of the girl's husband both earned the *jinshi* degree in 1190.

74 *Yijian zhi* zhijing.1.886–87.

75 *Yijian zhi* zhigeng.6.1179–80.

CONCLUSION

1 "Beishi tongzhi hunli, yiyuan pi fangzong," *Apple Daily*, August 26, 2006, https://tw.appledaily.com/headline/daily/20060826/2845963/.

2 Hymes, "Not Quite Gentlemen"; Wu, *Reproducing Women*, 11; Sivin, *Health Care in Eleventh-Century China*, 76.

3 Lochrie, *Heterosyncrasies*, 3; Hollywood, "The Normal, the Queer, and the Middle Ages," 176.

4 Rich, "Compulsory Heterosexuality," 133.

5 Sang, *The Emerging Lesbian*, 49–52, 63–65, 92.

6 Rich, "Compulsory Heterosexuality," 134.

BIBLIOGRAPHY

ABBREVIATIONS

CSJC   *Congshu jicheng, chubian* 叢書集成, 初編. Beijing: Zhonghua Shuju, 1985.

DZ   *Daozang* 道藏. Beijing: Wenwu Chubanshe; Shanghai: Shanghai
        Shudian; Tianjin: Tianjin Guji Chubanshe, 1988.

HWLC   *Han Wei Liuchao biji xiaoshuo daguan* 漢魏六朝筆記小說大觀. Shanghai:
        Shanghai Guji Chubanshe, 1999.

HY   *Combined Indices to the Authors and Titles of Books in Two Collections
        of Taoist Literature*. Harvard-Yenching Institute Sinological Index
        Series No. 25. Taipei: Chengwen Chubanshe, 1966.

SBCK   *Sibu congkan* 四部叢刊. Shanghai: Shangwu Yinshuguan, 1922–36.

SKQS   *Siku quanshu* 四庫全書. Taipei: Taiwan Shangwu Yinshuguan, 1983–86.

SS   *Scripta Sinica: Hanji dianzi wenxian ziliaoku* 漢籍電子文獻資料庫.
        Taipei: Academia Sinica, 1984–present.

SYBJ   *Song Yuan biji xiaoshuo daguan* 宋元筆記小說大觀. Shanghai: Shanghai
        Guji Chubanshe, 2001.

T   *Taishō shinshū daizōkyō* 大正新修大藏経. Takakusu Junjiro et al., eds.
        100 vols. Tokyo: Daizo Shuppankai, 1922–33.

XSKQS   *Xuxiu siku quanshu* 續修四庫全書. Shanghai: Shanghai Guji Chubanshe,
        1995–2002.

PRIMARY SOURCES (LISTED BY TITLE)

Beiji qianjin yaofang 備急千金要方, by Sun Simiao 孫思邈 (581–682). Taipei:
    Zhongguo Yiyao Yanjiusuo, 1990.

Bencao yanyi 本草衍義, by Kou Zongshi 寇宗奭. First pub. 1116. XSKQS.

Biqiuni zhuan 比丘尼傳, by Shi Baochang 釋寶唱 (b. ca. 466). T. 2063.

Chaoye qianzai 朝野僉載, by Zhang Zhuo 張鷟 (ca. 650–730). SKQS.

Chushi yishu jiaoshi 褚氏遺書校釋, attributed to Chu Cheng 褚澄 (d. 483). Collated
    and annotated by Zhao Guohua. Zhengzhou: Henan Kexue Jishu Chubanshe,
    1986.

Da Jin guozhi jiaozheng 大金國志校證, attributed to Yuwen Maozhao 宇文懋昭. Collated by Cui Wenyin. Beijing: Zhonghua Shuju, 1986.

Da Song sengshi lüe 大宋僧史略, by Zanning 贊寧 (919–1001). T. 2126.

Danxi yiji 丹溪醫集, by Zhu Zhenheng 朱震亨 (1281–1358). Beijing: Renmin Weisheng Chubanshe, 1999.

Daofa huiyuan 道法會元. HY 1210. DZ.

Dongxuan lingbao ziran jiutian shengshen yuzhang jingjie 洞玄靈寶自然九天生神玉章經解. HY 397. DZ.

Du Guangting jizhuan shizhong jijiao 杜光庭記傳十種輯校, by Du Guangting 杜光庭 (850–933). Collated by Luo Zhengming. Beijing: Zhonghua Shuju, 2013.

Fahai yizhu 法海遺珠. HY 1158. DZ.

Foshuo Longshi nü jing 佛說龍施女經, by Zhi Qian 支謙 (222–280). T. 557.

Fu Qingzhu nüke 傅青主女科, by Fu Shan 傅山 (1607–1684). Haishan xianguan congshu, 1849.

Furen daquan liangfang 婦人大全良方, by Chen Ziming 陳自明 (1190–1272). Prefaced in 1237. Punctuated and collated by Yu Ying'ao et al. Beijing: Renmin Weisheng Chubanshe, 1985.

Guang hongming ji 廣弘明集, by Daoxuan 道宣 (596–667). T. 2103.

Huangdi neijing lingshu yijie 黃帝內經靈樞譯解, edited by Yang Weijie 楊維傑. Taipei: Tailian Guofeng Chubanshe, 1984. SS.

Ishinpō 医心方, by Tanba no Yasuyori 丹波康賴 (912–995). Finished in 982. Annotated by Zhao Mingshan et al. Shenyang: Liaoning Kexue Jishu Chubanshe, 1996.

Jiaozhu furen liangfang 校註婦人良方. Originally compiled by Chen Ziming 陳自明. Edited and annotated by Xue Ji 薛己 (1487–1558). Shanghai: Shanghai Weisheng Chubanshe, 1956.

Jile ji 雞肋集, by Chao Buzhi 晁補之 (1053–1110). SBCK.

Jingyue quanshu 景岳全書, by Zhang Jiebin 張介賓 (ca. 1563–1640). SKQS.

Jinkui yaolüe 金匱要略, by Zhang Ji 張機 (145–208). In *Sibu beiyao* 四部備要. Taipei: Taiwan Zhonghua Shuju, 1966.

Kuoyi zhi 括異志, by Zhang Shizheng 張師正 (b. 1017). Compiled ca. 1070–90s. Beijing: Zhonghua Shuju, 2006.

Liexian zhuan 列仙傳, attributed to Liu Xiang 劉向 (ca. 77–6 BCE). HY 294. DZ.

Lingbao lingjiao jidu jinshu 靈寶領教濟度金書. HY 466. DZ.

Maijing jiaozhu 脈經校注, by Wang Shuhe 王叔和 (3rd century). Edited by Shen Yannan. Beijing: Renmin Wishing Chubanshe, 1991.

Mengzi zhushu 孟子注疏, by Meng Ke 孟軻 (372–289 BCE). Annotated by Zhao Qi and Sun Shi. *Shisanjing zhushu* edition. Taipei: Yiwen Yinshuguan, 1965.

Nüke baiwen 女科百問, by Qi Zhongfu 齊仲甫. Prefaced in 1220. XSKQS.

Qingsuo gaoyi 青瑣高議, by Liu Fu 劉斧 (11th century). SYBJ.

Rumen shiqin 儒門事親, by Zhang Congzheng 張從正 (1156–1228). SKQS.

Shangqing lingbao dafa 上清靈寶大法, compiled by Wang Qizhen 王契真; transmitted by Ning Quanzhen 寧全真 (1101–1181). HY 1211. DZ.

Shengji zonglu 聖濟總錄, by Shen Fu 申甫 et al. Compiled in 1111–1117. 1919 reprint of Shanghai Wenruilou 文瑞樓 edition. SS.

Shenxian zhuan jiaoshi 神仙傳校釋, by Ge Hong 葛洪 (283–343). Edited and annotated by Hu Shouwei. Beijing: Zhonghua Shuju, 2010.

Shiji (Xin jiaoben Shiji sanjia zhu) 新校本史記三家注, by Sima Qian 司馬遷 (145–86 BCE). Taipei: Dingwen Shuju, 1981.

Song da zhaoling ji 宋大詔令集, edited by Song Shou 宋綬 (991–1040). Beijing: Zhonghua Shuju, 2009.

Song huiyao jigao 宋會要輯稿, compiled by Xu Song 徐松 (1781–1848). Beijing: Zhonghua Shuju, 1957.

Songdai chuanqi ji 宋代傳奇集, edited by Li Jianguo 李劍國. Beijing: Zhonghua Shuju, 2001.

Soushen houji (Xinji soushen houji) 新輯搜神後記, by Tao Qian 陶潛 (365–427). Reconstituted and collated by Li Jianguo. Beijing: Zhonghua Shuju, 2007.

Soushen ji (Xinji soushen ji) 新輯搜神記, by Gan Bao 干寶 (fl. ca. 317). Reconstituted and collated by Li Jianguo. Beijing: Zhonghua Shuju, 2007.

Taiping guangji 太平廣記, compiled by Li Fang 李昉 (925–996). Beijing: Zhonghua Shuju, 2008.

Taiping shenghui fang 太平聖惠方, by Wang Huaiyin 王懷隱 et al. Compiled in 978–992. Taipei: Xinwenfeng Chubanshe, 1980. SS.

Taiping yulan 太平御覽, by Li Fang 李昉 (925–996) et al. SBCK.

Taiqing jinque yuhua xianshu baji shenzhang sanhuang neimiwen 太清金闕玉華仙書八極神章三皇內祕文. HY 854. DZ.

Touxia lu 投轄錄, by Wang Mingqing 王明清 (b. 1127). Compiled in 1159. SYBJ.

Waitai miyao 外臺秘要, by Wang Tao 王燾 (670–755). Compiled in 752. Taipei: Zhongguo Yiyao Yanjiusuo, 1965. SS.

Wangsheng ji 往生集, by Zhuhong 袾宏 (1535–1615). T. 2072.

Weisheng jiabao chanke beiyao 衛生家寶產科備要, by Zhu Duanzhang 朱端章. Compiled in 1184. CSJC.

Wenzhou fuzhi 溫州府志. First printed in 1760. Reprinted in 1914.

Wushang jiuxiao yuqing dafan ziwei xuandu leiting yujing 無上九霄玉清大梵紫微玄都雷霆玉經. HY 15. DZ.

Xu Shuwei yixue quanshu 許叔微醫學全書, edited by Liu Jingchao 劉景超 and Li Jushuang 李具雙. Beijing: Zhongguo Zhongyiyao Chubanshe, 2006.

Xu xian zhuan 續仙傳, by Shen Fen 沈汾 (937–975). SKQS.

Xueshi yi' an 薛氏醫案, by Xue Ji 薛己 (1487–1558). SKQS.

Yangxing yanming lu (Xinyi yangxing yanming lu) 新譯養性延命錄, attributed to Tao Hongjing 陶弘景 (452–536). Compiled ca. 7th–8th centuries. Annotated and translated by Zeng Zhaonan. Taipei: Sanmin Shuju, 2009.

Yijian zhi 夷堅志, by Hong Mai 洪邁 (1123–1202). Punctuated and collated by He Zhuo. Beijing: Zhonghua Shuju, 2006.

Yixue zhengchuan 醫學正傳, by Yu Tuan 虞搏. Prefaced in 1515. XSKQS.

Yiyuan 異苑, by Liu Jingshu 劉敬叔 (5th century). HWLC.

Youming lu 幽明錄, by Liu Yiqing 劉義慶 (403–444). HWLC.

Youyang zazu 酉陽雜俎, by Duan Chengshi 段成式 (d. 863). Beijing: Zhonghua Shuju, 1981.

Yuanshi wuliang duren shangpin miaojing tongyi 元始無量度人上品妙經通義. HY 89. DZ.

Yunji qiqian 雲笈七籤, by Zhang Junfang 張君房. Beijing: Zhonghua Shuju, 2003.

Za piyu jing 雜譬喻經, translated by Kumārajīva 鳩摩羅什 (ca. 401–413), collected by Daolüe 道略. T. 207.

Zhen gao 真誥, by Tao Hongjing 陶弘景 (452–536). Completed in 499. HY 1010. DZ.

Zhenglei bencao 證類本草, compiled by Tang Shenwei 唐慎微. Collated by Cao Xiaozhong 曹孝忠. Expanded by Kou Zongshi 寇宗奭. SKQS.

Zhouhou fang (*Buji Zhouhou fang*) 補輯肘後方, by Ge Hong 葛洪 (283–343). Supplemented by Tao Hongjing 陶弘景 (452–536). Edited by Shang Zhijun 尚志鈞. Hefei: Anhui Kexue Jishu Chubanshe, 1996.

Zhubing yuanhou lun jiaoshi 諸病源候論校釋, by Chao Yuanfang 巢元方. Prefaced in 610. Collated and edited by Nanjing Zhongyi Xueyuan 南京中醫學院. Beijing: Renmin Weisheng Chubanshe, 1980.

Zhuzi yulei 朱子語類, edited by Li Jingde 黎靖德. Collated and punctuated by Wang Xingxian. Beijing: Zhonghua Shuju, 1986.

SECONDARY SOURCES (LISTED BY AUTHOR)

Allen, Sarah M. *Shifting Stories: History, Gossip, and Lore in Narratives from Tang Dynasty China.* Cambridge, MA: Harvard University Asia Center, 2014.

Balkwill, Stephanie. "The Sutra on Transforming the Female Form: Unpacking an Early Medieval Chinese Buddhist Text." *Journal of Chinese Religions* 44, no. 2 (2016): 127–48.

———. "When Renunciation Is Good Politics: The Women of the Imperial Nunnery of the Northern Wei (386–534)." *Nan Nü* 18, no. 2 (2016): 224–56.

———. "Why Does a Woman Need to Become a Man in Order to Become a Buddha? Past Investigations, New Lead." *Religion Compass* 12 (2018): e12270.

Barlow, Tani. *The Question of Women in Chinese Feminism.* Durham: Duke University Press, 2004.

Bernhardt, Katheryn. *Women and Property in China, 960–1949.* Stanford: Stanford University Press, 1999.

Birge, Bettine. *Women, Property, and Confucian Reaction in Sung and Yüan China, 960–1368.* Cambridge: Cambridge University Press, 2002.

Blanchard, Lara C. W. *Song Dynasty Figures of Longing and Desire: Gender and Interiority in Chinese Painting and Poetry.* Leiden: Brill, 2018.

Bokenkamp, Stephen R. "Declarations of the Perfected." In *Religions of China in Practice*, edited by Donald S. Lopez, Jr., 166–79. Princeton: Princeton University Press, 1996.

———. *Early Daoist Scriptures.* Berkeley: University of California Press, 1997.

———. "Sisters of the Blood: The Lives behind the Xie Ziran Biography." *Daoism: Religion, History and Society* 8 (2016): 7–33.

———. "Sources of the Ling-Pao Scriptures." In *Tantric and Taoist Studies*, edited by Michel Strickmann, 434–86. Brussels: Institut Belge des Hautes Études Chinoises, 1983.

———. "Tianshi dao hunyin yishi 'heqi' zai Shangqing, Lingbao xuepai de yanbian" 天師道婚姻儀式"合氣"在上清, 靈寶學派的演變. In *Daojia wenhua yanjiu* 道家文化研究, edited by Chen Guying, 16:241–48. Hong Kong: Sanlian Shudian, 1999.

Bossler, Beverly. *Courtesans, Concubines, and the Cult of Female Fidelity: Gender and Social Change in China, 1000–1400.* Cambridge, MA: Harvard University Asia Center, 2013.

———. *Powerful Relations: Kinship, Status, and the State in Sung China (960–1279).* Cambridge, MA: Council on East Asian Studies, Harvard University, 1998.

Bray, Francesca. *Technology and Gender: Fabrics of Power in Late Imperial China.* Berkeley: University of California Press, 1997.

Bumbacher, Stephan Peter. *The Fragments of the* Daoxue zhuan: *Critical Edition, Translation, and Analysis of a Medieval Collection of Daoist Biographies.* Frankfurt am Main: Peter Lang, 2000.

Cahill, Suzanne E. "Discipline and Transformation: Body and Practice in the Lives of Daoist Holy Women of Tang China." In *Women and Confucian Cultures in Premodern China, Korea, and Japan*, edited by Dorothy Ko et al., 251–78. Berkeley: University of California Press, 2003.

———. *Divine Traces of the Daoist Sisterhood: "Records of the Assembled Transcendents of the Fortified Walled City" by Du Guangting.* Magdalena, NM: Three Pines Press, 2006.

———. "Practice Makes Perfect: Paths to Transcendence for Women in Medieval China." *Taoist Resources* 2, no. 2 (1990): 23–42.

Campany, Robert Ford. *To Live as Long as Heaven and Earth: A Translation and Study of Ge Hong's Traditions of Divine Transcendents.* Berkeley: University of California Press, 2002.

———. *Making Transcendents: Ascetics and Social Memory in Early Medieval China.* Honolulu: University of Hawai'i Press, 2009.

———. *Signs from the Unseen Realm: Buddhist Miracle Tales from Early Medieval China.* Honolulu: University of Hawai'i Press, 2012.

———. *Strange Writing: Anomaly Accounts in Early Medieval China.* Albany: State University of New York Press, 1996.

Chaffee, John W. *The Thorny Gates of Learning in Sung China: A Social History of Examinations.* Albany: State University of New York Press, 1995.

Chang Bide 昌彼得 et al. *Songren zhuanji ziliao suoyin* 宋人傳記資料索引. Taipei: Dingwen Shuju, 2001.

Chang Chaojan [Zhang Chaoran] 張超然. *Xipu, jiaofa, ji qi zhenghe: Dong Jin Nanchao Daojiao Shangqing jingpai de jichu yanjiu* 系譜, 教法及其整合: 東晉南朝道教上清經派的基礎研究. PhD diss., National Chengchi University, 2007.

Chang Hsun [Zhang Xun] 張珣. "Jizhong Daojing zhong dui nüren shenti miaoshu zhi chutan" 幾種道經中對女人身體描述之初探. *Si yu yan* 思與言 35, no. 2 (1997): 235–65.

Chao, Shin-yi. "Good Career Moves: Life Stories of Daoist Nuns of the Twelfth and Thirteenth Centuries." *Nan Nü* 10 (2008): 121–51.

Chen, Hsiu-fen 陳秀芬 "Between Passion and Repression: Medical Views of Demon Dreams, Demonic Fetuses, and Female Sexual Madness in Late Imperial China." *Late Imperial China* 32, no. 1 (2011): 51–82.

———. "Dang bingren jiandao gui: Shilun Ming Qing yizhe duiyu 'xiesui' de taidu" 當病人見到鬼: 試論明清醫者對於 "邪祟" 的態度. *Guoli zhengzhi daxue lishi xuebao* 30 (2008): 43–86.

———. "Zai mengmei zhi jian: Zhongguo gudian yixue duiyu 'meng yu gui jiao' yu nüxing qingyu de gouxiang" 在夢寐之間: 中國古典醫學對於 "夢與鬼交" 與女性情欲 的構想. *Zhongyang yanjiuyuan lishi yuyan yanjiusuo jikan* 中央研究院歷史語言研 究所集刊 81, no. 4 (2010): 701–36.

Chen, Jinhua. "Family Ties and Buddhist Nuns in Tang China: Two Studies." *Asia Major 3rd ser.* 15, no. 2 (2002): 51–85.

Chen Yuanpeng 陳元朋. *Liang Song de shangyi shiren yu ruyi: Jianlun qi zai Jin Yuan de liubian* 兩宋的尚醫士人與儒醫: 兼論其在金元的流變. Taipei: Guoli Taiwan Daxue Chuban Weiyuanhui, 1997.

Cheng, Hsiao-wen. "Before Sexual and Normal: Shifting Categories of Sexual Anomaly from Ancient to Yuan China." *Asia Major 3rd ser.* 31, no. 2 (2018): 1–39.

Cheng Su-Chun [Zheng Suchun] 鄭素春. "Tang Song shiqi Wei Huacun xinyang yanjiu" 唐宋時期魏華存信仰研究. In *Daojiao nüshen xinyang yanjiu* 道教女神信仰 研究, edited by Zhuang Hongyi, 1–69. Xinbeishi: Fuda Shufang, 2014.

Cheng Ya-ru [Zheng Yaru] 鄭雅如. *Qinggan yu zhidu: Wei Jin shidai de muzi guanxi* 情感與制度: 魏晉時代的母子關係. Taipei: Taida Chuban Zhongxin, 2001.

———. "Lixiang rensheng de xin xiangdu: Beichao Suidai zaijia nüxing muzhi zhong de xinyang miaoshu" 理想人生的新向度: 北朝隋代在家女性墓誌中的信仰描述. *Zaoqi Zhongguo yanjiu* 早期中國研究 10, no. 1 (2018): 1–90.

Chern Meei-hwa [Chen Meihua] 陳美華. "Jiedu 'biqiuni' zai xifangren yanzhong de yinhan" 解讀 "比丘尼" 在西方人眼中的隱含. *Zhonghua foxue xuebao* 中華佛學學報 11 (1998): 311–27.

Cho, Philp S. "Healing and Ritual Imagination in Chinese Medicine: The Multiple Interpretations of *Zhuyou*." *EASTAM* 38 (2014): 71–112.

———. "Ritual and the Occult in Chinese Medicine and Religious Healing: The Development of Zhuyou Exorcism." PhD diss., University of Pennsylvania, 2005.

Chu Pingyi [Zhu Pingyi] 祝平一. "Song Ming zhiji de yishi yu 'ruyi'" 宋明之際的醫史與 "儒醫". *Zhongyang yanjiuyuan lishi yuyan yanjiusuo jikan* 77, no. 3 (2006): 401–49.

Chuang Hung-I [Zhuang Hongyi] 莊宏誼. "Songdai Daojiao yiliao: Yi Hong Mai Yijian zhi weizhu zhi yanjiu" 宋代道教醫療: 以洪邁夷堅志為主之研究. *Furen zongjiao yanjiu* 輔仁宗教研究 12 (2005): 73–147.

Davis, Edward L. *Society and the Supernatural in Song China*. Honolulu: University of Hawai'i Press, 2001.

de Groot, J. J. M. *The Religious System of China, Its Ancient Forms, Evolution, History and Present Aspect, Manners, Customs and Social Institutions Connected Therewith*. Leiden: Brill, 1892–1910.

Despeux, Catherine, and Livia Kohn. *Women in Daoism*. Cambridge, MA: Three Pines Press, 2003.

Dikötter, Frank. *Sex, Culture, and Modernity in China: Medical Science and the Construction of Sexual Identities in the Early Republican Period*. Honolulu: University of Hawai'i Press, 1995.

Du Zhengzhen 杜正貞. "Beike zhong de difang jiceng zuzhi yu quanli jiegou: Yi Shanxi Jincheng Fuchengcun Yuhuangmiao Song Jin Yuan beike timing mingxian weili" 碑刻中的地方基層組織與權力結構: 以山西晉城府城村玉皇廟宋金元碑刻題名名銜為例. In *Hanxue yanjiu yu Zhongguo shehui kexue de tuijin guoji xueshu yantaohui lunwenji* 漢學研究與中國社會科學的推進國際學術研討會論文集, 366–80. Beijing: Zhongguo Shehui Kexue Chubanshe, 2012.

Dudbridge, Glen. *Religious Experience and Lay Society in T'ang China: A Reading of Tai Fu's Kuang-i chi*. Cambridge: Cambridge University Press, 1995.

Ebrey, Patrica Buckley. *The Inner Quarters: Marriage and the Lives of Chinese Women in the Sung Period*. Berkeley: University of California Press, 1993.

———. *Women and the Family in Chinese History*. New York: Routledge, 2002.

Egan, Ronald. "Crime, Violence, and Ghosts in the Lin'an Stories in *Yijian zhi*." In *Senses of the City: Perceptions of Hangzhou and Southern Song China, 1127–1279*, edited by Joseph S. C. Lam et al., 149–78. Hong Kong: Chinese University Press, 2017.

Eskildsen, Stephen. *Daoism, Meditation, and the Wonders of Serenity: From the Latter Han Dynasty (25–220) to the Tang Dynasty (618–907)*. Albany: State University of New York Press, 2015.

———. *The Teachings and Practices of the Early Quanzhen Taoist Masters*. Albany: State University of New York Press, 2004.

Fan Ka Wai [Fan Jiawei] 范家偉. *Bei Song Jiaozheng yishu ju xintan* 北宋校正醫書局新探. Hong Kong: Zhonghua Shuju, 2014.

Furth, Charlotte. *A Flourishing Yin: Gender in China's Medical History, 960–1665*. Berkeley: University of California Press, 1999.

———. "Rethinking Van Gulik: Sexuality and Reproduction in Traditional Chinese Medicine." In *Engendering China: Women, Culture and the State*, edited by Christina K. Gilmartin et al., 125–46. Cambridge, MA: Harvard University Press, 1994.

Georgieva, Valentina. "Representation of Buddhist Nuns in Chinese Edifying Miracle Tales during the Six Dynasties and the Tang." *Journal of Chinese Religions* 24, no. 1 (1996): 47–76.

Gerritsen, Anne. "Visions of Local Culture: Tales of the Strange and Temple Inscriptions from Song-Yuan Jizhou." *Journal of Chinese Religions* 28 (2000): 69–92.

Goldin, Paul Rakita. "The Culture and Religious Background of Sexual Vampirism in Ancient China." *Theology and Sexuality* 12, no. 3 (2006): 285–308.

Goldman, Andrea S. "The Nun Who Wouldn't Be: Representations of Female Desire in Two Performance Genres of 'Si Fan.'" *Late Imperial China* 22, no. 1 (2001): 71–138.

Goldschmidt, Asaf. *The Evolution of Chinese Medicine, Song Dynasty, 960–1200.* New York: Routledge, 2009.

Goossaert, Vincent. "The Invention of an Order: Collective Identity in Thirteenth-Century Quanzhen Taoism." *Journal of Chinese Religions* 29, no. 1 (2001): 111–38.

Grant, Beata. "Da Zhangfu: The Gendered Rhetoric of Heroism and Equality in Seventeenth-Century Chan Buddhist Discourse Records." *Nan Nü* 10 (2008): 177–211.

Gross, Rita M. *Buddhism after Patriarchy: A Feminist History, Analysis, and Reconstruction of Buddhism.* New York: State University of New York Press, 1993.

Halperin, Mark. "Domesticity and the Dharma: Portraits of Buddhist Laywomen in Sung China." *T'oung Pao* 92 (2006): 50–100.

Hansen, Valerie. *Changing Gods in Medieval China, 1127–1276.* Princeton: Princeton University Press, 1990.

Heirman, Ann. "Chinese Nuns and Their Ordination in Fifth-Century China." *Journal of the International Association of Buddhist Studies* 24, no. 2 (2001): 275–304.

Hollywood, Amy. "The Normal, the Queer, and the Middle Ages." *Journal of the History of Sexuality* 10, no. 2 (2001): 173–79.

Hsieh, Daniel. *Love and Women in Early Chinese Fiction.* Hong Kong: Chinese University Press, 2008.

Hsieh, Ding-hwa. "Buddhist Nuns in Sung China." *Journal of Song-Yuan Studies* 30 (2000): 63–96.

Hsu, Elizabeth. *Pulse Diagnosis in Early Chinese Medicine: The Telling Touch.* Cambridge: Cambridge University Press, 2010.

Huang, Debby Chih-Yen, and Paul R. Goldin. "Polygyny and Its Discontents: A Key to Understand Traditional Chinese Society." In *Sexuality in China: Histories of Power and Pleasure*, edited by Howard Chiang, 16–33. Seattle: University of Washington Press, 2018.

Huang, Shih-shan Susan. "Tianzhu Lingqian: Divination Prints from a Buddhist Temple in Song Hangzhou." *Artibus Asiae* 7, no. 2 (2007): 243–96.

Huang Minzhi 黃敏枝. "Songdai funü de lingyi cemian: Guanyu Songdai de biqiuni" 宋代婦女的另一側面: 關於宋代的比丘尼. In *Tang Song nüxing yu shehui* 唐宋女性與社會, edited by Deng Xiaonan, 567–655. Shanghai: Shanghai Cishu Chubanshe, 2003.

Huntington, Rania. *Alien Kind: Foxes and Late Imperial Chinese Narrative.* Cambridge, MA: Harvard University Asia Center, 2003.

———. "Foxes and Sex in Late Imperial Chinese Narrative." *Nan Nü* 2, no. 1 (2000): 78–128.

Hymes, Robert. "Getting the Words Right: Speech, Vernacular Language, and Classical Language in Song Neo-Confucian 'Records of Words.'" *Journal of Song-Yuan Studies* 36 (2006): 25–55.

———. "Not Quite Gentlemen? Doctors in Sung and Yuan." *Chinese Science* 8 (1987): 9–76.

———. "Truth, Falsity, and Pretense in Song China: An Approach through the Anecdotes of Hong Mai." *Chūgoku shigaku* 中国史学 15 (2005): 1–26.

Inglis, Alister D. "Hong Mai's Informants for the 'Yijian zhi.'" *Journal of Sung-Yuan Studies* 32 (2002): 83–125.

———. *Hong Mai's* Record of the Listener *and Its Song Dynasty Context.* Albany: State University of New York Press, 2006.

———. "Narratological Ambiguity in Hong Mai's *Yijian zhi.*" *Transactions of the International Conference of Eastern Studies* 59 (2014): 24–46. Tokyo: Tōhō Gakkai.

———. "A Textual History of Hong Mai's *Yijian zhi.*" *T'oung Pao* 93 (2007): 283–368.

Jia, Jinhua. *Gender, Power, and Talent: The Journey of Daoist Priestesses in Tang China.* New York: Columbia University Press, 2018.

Kang, Xiaofei. *The Cult of the Fox: Power, Gender, and Popular Religion in Late Imperial and Modern China.* New York: Columbia University Press, 2006.

Kleeman, Terry F. *Celestial Masters: History and Ritual in Early Daoist Communities.* Cambridge, MA: Harvard University Asia Center, 2016.

———. "The Performance and Significance of the Merging the Pneumas (*Heqi*) Rite in Early Daoism." *Daoism: Religion, History and Society* 6 (2014): 85–112.

Ko, Dorothy. *Cinderella's Sisters: A Revisionist History of Footbinding.* Berkeley: University of California Press, 2005.

Komjathy, Louis. *Cultivating Perfection: Mysticism and Self-Transformation in Early Quanzhen Daoism.* Leiden: Brill, 2007.

———. "Sun Buer: Early Quanzhen Matriarch and the Beginnings of Female Alchemy." *Nan Nü* 16, no. 2 (2014): 171–238.

Kuriyama, Shigehisa. "Angry Women and the Evolution of Chinese Medicine." In *National Health: Gender, Sexuality and Health in a Cross-Cultural Context,* edited by Michael Worton and Nana Wilson-Tagoe, 179–89. London: UCL, 2004.

Lee, Jen-der 李貞德. "Han Tang zhijian qiuzi yifang shitan: Jianlun fuke lanshang yu xingbie lunshu" 漢唐之間求子醫方試探: 兼論婦科濫觴與性別論述. *Zhongyang yanjiuyuan lishi yuyan yanjiusuo jikan* 68, no. 2 (1997): 283–367.

———. "*Yixinfang* lun 'furen zhubing suoyou' ji qi xiangguan wenti" 醫心方論 "婦人諸病所由" 及其相關問題. *Qinghua xuebao* 清華學報 34, no. 2 (2004): 479–511.

Leung, Angela Ki-che. "Medical Learning from the Song to the Ming." In *The Song-Yuan-Ming Transition in Chinese History,* edited by Paul Smith and Richard von Glahn, 374–98. Cambridge, MA: Harvard University Asia Center, 2003.

Levering, Miriam. "Miao-tao and Her Teacher Ta-hui." In *Buddhism in the Sung Dynasty*, edited by Peter N. Gregory and Daniel A. Getz, Jr., 188–219. Honolulu: University of Hawai'i Press, 1999.

———. "Women Ch'an Masters: The Teacher Miao-tsung as Saint." In *Women Saints in World Religions*, edited by Arvind Sharma, 181–204. Albany: State University of New York Press, 2000.

Li Guoling 李國玲. *Songren zhuanji ziliao suoyin bubian* 宋人傳記資料索引補編. Chengdu: Sichuan Daxue Chubanshe, 1994.

Li Jianguo 李劍國. *Songdai zhiguai chuanqi xulu* 宋代志怪傳奇敘錄. Tianjin: Nankai Daxue Chubanshe, 1997.

———. *Tang Wudai zhiguai chuanqi xulu* 唐五代志怪傳奇敘錄. Tianjin: Nankai Daxue Chubanshe, 1992.

Li Jianmin 李建民. "Dumai yu Zhongguo zaoqi yangsheng shijian: Qijing bamai de xin yanjiu zhi er" 督脈與中國早期養生實踐: 奇經八脈的新研究之二. *Zhongyang yanjiuyuan lishi yuyan yanjiusuo jikan* 76, no. 2 (2005): 249–313.

———. *Fangshu, yixue, lishi* 方術, 醫學, 歷史. Taipei: Nantian Shuju, 2000.

———. "Suibing yu changsuo: Chuantong yixue dui suibing de yizhong jieshi" 祟病與場所: 傳統醫學對祟病的一種解釋. *Hanxue yanjiu* 漢學研究 12, no. 1 (1994): 101–48.

Li Yu-chen [Li Yuzhen] 李玉珍. "Fojiao piyu (Avadāna) wenxue zhong de nan nü meise yu qingyu: Zhuiqiu meili de zongjiao yihan" 佛教譬喻(Avadāna)文學中的男女美色與情慾: 追求美麗的宗教意涵. *Xin shixue* 新史學 10, no. 4 (1999): 31–66.

Liao, Hsien-hui. "Popular Religion and the Religious Beliefs of the Song Elite." PhD diss., University of California, Los Angeles, 2001.

Lin Fu-shih [Lin Fushi] 林富士. "Lüelun zaoqi Daojiao yu fangzhongshu de guanxi" 略論早期道教與房中術的關係. *Zhongyang yanjiuyuan lishi yuyan yanjiusuo jikan* 72, no. 2 (2001): 233–300.

———. "Renjian zhi mei: Han Tang zhijian 'jingmei' gushi xilun" 人間之魅: 漢唐之間 "精魅" 故事析論. *Zhongyang yanjiuyuan lishi yuyan yanjiusuo jikan* 78, no. 1 (2007): 107–82.

———. "Shi mei: Yi xian Qin zhi Liuchao shiqi de wenxian ziliao weizhu de kaocha" 釋 "魅": 以先秦至六朝時期的文獻資料為主的考察. In *Gui mei shen mo: Zhongguo tongsu wenhua cexie* 鬼魅神魔: 中國通俗文化側寫, edited by Pu Muzhou (Mu-chou Poo), 109–34. Taipei: Maitian Chuban, 2005.

———. "Zhongguo gudai wuxi de shehui xingxiang yu shehui diwei" 中國古代巫覡的社會形象與社會地位. In *Zhongguo shi xinlun: Zongjiao shi fence* 中國史新論: 宗教史分冊, edited by Lin Fushi, 65–134. Taipei: Lianjing Chuban Shiye Gongsi, 2011.

Liu Ching Cheng [Liu Jingzhen] 劉靜貞. *Bujuzi: Songren de shengyu wenti* 不舉子: 宋人的生育問題. Taipei: Daoxiang Chubanshe, 1998.

Liu Yuan-ju [Liu Yuanru] 劉苑如. *Shenti, xingbie, jieji: Liuchao zhiguai de changyi lunshu yu xiaoshuo meixue* 身體, 性別, 階級: 六朝志怪的常異論述與小說美學. Taipei: Zhongyang Yanjiuyuan Zhongguo Wenzhe Yanjiusuo, 2002.

Lochrie, Karma. *Heterosyncrasies: Female Sexuality When Normal Wasn't.* Minneapolis: University of Minnesota Press, 2005.

Loewe, Michael. "The Physician Chunyu Yi and His Historical Background." In *En suivant la voie royale: Mélanges en hommage à Léon Vendermeersch: Études thématiques 7*, edited by J. Gernet and M. Kalinowski, 297–313. Paris: École Française d'Extrême-Orient, 1997.

Luo, Manling. *Literati Storytelling in Late Medieval China.* Seattle: University of Washington Press, 2015.

———. "Tangdai xiaoshuo zhong yishi xingtai yiyi de 'yao'" 唐代小說中意識形態意義的妖. *Beijing Daxue xuebao* 北京大學學報 50, no. 6 (2013): 97–105.

Luo Zhengming 羅爭鳴. *Du Guangting Daojiao xiaoshuo yanjiu* 杜光庭道教小說研究. Chengdu: Bashu Shushe, 2005.

Ma Jixing 馬繼興. "Yixin fang zhong de gu yixue wenxian chutan" 医心方中的古医学文献初探. *Nihon ishigaku zasshi* 日本医史学雑誌 31, no. 3 (1985): 30–74.

Marcus, Sharon. "The State's Oversight: From Sexual Bodies to Erotic Selves." *Social Research: An International Quarterly* 78, no. 2 (2011): 509–32.

McDermott, Joseph P., and Shiba Yoshinobu. "Economic Change in China, 960–1279." In *The Cambridge History of China Volume 5, Part 2: Sung China, 960–1279*, edited by John W. Chaffee and Denis Twichett, 321–437. Cambridge: Cambridge University Press, 2015.

Mei Chia-ling [Mei Jialing] 梅家玲. "Liuchao zhiguai ren gui yinyuan gushi zhong de liangxing guanxi: Yi 'xingbie' wei zhongxin de kaocha" 六朝志怪人鬼姻緣故事中的兩性關係: 以 "性別" 問題為中心的考察. In *Gudian wenxue yu xingbie yanjiu* 古典文學與性別研究, edited by Hong Shuling et al., 95–127. Taipei: Liren Shuju, 1997.

Mohanty, Chandra Talpade, Ann Russo, and Lourdes Torres, eds. *Third World Women and the Politics of Feminism.* Bloomington: Indiana University Press, 1991.

Nakamura Jihē 中村治兵衛. *Chūgoku shamanizumu no kenkyū* 中国シャーマニズムの研究. Toyko: Tōsui Shobō, 1992.

Ng, Margaret Wee Siang. "Male Brushstrokes and Female Touch: Medical Writings on Childbirth in Imperial China." PhD diss., McGill University, 2013.

Okanishi Tameto 岡西為人. *Song yiqian yiji kao* 宋以前醫籍考. Prefaced 1948. Taipei: Nantian Shuju, 1977.

Owen, Lisa Battaglia. "Toward a Buddhist Feminism: Mahayana Sutras, Feminist Theory, and the Transformation of Sex." *Asian Journal of Women's Studies* 3, no. 4 (1996): 8–51.

Pang, Shiying. "Eminent Nuns And/Or/As Virtuous Women: The Representation of Tang Female Renunciants in Tomb Inscriptions." *T'ang Studies* 28 (2010): 77–96.

Paul, Diana Y. *Women in Buddhism: Images of the Feminine in the Mahayana Tradition.* Berkeley: University of California Press, 1985.

Pfister, Rudolf. "Gendering Sexual Pleasures in Early and Medieval China." *Asian Medicine* 7, no. 1 (2012): 34–64.

Pi Qingsheng 皮慶生. *Songdai minzhong cishen xinyang yanjiu* 宋代民眾祠神信仰研究. Shanghai: Shanghai Guji Chubanshe, 2008.

Rao Zongyi 饒宗頤. *Laozi Xiang'er zhu jiaojian* 老子想爾注校箋. Hong Kong: Tong Nam, 1956.

Raz, Gil. *The Emergence of Daoism: Creation of Tradition*. New York: Routledge, 2012.

Rich, Adrienne. "Compulsory Heterosexuality and Lesbian Existence." In *Feminism and Sexuality: A Reader*, edited by Stevi Jackson and Sue Scott, 130–41. New York: Columbia University Press, 1996.

Robinet, Isabelle. *Taoism: Growth of a Religion*. Translated by Phyllis Brooks. Stanford: Stanford University Press, 1997.

Rocha, Leon Antonio. "Xing: The Discourse of Sex and Human Nature in Modern China." *Gender and History* 22, no. 3 (2010): 603–28.

Salgado, Nirmala S. *Buddhist Nuns and Gendered Practice: In Search of the Female Renunciant*. New York: Oxford University Press, 2013.

Sang, Tze-lan D. *The Emerging Lesbian: Female Same-Sex Desire in Modern China*. Chicago: University of Chicago Press, 2003.

Schafer, Edward H. *The Divine Woman: Dragon Ladies and Rain Maidens in T'ang Literature*. Berkeley: University of California Press, 1973.

Scheid, Volker. *Chinese Medicine in Contemporary China: Plurality and Synthesis*. Durham: Duke University Press, 2002.

Seidel, Anna. "Post-Mortem Immortality or: The Taoist Resurrection of the Body." In *Gilgul: Essays on Transformation, Revolution and Permanence in the History of Religions*, edited by S. Shaked, D.Shulman and G. G. Stroumsa. Leiden: E. J. Brill, 1987.

Sivin, Nathan. *Health Care in Eleventh-Century China*. New York: Springer, 2015.

———. *Medicine, Philosophy and Religion in Ancient China: Researches and Reflections*. Aldershot, UK: Variorum, 1995.

———. "Text and Experience in Classical Chinese Medicine." In *Knowledge and the Scholarly Medical Traditions*, edited by Don Bates, 177–204. Cambridge: Cambridge University Press, 1995.

Sommer, Matthew. *Sex, Law, and Society in Late Imperial China*. Stanford: Stanford University Press, 2000.

Stanley-Baker, Michael. "Cultivating Body, Cultivating Self: A Critical Translation and History of the Tang Dynasty *Yangxing yanming lu*." Master's thesis, Indiana University, 2006.

Tanba no Mototane 丹波元胤. *Zhongguo yiji kao* 中國醫籍考 (1819). Beijing: Renmin Weisheng Chubanshe, 1956.

ter Haar, Barend J. "Newly Recovered Anecdotes from Hong Mai's (1123–1202) *Yijian zhi*." *Journal of Song-Yuan Studies* 23 (1993): 19–41.

Tsai, Kathryn Ann. *Lives of the Nuns: Biographies of Chinese Buddhist Nuns from the Fourth to Sixth Centuries*. Honolulu: University of Hawai'i Press, 1994.

Unschuld, Paul U. *Huang Di Nei Jing Ling Shu: The Ancient Classic on Needle Therapy*. Berkeley: University of California Press, 2016.

Valussi, Elena. "Blood, Tigers, Dragons: The Physiology of Transcendence for Women." *Asian Medicine* 4 (2009): 46–85.

———. "Female Alchemy and Paratext: How to Read *nüdan* in a Historical Context." *Asia Major* 21, no. 2 (2008): 153–93.

———. "Men and Women in He Longxiang's *Nüdan hebian*." *Nan Nü* 10 (2008): 242–78.

von Glahn, Richard. *The Sinister Way: The Divine and the Demonic in Chinese Religious Culture*. Berkeley: University of California Press, 2004.

Waltner, Ann. "Life and Letters: Reflections on Tanyangzi." In *Beyond Exemplar Tales: Women's Biography in Chinese History*, edited by Joan Judge and Hu Ying, 212–29. Berkeley: University of California Press, 2011.

Wang, Jinping. *In the Wake of the Mongols: The Making of a New Social Order in North China, 1200–1600*. Cambridge, MA: Harvard University Asia Center, 2018.

Wang Rutong 王孺童. *Biqiuni zhuan jiaozhu* 比丘尼傳校註. Beijing: Zhonghua Shuju, 2006.

Weeks, Jeffrey. *Sexuality*. 2nd edition. New York: Routledge, 2003.

Wright, Arthur F. "Biography of the Nun An-ling-shou." *Harvard Journal of Asiatic Studies* 15, no. 1/2 (1952): 193–96.

———. "Fo-t'u-teng: A Biography." *Harvard Journal of Asiatic Studies* 11, no. 3/4 (1948): 321–71.

Wu, Yi-Li. "Ghost Fetuses, False Pregnancies, and the Parameters of Medical Uncertainty in Classical Chinese Gynecology." *Nan Nü* 4, no. 2 (2002): 170–206.

———. *Reproducing Women: Medicine, Metaphor, and Childbirth in Late Imperial China*. Berkeley: University of California Press, 2010.

Xu, Man. *Crossing the Gate: Everyday Lives of Women in Song Fujian (960–1279)*. Albany: State University of New York Press, 2016.

Yao, Ping. "Good Karmic Connections: Buddhist Mothers in Tang China." *Nan Nü* 10 (2008): 57–85.

———. "Tang Women in the Transformation of Buddhist Filiality." In *Gendering Chinese Religion: Subject, Identity, and Body*, edited by Jinhua Jia et al., 25–46. Albany: State University of New York Press, 2014.

Yates, Robin D. S. "Medicine for Women in Early China: A Preliminary Survey." *Nan Nü* 7, no. 2 (2005): 127–81.

Yü, Chün-fang. *Kuan-yin: The Chinese Transformation of Avalokiteśvara*. New York: Columbia University Press, 2001.

Zeitlin, Judith T. *The Phantom Heroine: Ghosts and Gender in Seventeenth-Century Chinese Literature*. Honolulu: University of Hawai'i Press, 2007.

Zheng Canshan 鄭燦山. *Liuchao Sui Tang Daojiao wenxian lunkao* 六朝隋唐道教文獻論考. Taipei: Xinwenfeng, 2012.

INDEX

Barlow, Tani, 196n5

bedchamber (*fangzhong*) literature and techniques: compared with medical texts, 35, 39, 40–41, 43, 45, 182n64; on conception, 34, 180n37; criticism of, 144; descriptions of women's enchantment disorders, 80; female sexuality in, 45, 94, 139, 200n2; mentioned, 5, 75, 144–45, 149–50; narrative formula, 81; "Nourishment and Benefit in the Bedchamber" (Sun Simiao), 34, 181n43; on sexual arts, 34, 145; on women's ghost intercourse, 39, 49–50, 51, 54, 100, 165; on women's sexual desire, 22, 34

biji (miscellaneous jottings), 5

bijiang (descend through writing), 159–60

Biographies of Exemplary Women (Lienü zhuan), 122, 130

"Biography of the Director of Granaries" (Chunyu Yi), 23, 24, 27

Bokenkamp, Stephen, 201n19, 201n22, 203n52

bone fever (*guzheng*), 52–53, 184n27

Book of Changes (Yijing), 24, 29, 43; on male and female essences, 23, 30; notion of *shengsheng*, 12–13; recitation of, as treatment, 105

Book of Rites (Liji), 120–21

Buddhism: achieving Buddhahood, 136; Chan, 137, 138; female practitioners, 9, 136; hagiographies, 5; monks, 41, 120, 128, 129, 134, 142–43, 144, 189n40; and patriarchy, 136–37; Pure Land, 124, 136, 137–38; rebirth, 136–38; Song, 142, 147, 200n14. *See also* Buddhist nuns

Buddhist nuns: in Avadāna texts, 135; biographies of, 122–30; fad of vanity and competition, 129; dreams of intercourse, 40; gender

identity of, 119–20, 130, 138; ordination of, 120, 125, 127–29, 197n19; "second ordination," 127, 127–29; self-disfiguration by, 81, 135; Sri Lankan, 119–20, 128; story of Fawu, 142–44

Bureau for Revising Medical Texts, 53, 184n30

Cahill, Suzanne, 17, 137

Cai Jing, 106–7, 195n79

Cainü, 37

caiqi (adopt *qi*), 35

Campany, Robert, 151, 188n12, 188n22, 192n27, 203n51

Cao Pi, *Arrayed Marvels* (Lieyi zhuan), 74

Celestial Masters, 62, 63, 94, 106, 144–46, 158

celestial physicians, 63–64

celestial seal script, 159

celibacy: Buddhist, 140, 141–42, 200n13; Daoist, 146–47, 148–49, 150, 157–58; and family expectations of marriage, 140–41, 149; and fasting, 160–62; female, 16, 44, 135, 148, 151–52, 159, 200n3; male, 36, 139, 150, 199–200n1; male and female, 140, 151–52. *See also* Buddhist nuns; female renunciants; widows

Chan Buddhism, 137, 138

Chang Hsun, 136

Chao Buzhi, 201n15

Chao Yuanfang. See *On the Origins and Symptoms of Various Illnesses*

Chaoye qianzhai (Complete Record of Court and Country; Zhang Zhuo), 82–83, 98, 190n46

Chen, Hsiu-fen, 44, 183n74

Chen Shao, *Records of Penetrating the Mysterious* (Tongyou ji), 78, 81

Chen Yanzhi, *Xiaopin fang*, 181n41, 183n5

Chen Zhi, 31

Chen Ziming: citation of Chunyu Yi and Chu Cheng, 32–33; discussion on husbandless women, 23–25, 27, 40, 182n69; drew from Xu Shuwei, 24–25, 28–29, 179n15; *Good Formulas for Women* (Furen daquan langfang), 23–25, 43, 51, 54, 57; medical category of husbandless women (*guafu*), 9, 22, 25, 29, 40, 164; medical view of female sexuality, 21–22, 163–64; and sex-desire-procreation link, 22, 31, 45; on symptoms of manless women, 97–98; ties with Daoxue, 31

Cheng Ya-ru, 200n12

Chenggong Zhiqiong (deity), 12

childbirth, 41, 99; monstrous, 55, 57, 58, 59, 76, 99

Cho, Philip S., 186n63

Chu Cheng, 23, 25, 28, 32–33, 41; interpreted in *Sacred Benevolence*, 41–42. See also *Chu's Posthumous Work*

Chu Yong, *Quyi shuo*, 179n26

Chuang Hung-I, 186n63

chuanqi (tales of the marvelous), 72. *See also* anomaly accounts

Chunyu Yi, 25, 26, 32, 44; biography of, 23, 24, 27; diagnosis of ailment caused by *yu*, 26, 27, 28

Chu's Posthumous Work (Chushi yishu; Chu Cheng), 24, 32–33, 35, 42–43, 178n8, 179n26; "Asking for Progeny" (Wen zi) section, 33–34, 180n28; "Essence and Blood" (Jing xie) section, 33; on having sex too early, 33–34, 35. *See also* Chu Cheng

cinnabar, 38, 48, 65

Classic of Great Purity (Daqing jing), 38, 39, 181n55

Complete Record of Court and Country (Chaoye qianzhai; Zhang Zhuo), 82, 98, 190n46

Comprehensive Record of Strange Hearsay (Yiwen zonglu), 89

conception, 13–14, 34, 35, 180n37

concubines, 12, 24, 41, 58, 99, 150, 161–62

Confucian family system, 4, 29, 119, 150, 177n27. *See also* marriage

Continued Traditions of Transcendents (Xu xian zhuan; Shen Fen): biography of Pei Xuanjing, 3, 149, 156–58; biography of Qi Xiaoyao, 149, 154–56, 158

corpse transmission (*chuanshi*), 52–53, 184n27

court ladies, 31, 32, 37, 40, 60, 149

courtesans and prostitutes, 25–26, 57, 75, 177n28, 179n10

Cui's Important Formulas (Cuishi zuanyao fang), 39, 50

Cultivating Nature and Prolonging Life (Yangxing yanming lu), 36, 37; "Damages and Benefits of Dominating Women" chapter, 34–35

da zhangfu. See "great gentleman"

Dai Fu, *Wide-Ranging Records of the Strange* (Guangyi ji), 78, 189n26

dan (elixir; Daoist alchemy), 48, 50, 132, 150, 154, 189n40; *nüdan* (female alchemy), 136, 199n52

Daoism: Celestial Master, 63, 144–46, 158; Complete Perfection (Quanzhen), 147–48, 203n49; Divine Empyrean (Shenxiao), 67; Five Thunder Rites, 110; Huangting meditation, 154; illness in, 63, 186n63; "new therapeutic movements," 63; number of monks

Daoism (continued)
and nuns in Song, 147; ordination,
147; Orthodox Unity (Zhengyi),
63, 94, 192n32; rite for entering the
oratory, 158; ritual masters, 63–66,
102, 107, 109, 186n63, 193n43; Seven
Perfected, 147–48; sexual practices,
62–63, 144–46, 149–50, 180n30,
201n22, 202n47; Supreme Purity
(Shangqing), 130, 131, 134, 145,
146–47, 148–49, 153, 154, 158, 201n25;
talismans, 62, 64, 65–66. *See also*
Daoist practitioners; Daoist texts
Daoist practitioners: ascent to
heaven, 130, 133, 149, 150, 151,
154, 155, 157, 202n46; diet of, 130,
151; female, 8, 17, 136, 137, 147;
liberation from the corpse, 150,
202n48. *See also* exorcism; female
transcendents
Daoist texts: on bodily cultivation, 154;
exorcism manuals, 61–62, 63–64,
65–67; on female alchemy, 136;
hagiographies, 5, 102, 130, 148–49, 151,
153, 160; on immortality cultivation,
61–62; Lingbao scriptures and
rites, 62, 63, 65, 145–46, 199n53;
Students of the Dao, 130–31, 148;
*Uncollected Pearls from the Ocean
of Rituals*, 65. See also *Assembled
Transcendents*; *Continued Traditions
of Transcendents*
Daoxue, 22, 30, 31. *See also* Neo-
Confucian philosophy
Dark Book of the Divine Thearch
(Zichen xuanshu; Zhang Shunlie),
66–67
Dark Purity, Madam (deity), 146
Davis, Edward, 87–88, 100–101, 193n43,
195n72
Declarations of the Perfected (Zhen gao;
comp. Tao Hongjing), 146
deer antler, 47, 183n2

deities: benign relationships with,
96–97; demonic, 97, 98–99; female,
12, 96, 177n28. *See also* female
transcendents; ghosts; spirits;
transcendents
Deng Zhi (source-informant for
Yijian zhi), 193n47, 196n87, 196n95,
203n51
Deng Zhiqing (source-informant for
Yijian zhi), 193n38
depletion, 39, 40, 42, 47, 48–49, 56,
182n69
desire: as cause of illness, 38, 51;
connection with ghost fetuses,
60–61; female, 37, 38; male, 36;
meanings of *yu*, 26–27, 30; in
Neo-Confucian philosophy, 6,
29–30, 45; as "primordial force," 13;
same-sex, 165; as sexual thoughts
(*yuxin*), 23, 27, 28, 31, 33, 44, 45;
unfulfilled, 22, 23–24. *See also*
female sexuality; sex-desire-
procreation link
dihuang pill, 24, 28
discourse, unstable, 9–10, 165–66
divination, 24, 100, 194n51; by
examination takers, 176n9. See also
wu
Divine Farmer's Materia Medica
(Shennong bencao jing), 50
Divine Matriarch of the West
(Xiwangmu), 131, 157
Divine Patriarch of the East, 131
divorce, 124, 141, 148
Dong Feng (transcendent; physician),
75
Dong Jingchen, 192n31
Dong Shangxian (Supreme
Transcendent Dong), 133, 135
Dong Zhongfu (Daoist priest), 110
Dongling Shengmu (Holy Mother of
Dongling), 154
Dou Weiwu/Weixian, 83, 190n47

dreams, 8, 59, 82, 113, 127, 159; of ghost intercourse, 37, 39–40, 48–54, 62, 64–67, 183n2, 184n21; of intercourse with malign *qi*, 32, 39, 40, 47, 51; of sexual intercourse, 47, 61

Du Guangting, 198n33. See also *Assembled Transcendents*

Du Zhengzhen, 176n10

dual *bhikṣuṇī* ordination, 120–21

Duan Chengshi, *Youyang Morsels* (Youyang zazu), 79, 189n40

Dudbridge, Glen, 177n28

efficacious narratives, 106–7, 195n84

Egan, Ronald, 175n7

elite and commoner religious practices, 7, 176n9

enchantment disorders: agents of, 73, 80, 187n6; associated with Wutong, 64–65, 99–100; in bedchamber literature, 80; conflation with female sorcerers and transcendents, 10, 17, 102, 150–51, 152, 160, 162; diagnosis of, 54; and female sexuality, 72, 77, 80; in folk and literary tales, 10, 71–72, 74, 77, 165; narratives of failure, 10, 114–16; popular beliefs on, 79; in Song anecdotes, 10, 86–87, 93–95; treatment for, 74, 79–80, 189–90n40; women's accounts of, 84; and women's lack of interest in marriage, 80–81, 140; and women's literacy, 81–82; and women's marital status, 74–75; women's responses to, 75–76, 188n15; and women's secrets, 82–85; women's symptoms, 72, 78, 79, 93, 94, 97–98, 152

epigraphic writings, 141, 150, 200n3, 200n12

epistemology, 4, 10

ethnographic interviews, 9, 176n20

excessive thoughts, 21, 44, 45. See also desire

exemplary biographies and tales, 83, 122, 130

exhaustion, 41, 42, 48, 182n69; *laozhai* (exhaustion plague), 66–67. See also depletion

exorcism, 7, 82–83, 93, 104, 107, 184n14, 187n2; in Daoist traditions, 63, 65–66, 94–95, 106, 186n56; for demonic enchantment, 71–72, 79–80, 85, 189–90n40; manuals and texts, 5, 61–62, 63–64, 65–67; recipes related to, 48; in Song, 103, 195n72

Fabian (Buddhist nun), 122

family system, 4, 29, 119, 150, 177n27. *See also* marriage

Fan, Madam (transcendent), 146, 149

fantastique, 92

Faquan (Buddhist nun), 123

Fasheng (Buddhist nun), 197–98n21

fasting, 62, 132, 151, 153, 154, 155, 160–62

Fawu (Buddhist nun), 142–44

Faying, Vinaya Master, 129

female body, 41, 120, 135, 199n49; in bedchamber and popular literature, 44, 75; divine, 160–62; transformation of, 5, 136–38

female fidelity, 9, 25, 44, 82. *See also* widows, chastity of

female ghosts, 73–74, 188n16

female renunciants: agency of, 16–17; community nunnery for, 8; Daoist, 148, 203n49; epitaphs of, 141, 150, 175n5, 200n3, 200n12; and family life, 16; gendered identity of, 17, 119–20, 123, 127, 130–31; issue of marriage, 123–24; political motivation, 141; scholarly analysis, 178n40. *See also* Buddhist nuns; celibacy; manless women female sexuality: association with Heaven and Earth, 21–22, 43, 44, 45; in bedchamber literature, 45, 94, 139, 200n2; and enchantment disorders, 72, 77, 80, 152; and independent women, 102; late imperial perspectives, 44, 182n66; of maids, 76; medical view of, 21–22, 31, 32; in Wutong lore, 100. *See also* desire; manless women

female transcendents: admonishments of male practitioners, 146; assaulted by Buddhist monks, 134; celibacy and isolation of, 148, 151–52; conflation with enchanted women, 10, 17, 103, 150–51, 152, 162; definition of, 151; grannies, 133–34; hagiographies of, 102, 121, 131–35, 148–49, 151, 153, 160; illness of, 102–3, 150–51; stories of unexpected talent, 82. See also *Assembled Transcendents*; *Continued Tradition of Transcendents*; Daoist practitioners

fever, 95, 97; bone, 52–53, 184n27

filiality, 16, 124, 125, 142

fire, 42, 44

five phases, 42, 49

five viscera, 39, 48–49

foot-*qi*, 41

footbinding, 176n20

Formulary of the Medical Bureau (Taiping huimin hejiju fang), 104

Formulas at Hand (Zhouhou beiji fang; Ge Hong), 47, 51, 52

Fotucheng (Buddhist monk), 124, 141, 143

fox spirits: compared with Wutong, 100; possession by, 3, 48, 74, 86–87, 189n40; vixen as embodiment of lust, 74, 188n17

fox stories: pre-Song, 80–81, 85; in *Record of the Listener*, 92;

seventeenth and eighteenth century, 74; Song anecdotes, 86–87; in Tang tales, 78, 84, 189n26

Fu Shan, 61

fuke (women's medicine), 29

Furth, Charlotte, 21

Further Records of an Inquest into the Spirit-Realm (Soushen houji), 13, 75–76, 80, 96–97; authorship and date, 188n22

Gan Bao, *Inquest into the Spirit-Realm* (Soushen ji), 12, 13, 75, 92, 177n29

ganyun (affected pregnancy), 13–14, 55, 185n43

Gaoseng zhuan, 197n10

Garden of Marvels (Yiyuan; Liu Jingshu), 74, 76

gazetteers, 7, 89

Ge Hong: *Formulas at Hand*, 47, 51, 52; *Traditions of Divine Transcendents*, 75, 148, 151, 203n51

gender and religion, 119–22, 137–38. *See also* Buddhist nuns; female renunciants; female transcendents

Gerritsen, Anne, 176n10

ghost fetuses (*guitai*): connected with excessive desire, 21, 60–61; Daoist rituals for, 64; diagnosis of, 57, 58–59; late imperial medical debates on, 185n41; of married and unmarried women, 57–58, 60, 61; mechanism of formation, 56; in medical texts, 21, 40, 46, 56–57, 59, 60–61; and monstrous births, 58, 59–60; recipes for purging, 56–57, 103, 185n39; as result of ghost intercourse, 46, 55, 59–60; in tales and anecdotes, 57–59; use of term, 55–56. *See also* intercourse with ghosts

ghosts. *See* intercourse with ghosts; spirits

infertility, 51, 180n37, 184n21

Inglis, Alister D., 191n13, 192n29

Inquest into the Spirit-Realm (Soushen ji; Gan Bao), 12, 13, 75, 92, 177n29

intercourse with buried corpses, 66

intercourse with ghosts: association with ghost fetuses, 46, 55, 59–60; attachment of ghost *qi*, 51; in bedchamber versus medical texts, 39; in Chao Yuanfang's *On the Origins*, 48–49; in Daoist texts and exorcism manuals, 46, 61–62; dreaming of, 37, 39–40, 48–49, 51, 64–67, 183n2; elixirs for, 50; gendered symptoms, 49–50, 52; leading to delirium, 47; and leaking of *jing*, 47, 52; material benefits, 96, 97; medical explanations, 21, 37, 44, 46, 79, 164; in Qi Zhongfu's *One Hundred Questions*, 39–40; Tang recipes, 50; treatment for women, 37, 39, 64, 181nn52–53; types of women affected, 40, 51; women's symptoms, 53–54, 79. *See also* dreams; ghost fetuses

Invaluable Formulas (Beiji qianjin yaofang; Sun Simiao), 28, 34–36, 38–39, 48, 79, 181n43; supplement to, 53

Ishinpō (Heart of Medicine; Tanba no Yasuyori), 34, 36–37, 38, 48, 50, 180n32, 181n49, 181n54

jealousy, 139–40, 143, 145; of female gods and demons, 12, 87; of husbands, 135, 149

Jia Jinhua, 198n37

jian (illicit sex), 11, 14

Jiang Guan, *Ming yi lei an*, 185n49

Jiang Zhiqi, 159

jiao rites, 109, 110

jiaoqi (foot-*qi*), 41

jing (essence): in Celestial Master Daoism, 144; of demons and ghosts, 56, 99; irregular circulation of, 33; leaking of, in dreams, 47, 52, 183n3; and men's desire for a mate, 24, 28; use in sexual arts, 34–36

Jing Huan, *Leisure Tales of a Humble Man* (Yeren xianhua), 79

Jinggui (Buddhist nun), 122

Jingjian (Buddhist nun), 122, 127–29

jingmei (nonhuman monstrous creatures), 74, 188n10

Jingxiu (Buddhist nun), 127, 141

Kang Minggan (Buddhist nun), 125–26

Ko, Dorothy, 176n20

Kou Zongshi, 182n69; *Expanded Commentaries of Materia Medica* (Bencao yanyi), 42

Kuriyama, Shigehisa, 44

laozhai (exhaustion plague), 66–67

legal system and sexuality, 11, 14, 15, 147

LGBT movement, 163

Li Jianguo, 190n3

Li Zhenduo (transcendent), 134

Lin Fu-shih, 187n6, 189n27, 193n51

Lingbao scriptures, 62, 63, 65, 145–46, 199n53

Lingshu (Yellow Emperor's Inner Canon: Numinous Pivot), 47, 48

literary tales, 10, 71–72, 74, 76–77, 103, 165. *See also* anomaly accounts (*zhiguai*)

Liu Fu, *Elevated Discussions from the Eminent Households* (Qingsuo gaoyi), 3, 86–88, 94, 101, 102, 190n3, 191n8

Liu Jingshu, *Garden of Marvels* (Yiyuan), 74, 76

Liu Yiqing, *Records of the Hidden and the Visible Worlds* (Youming lu), 75, 76

Liu Yuan-ju, 11–13, 177n25

Lives of the Nuns (Biqiuni zhuan; Baochang): biographies of Huiguo, Sengguo, and Baoxian, 129; biography of An Lingshou, 123–24, 140–41, 143; biography of Jingjian, 127–29; biography of Jingxiu, 127; biography of Nun Kang Minggan, 125–26; biography of Nun Miaoxiang, 123, 124, 141; biography of Shi Huimu, 124–25, 128; compared with *Lives of the Eminent Monks*, 197n10; family expectations for marriage in, 140–41; perspective on gender, 120–30, 126–28, 137; preface, 122; virtues associated with nuns, 123, 126–27

local cults, 7, 133, 203n51

Longshi (Buddhist female devotee), 136

Lu Dangke (exorcist), 107

Lü Fu, 60–61

Lu Yanghao, 67

Luo, Manling, 190n46

Luo Jin (Luo the Interdictor), 93, 104, 192n31

Ma Shu, *Students of the Dao* (Daoxue zhuan), 121, 130–31, 148

Ma Yu, 148

Mahāprajāpatī, 122

maids, 8, 12, 13, 73, 76, 77, 157; of the king of Jibei, 26–27, 28, 44

manless women, 3–5; associated with demons, 5, 8–9; divine, 162; and enchantment, 54, 77; fear of, 37, 94, 139, 165–66; and the female body, 137–38; religious devotees, 5, 16; versus same-sex intimacy, 16; and sexual desire, 28; during the Song, 7–9; sources on, 5–6, 9–10;

as subject of unstable discourses, 165–66; subjectivity of, 159, 162; symptoms associated with, 23–24, 29, 43–44, 54, 97–98. See also *guafu*; heterosexual inactivity

marital status: and ghost intercourse, 58; and the *guafu* category, 22, 25; of renunciants, 139, 150; in stories and tales, 74–75, 95; used in diagnosing pregnancy, 32, 40; and *xian*, 162

marriage: depictions of, 110; after enchantment, 75, 114–15, 116, 165; family expectations of, 140–41, 155, 157, 158; incompatibility with spirit possession, 160–61; as issue for female renunciants, 123–24; as possible cure for enchantment, 114, 116; premodern system, 165; resistance of, 80–81, 130–31; same-sex, 163; and two-gender model, 121

matchmakers, 155; for demons, 72, 86, 94

medical knowledge: buttressed by Confucian classics, 29, 163; and Confucian ethics, 6, 163–64; on homosexuality and AIDS, 163. *See also* medical texts; physicians

medical recipes, 24, 28, 38, 47–48, 50, 103–4, 190n41

medical texts: compared with anomaly accounts, 72, 187n5; compared with bedchamber tradition, 35, 39, 40–41, 43, 45, 182n64; Song, 39–43, 51, 53; later imperial compilations, 43; as source of information on manless women, 5, 54. *See also* Chen Ziming; *Heart of Medicine*; *Invaluable Formulas*; medical recipes; *On the Origins and Symptoms of Various Illnesses*; *One Hundred Questions on Women's Medicine*; Zhu Zhenheng

puragatory therapies, 103, 194n64. *See also* abortion

Pure Land Buddhism, 124, 136, 137–38

qi: congealing in the spleen, 43–44; excessive and deviated, 47; of the five phases, 49; ghostly, 79; malign, 32, 39, 40, 47, 48, 51; of the *shen*-spirits in the five viscera, 49; treatments to fortify, 79; water and wood, 42; women's foot, 41; of *yuan* and *kuang*, 181n54

Qi Xiaoyao (transcendent), 149, 154–56, 158

Qi Zhongfu, 39–41. See also *One Hundred Questions on Women's Medicine*

Qian Miaozhen (transcendent), 148

Qin Jingjian (Buddhist nun), 137–38

Qingsuo gaoyi. See Liu Fu

Qiu Chuji, 147, 148

Quanzhen (Complete Perfection) Daoism, 147–48, 203n49

quiet chambers (*jingshi*), 158–59, 161, 203n66

Quyi shuo (Chu Yong), 179n26

Raz, Gil, 201n22, 201n25

realgar, 47, 48, 50, 183n2

Record of the Listener (Yijian zhi; Hong Mai): as account of everyday lives, 6; amateurs' narratives, 108–10; anecdotes of divine female body, 160–62; belief in ubiquity of spirits, 176n9; case history of Xiong Bangjun, 105; "Chen the Female *Wu*," 101–2; "Chen's Wife," 108; circulation and preservation, 89, 191n10; "Clay Fetus," 104, 106; comparison with *Records of an Inquest into the Spirit-Realm*, 92; "deferral of truth," 97; distinguished from anomaly accounts, 88, 89, 91–92; efficacious narratives, 106–7; "The Fangs' Daughter," 94–95, 106; on ghost fetuses, 58, 59, 61, 185n46; as hearsay, 6, 10, 90–91, 92, 192n29; "Lady by the West Lake," 104, 106; later adaptations of, 103; narratives of failure, 110–16; narratological ambiguity in, 92–93; prefaces to, 89–90, 91, 191n18; as records not fit for orthodox histories, 175n7; "Red Leaf in the Arms," 111–12; "Sir Candlenut of Xincheng," 108; "Sir Wulang," 95–97, 110, 113; "Snake Anomaly in the Yu Family," 112–14, 196n96; and Song anecdotal writings, 88–89; as source on manless women, 6, 7–9; sources of, 89–91, 109, 161, 191n13, 191n22, 192n35, 193n47, 195n86, 196nn87–88, 196n93, 196nn95–97, 203n51; stories about Wutong, 95–96; stories of material benefits from spirit relationships, 97; story of Chen Daoguang's relationship with female deity, 96; story of Wen and Yang who practiced the Dao, 7–8; style and language of, 91, 93, 191n21; "The Tree Lodgers in Jiangnan," 98–100, 101, 102, 150–51, 152, 160; women 's own accounts in, 84; "Yong's Daughter," 7, 114–16

Records of the Grand Historian (Shiji; Sima Qian), 23, 24, 27, 90

Renzong, Song Emperor, 159

replenishing medicines, 103, 104, 194n64

Rich, Adrienne, 165–66

Rites of Impure Traces (Huiji Fa), 107

Rites of the Three Altars (Santan Fa), 107, 195n75

Yang Daozhen (physician), 58–59, 60

Yang Gaoshang (exorcist), 107, 115

yangsheng (body cultivation), 181n55

Yangxing yanming lu (Records of Cultivating Nature and Prologing Life), 34–35, 36, 37

Yanhua (deity), 159–60

yasheng (conquering the enemy with occult means), 100

yao (demonic), 73, 74

Yao, Emperor, birth of, 13

Yao, Ping, 220n13

Yellow Emperor, birth of, 13

yi (physicians), 67, 80, 103–4, 184n14, 187n5, 194n65; *ruyi*, 5, 6, 29; and *wu*, 100, 101, 195n70

Yijian zhi. See *Record of the Listener*

yin and *yang*, 13, 14, 35, 37, 49, 80, 131–32; *qi*, 35, 38, 39, 55, 194

yinyu (lust), 62, 186n58

Yongzheng, Qing Emperor, 11

Youyang Morsels (Youyang zazu; Duan Chengshi), 79, 189n40

yu. See desire

Yu Tuan, 60

Yu Zhongyong (source-informant for *Yijian zhi*), 196n96

Yuhuang Temple (Jincheng, Shanxi), 176n10

yuxin (thoughts of *yu*), 27, 28, 31

Zhan Daozi (Kangzong; source-informant for *Yijian zhi*), 192n33

Zhang, Celestial Master, of Dragon-Tiger Mountain, 94, 106

Zhang Congzheng (source-informant for *Yijian zhi*), 51, 184n21

Zhang Ji: *Discussion of Cold Damage* (Shanghan lun), 53; *Synopsis Recipes from the Golden Cabinet* (Jinkui yaolüe), 53, 54

Zhang Shizheng, *Collection of Anomaly Accounts* (Kuoyi zhi), 93–94, 192n31

Zhang Shunlie, *Dark Book of the Divine Thearch* (Zichen xuanshu), 66–67

Zhang Xujing, Celestial Master, 106–7

Zhang Yuchu, Celestial Master, 62

Zhang Zhuo, *Complete Record of Court and Country* (Chaoye qianzhai), 82–83, 98, 190n46

Zhen Quan, 39

zheng and *jia* conglomerates, 32, 40, 56, 179n24

Zhenglei bencao, 183n2

Zhenwu, temple of, 114, 115

zhiguai. See anomaly accounts

Zhou Shaolu (source-informant for *Yijian zhi*), 58

Zhu Conglong (source-informant for *Yijian zhi*), 109, 110, 192n35, 196n88

Zhu Duanzhang, *Handbook for Childbirth* (Weisheng jiabao chanke beiyao), 56, 57

Zhu Xi, 30, 31

Zhu Zhenheng, 31, 43–44, 51–52, 61, 164, 183n74

Zhuanxu, Emperor, birth of, 13

Zhuhong (Buddhist monk), *Assembled Record of Rebirth*, 137–38